PRAISE FOR PROCU|
O>AGIE

Procurement Mojo is extremely relevant and very well-written. Sigi Osagie hits the nail on the head; this book really resonates with my own experience. It convincingly lays out solutions to the difficulties and frustrations Procurement executives and practitioners face – engaging with stakeholders; trying to sell Procurement to the wider business; fighting for investment; and so on. Crucially, Sigi is absolutely right that 'people' are the number one factor. I loved the simplicity of the language and the sensible, clear-cut guidance – indispensable advice.

Paul Farrow, VP Supply Management, Hilton Worldwide

There are lots of purchasing books out there, but none of them show how to create a lasting and sustainable Procurement brand. *Procurement Mojo*, at last, provides an effective and definitive guide. Sigi Osagie's vast Procurement experience shines through. Insightful, illuminating and inspiring!

Jonathan Patrick, Former European Procurement Director, Sony

A much-needed book that articulates the fundamentals of creating Procurement success. *Procurement Mojo* brilliantly outlines pragmatic answers to the key problems of building a credible Procurement brand and a capability to match. A great book with sound examples, shrewd approaches and loads of smart advice. Read it!

James Cowley, Procurement and Supply Chain Director, Balfour Beatty Services

Sigi Osagie's personal story of career success – from penniless, near-barefoot immigrant to global supply executive in fourteen years – is as inspiring as the knowledge he shares here. *Procurement Mojo* is as much about Procurement success as individual success for purchasing people. Buy this book, read it, and you'll be delighted!

Ray Packe, Former Head of Global Purchasing, Marconi plc

...[Sigi] has been instrumental in aligning our Procurement function to Gatwick's new priorities, and instigated a number of developments to improve our supply base and procurement capability... [he] brings clarity, direction and focus to organisational development issues and supply management challenges... and is able to articulate ideas effectively and secure stakeholder alignment.

Scott Stanley, COO, Gatwick Airport

True Procurement success is not about category management, e-sourcing and so on; it's about building foundational capability, and Sigi Osagie explains this in a powerfully persuasive manner. *Procurement Mojo* underscores the importance of the single most critical factor in creating sustainable success – people. This is an invaluable guide for Procurement professionals and senior executives who want more from their Procurement.

Allan Stamper, Chief Executive, Water Division, Halma plc

Procurement Mojo gets to the core issues – Procurement talent, stakeholders, and Procurement's profile in the wider business. This book is superbly-focused and engaging. With stories from his own remarkable career, Sigi Osagie pulls together the secrets of success in Procurement. This book should be compulsory reading for all Procurement professionals and senior executives responsible for purchasing.

Chris Efstathiou, Vice President of Supply Chain, Kiva Systems

Procurement Mojo addresses the real concerns purchasing people grapple with; not least, improving capability, raising Procurement's profile and nurturing a great Procurement brand. Valuable insights and lots of pragmatic techniques. You must read it if you really want to boost your Procurement ability.

Stephen Faley, Global Director, Procurement & Supply Chain Management, David Brown Gear Systems

This is a superb book – a 'must read' for all Procurement people! Sigi Osagie lays out a structured approach to the most important Procurement issues, in straightforward language, with compelling models and examples. If you're in the Procurement field – whether you're a CPO or a Junior Buyer – read *Procurement Mojo* to really up your game. I loved it!

Roberto Troiolo, Senior Director of Global Procurement, Major telecoms manufacturer

I had the pleasure of working with Sigi on improving our Procurement... and he did more than educate me – he brought out a passion that I had lost. He has inspired me to take my Procurement function to a different level and drive greater profitability for the company.

Natalie Bouwer, Procurement Manager, David Brown Gear Systems, South Africa

What purchasing people need most is good practical guidance to tackle the problems they routinely face in the job. *Procurement Mojo* provides it. Sigi Osagie highlights the true essence of successful Procurement in simplified language, and offers informed advice on building a Procurement brand, which all purchasing people will get tremendous benefit from.

David Bradley, Supply Chain Director, Moog Tritech

The following figures are reproduced with the permission of the copyright-holder EPG Solutions Limited: Figures 1.3, 2.1, 2.4, 5.4 and 6.1

First published in 2014 by Management Books 2000 Ltd
36 Western Road
Oxford OX1 4LG
Tel: 0044 (0) 1865 600738
Email: info@mb2000.com
Web: www.mb2000.com

British Library Cataloguing in Publication Data is available

ISBN 9781852527457

PROCUREMENT MOJO

Strengthening the Function and Raising Its Profile

Sigi Osagie

Management Books 2000

For Heather.
Thank you for everything.
When I count my blessings I count you twice.

CONTENTS

Acknowledgements 9

Preface 11

Introduction 17

Why 'Procurement Effectiveness'? 20

STEP 1: Build an Effective Procurement Organisation 43
  Functional Leadership 49
  Functional Goals...................................... 57
  People Capability...................................... 67
  Individual Performance and Rewards................ 79
  Culture... 90

STEP 2: Deploy Fit-for-Purpose Enablers 102
  Basic Procurement Processes...................... 111
  Technology Enablement 123

STEP 3: Adopt Robust Supply Base Management 129
  Supplier Performance and Relationship Management............ 136
  Risk Management 146
  Beyond SPRM and Risk Management 157

STEP 4: Apply Appropriate Performance Frameworks 164
  Performance Management of Procurement Programmes....... 166
  Procurement Functional Performance.................. 176

STEP 5: Build Your Procurement Brand...................191
  Repositioning Procurement........................ 194
  *Managing Stakeholders – Communication and Customer
    Relationship Management* 200
  Procurement PR...................................... 218

Epilogue 232

References and Bibliography 239

Index 244

ACKNOWLEDGEMENTS

They say that it takes a whole village to raise a child. There have certainly been many wonderful villagers in my community who have helped bring this book to fruition. I am immensely grateful to every one of them, including those who have contributed to my learning and growth on my adventure in search of my personal mojo.

In particular, I'd like to express my gratitude to my two key career mentors – Hugh Humphrey, who taught me about 'results' and 'winning friends and influencing people', and Ray Packe, who schooled me in the art of leveraging interpersonal and organisational dynamics and aided my leadership development in many ways. Thanks to Malcolm Hewitt; Seka Nikolic; Lynn Saunders; and to Kathy Gayle, for her counsel when I first embarked on my writing odyssey all those years ago – her feedback was inspiring.

I'd also like to thank those who gave freely of their time on this project and provided me with the benefit of their experience in various ways, especially Bob Garvey; David Clutterbuck; Stuart Emmett; Sheila Cameron; Mike Buchanan; Christopher Barrat; Bryony Thomas; Obi Abuchi; Andrea Reynolds; Roy France; and Kate Pool at The Society of Authors, to whom I'll always be indebted for her tremendous assistance.

Special thanks to Roberto Troiolo, Paul Farrow and Paul Fitch, who kindly read my manuscript and provided valuable critique that helped polish my work. Of course, that work would never have morphed into the finished book without the efforts of Nicholas Dale-Harris and his team at Management Books 2000 – thank you!

Finally, I must pay tribute to my prime cheerleader, my wife, Heather. Her unwavering belief in me and her continuing encouragement have been indispensable sustenance on my adventure. When I count my blessings I count her twice.

PREFACE

I started writing this book a couple of years ago, soon after delivering a series of keynote speeches on 'Enhancing Procurement Effectiveness'. But, in truth, the seeds of the book were sown much earlier. Many years ago, a large jumbo jet touched down at Heathrow Airport one late evening in June. I stepped off the plane with my fellow passengers who had all boarded the flight in one of Africa's major cities about seven hours earlier. And thus began my adult life as an immigrant in England, a life that's been nearly as challenging as it's been rewarding.

The 'moving staircase' I encountered at Heathrow tube station was a marvel to my senses, like something from another planet. But getting used to the ubiquitous escalators on the London Underground network was a small challenge compared to what lay before me in transforming my life.

I didn't worry about the holes in my shoes that first day; those worries would come in a few months when I would feel the biting cold of winter clawing at my feet. But I was very aware of the few coins that jangled in my pocket, reminding me that I had to find a job fast or ... God knows what. Indeed, I soon found a job mopping floors in the Häagen-Dazs restaurant in Leicester Square.

Many years later, fourteen to be exact, I sat in my office in Coventry reading an organisation announcement on the company intranet. It announced several senior appointments in the company, including mine – as a director with global supply management responsibilities spanning thirteen or so countries. I was thirty-four at the time. I had achieved my career ambition of becoming a director in a blue-chip company by the age of thirty-five. You couldn't get more blue-chip than Marconi plc, the erstwhile GEC-Marconi – a multi-billion pound behemoth of a conglomerate with interests in several sectors and tentacles stretching to all corners of the globe.

The fourteen years between my arrival at Heathrow as a penniless, near-barefoot immigrant and reaching the upper echelons of leadership in the corporate world had been extremely educative indeed. My initial thirst for knowledge had centred on my desire to better myself and be successful in my career. But I soon learnt that success in my career and success in my personal life had more in common than I would have thought. Achieving both relied crucially on my ability to take appropriate actions towards my desires and goals, i.e. my ability to do *the right things* – my effectiveness.

I would come to learn that effectiveness was far more important than anything else in achieving long-term success. (Assuming, of course, that a healthy dose of ambition already exists.) It made no difference whether I was beating the pavements in London's West End hunting for my first menial job, or expending effort coaching and mentoring a member of my team when I'd started managing people; proactively *doing the right things* to get the outcome I wanted would always be a consistent requirement to successfully achieve my goals.

The career opportunities which gave me chances to develop or turn around functional organisations were particularly insightful in demonstrating the power and importance of effectiveness. In any realm of life, organisations, be they functional teams, small business ventures, charities, huge multinationals or even nation states, are only ever successful in the long term through effectiveness – focusing on the critical actions that create the outcomes they desire.

It took me several painful efforts trying to build successful functional teams before I truly appreciated this learning. And, like anyone who has tried to drive transformational change in organisations, I have a few battle-scars to show for my efforts. My first attempt would have been an excellent episode of the phantom sitcom, *How Not to Win Friends and Influence People!*

It was my first job straight out of university. I was recruited to set up the supply management function and introduce Materials Requirements Planning (MRP) in a small manufacturing business in South London. I was excited at the opportunity. My Manufacturing Systems Engineering degree course had been less about 'engineering' *per se*, but more about supply chain management – a study of the systems or techniques used to manage manufacturing operations, which is where the supply management disciplines we recognise today originated from. And I had just spent the preceding six months or so working on my final year project: setting up a simulation model of an MRP system. Here was a chance to put all that theoretical knowledge into practice. I was so elated when I read the offer letter from the company I nearly ran into the street to do a solo conga.

But, alas, my enthusiasm soon waned, as I struggled to influence the staff in the company to embrace the modern purchasing and materials management approaches I was introducing. I failed miserably, initially. And my failure was demoralising.

Thankfully, my boss – Harry Hughes, the Production Director – was a fantastic leader. He coached and mentored me in the ways of organisations and how to achieve my results through others; lessons that, perhaps, should be included in all tertiary education curricula. After all, organisations are really all about people first and foremost. Sadly, many of us repeatedly forget this as we get embroiled in the tasks and challenges of every-day life at work. I am just as guilty as anyone else, though less so these days.

I started to learn about 'people' and how critical this dimension was to my effectiveness in the workplace right from that first job working for Harry. And years later, as I took up increasingly senior roles in management, I continued to recognise how my success at my job was strongly related to my ability to align people to my agenda and nurture effective relationships.

Organisations are indeed about people. Unfortunately, far too many of us fail to understand and leverage this key factor. Our failure stems from a fundamental lack of effectiveness, whether we are talking about individuals or functional organisations. Reading through several issues of various hard-copy and electronic trade publications highlights that many Procurement functions today struggle with three critical challenges, all people-related: effective functional leadership; skills and competency of purchasing staff; and sub-optimal stakeholder relationships – all of which detract from Procurement's value-add in organisations.

These are challenges many of us recognise, nay, have experienced. I certainly have. My initial interest in these issues stemmed from my craving for success, right from the early stages my career. It became a growing force that compelled me to do my MBA dissertation research on 'management effectiveness and organisational performance' – a study of how the effectiveness of managers in an organisation impacts its performance and success. I used one of Marconi's businesses as my principal guinea-pig organisation.

The insights I gained from that research study cemented my evolving beliefs on the importance of 'leadership' and 'effectiveness' in organisations. And I continued to apply a lot of the knowledge I had gained as my management career in the corporate world grew. Nearly a decade after that study, when I started developing a second career as a writer and business speaker, I discovered that many others either share an identical ethos or thirst for such knowledge. Over the last few years, I have been delivering talks on effectiveness and success in the workplace to groups of purchasing professionals in several countries, including a series of keynote speeches at member conferences of the Chartered Institute of Purchasing & Supply (CIPS). In these forums I consistently hear the same clamour for knowledge on the appropriate approaches that enable purchasing professionals and Procurement functions to achieve sustainable success.

For Procurement leaders and staff, it appears the biggest frustration they face is the lack of appreciation of their value-add in their organisations, and, commonly, being 'denied' the opportunity to showcase their value proposition. As one purchasing manager put it in a recent blog entry, "Why should I have to constantly fight to be allowed to do my job?!"

Why indeed?

But here's something else to ponder: would you show up at a gunfight with a knife?

Few of us would. So why moan about the organisational contexts Procurement has to operate in? Our focus should instead be on being properly equipped for success, by taking the right actions to achieve the desired outcomes.

If you are familiar with the old 'effectiveness versus efficiency' debate you will probably recognise immediately the critical importance of Procurement effectiveness, considering the challenges most Procurement functions face and the organisational terrain they operate in today. Peter Drucker's guidance, nearly five decades ago, that effectiveness is what turns concepts, knowledge and intelligence into results still rings true today. In essence, effectiveness is what transmutes desires into actual outcomes. For Procurement functions and leaders seeking the path to long-term sustainable success, where the function's organisational capability is strengthened and it is highly regarded in the wider enterprise, there is no alternative but to enhance functional effectiveness – *do the right things* to create the outcome you desire.

Many Procurement functions continue to place overriding emphasis on the numbers, focusing on indicators such as cost savings, cost-to-procure, Procurement return on investment (ROI) and other efficiency measures. They forget that efficiency simply compares input effort or quantity to the amount of output achieved. But what if the output achieved is the wrong output? You might be highly efficient at climbing up a ladder, but what if the ladder is leaning against the wrong wall?

Procurement effectiveness, simply put, is about doing the right things to achieve the *desired* outcomes of the function. Focusing on Procurement effectiveness forces us to question what 'the right things' are. But answering that question demands that we have clarity on the outcomes we want – what does the Procurement function want to achieve really?

Judging by the plethora of articles, blog comments, case studies, roundtable discussions, expert panel opinions, etc., most purchasing people seem to agree that what Procurement wants boils down to three things fundamentally:

(1) The capability to deliver on its functional obligations
(2) The 'organisational space' to get on with delivering those obligations, and
(3) Recognition of Procurement's value-add across the wider organisation.

This book will show you how these functional desires can be fulfilled. It is not a 'Procurement book' that will teach you about purchasing – what it is and how to do it; many books and courses already exist to do that. This book focuses instead on illustrating how to find your 'Procurement mojo' by enhancing functional effectiveness. Although the term *mojo* has its roots in African voodoo, we don't all have to be of African heritage to connect with our mojo, that magic charm or special spark that embodies a combination of all the right stuff that creates lasting success. By adopting the approaches outlined in this book, you can create an effective Procurement function that delivers long-term sustainable success for your organisation and yourself as an individual.

For any doubters out there, I have one simple advice: try it and see.

I don't boast to be an 'expert' on enhancing Procurement effectiveness. But I have had many chances to create effective purchasing infrastructures in several organisations, spanning multiple industries and countries, while trying out those insights gained from my study of management effectiveness and organisational performance. This book is a culmination of those experiences, as well as countless dialogues, conferences, roundtable and expert panel discussions with professional peers who shared their own experiences.

The various exchanges I have had with purchasing professionals in many countries all over the world have been invaluable. Some of these folks were colleagues in my corporate career, personnel in client organisations, delegates at speaking events and readers who contacted me having read my articles in trade publications. I would like to use this opportunity to thank all those wonderful people who have shared their personal experiences with me and asked me so many questions, thought-provoking questions which enabled me to shape the delivery of my message and, ultimately, led me to the words I am writing now. In many places in this book, I use those experiences and 'war stories' from my own career to illustrate particular points. I have deliberately omitted or changed specific names in most cases to protect the anonymity of individuals and organisations and spare a few blushes.

The principles outlined in this book are based on first-hand experiences (which were sometimes painful!) and those innumerable discussions mentioned above. You will probably find some of what I say immediately intuitive. But even if you only learn one thing from reading this book and you are able to put it into practice successfully, thereby moving your Procurement function towards greater effectiveness, then you are already boosting your Procurement mojo.

Sigi Osagie
Enfield Town, Middlesex, England

INTRODUCTION

Many Procurement functions struggle to deliver long-term sustainable value to their organisations. This is typically down to a fundamental lack of functional effectiveness, which also hinders Procurement's standing in the enterprise. Purchasing professionals in such organisations are usually frustrated by the myriad of problems this brings in their organisational life. They sense that things can be better, and yearn for an organisational existence wherein their Procurement function can fulfil its true potential in the enterprise. This book reveals the basic steps Procurement functions can take to redress these issues and find their Procurement mojo.

Enhancing Procurement effectiveness is the only way to strengthen the function and raise its profile in the enterprise, thus providing the right organisational climate for purchasing staff to truly perform, develop and attain the fulfilment they yearn for.

This book will take you through the key principles to enhance Procurement effectiveness and illustrate practical solutions you can apply without boiling the ocean. The next chapter explains why Procurement effectiveness is the most fundamental requirement to build sustainable purchasing capability, and introduces the five-step model to achieve this. Each subsequent chapter covers one of the five individual steps in detail, uncovering the critical approaches to achieve effectiveness and how each step helps you find your Procurement mojo.

This is not a purchasing textbook to teach you what this important organisational activity is. If you know nothing about purchasing, then, perhaps, what you learn from this book will be of limited use. If you want to learn about the rudimentary elements of purchasing, you're probably better off gaining some practical experience, reading something else or attending relevant courses. This book is primarily for those who already know what purchasing is and want to learn how to unleash its true potential in the enterprise. Read it with an open mind, laying aside your conventional perspectives of what 'good purchasing' is about and how to achieve sustainable purchasing success.

If you really want to learn how to get a Procurement function to play its true role in the wider enterprise, read the whole book first; then go back and re-read the specific sections of particular relevance to your own organisational context to truly grasp any salient points you may have missed initially. If you already understand what true Procurement success is about but need to improve on a particular aspect, like managing stakeholders, for example, then delve into the relevant chapter to glean the insights that will help propel you towards your Procurement mojo.

Throughout the book I explain the principles and approaches as simply as possible, avoiding as much technical jargon as I can without detracting from the core messages; because I have learnt that simplicity greatly aids understanding.

The approaches expounded in this book may not be what you expect. They are certainly not the so-called "best-practice" purchasing approaches we are constantly inundated with – techniques like category management; spend analytics; e-procurement; lean purchasing; and so on. Many such methodologies are useful aids to develop an *efficient* purchasing capability, but without underlying *effectiveness* their value will always be limited. This book will show you how to develop that most fundamental requirement for long-term sustainable success: Procurement effectiveness.

Like all organisational activities, purchasing is carried out by people. They may be aided by technology and other enablers, but people are the fundamental creators or destroyers of organisational performance success. Understandably, many of the principles and approaches revealed in this book revolve around people, and the chapter on Building an Effective Procurement Organisation goes into greater depth than the others.

Purchasing people remain undecided on the most appropriate appellation for the function or profession – should it be "Purchasing" or "Procurement" or "Supply Management" or something else? The debate adds no value to the function's success in the enterprise. Indeed, the seeming identity crisis fans the flames of misunderstanding by those outside the profession. For these reasons,

I have adopted a simple approach in this book: throughout the book I use 'Procurement' to refer to the functional entity or department, while 'purchasing' and 'supply management' refer to the functional activity and are used interchangeably.

I hope this clarification helps you understand the concepts presented here. Gaining this understanding and putting it to use is vital for the success of your own Procurement function and the organisation it serves.

WHY 'PROCUREMENT EFFECTIVENESS'?

Effectiveness is not a requirement that is peculiar to Procurement. Rather, it is central to success in any realm of life. My own experiences are adequate evidence for me. I am sure that if many of us examine our personal experiences in successfully achieving things we truly desired in life, we will see clear evidence of the importance of taking the right actions, *doing the right things*, to get what we want. In some senses, it's quite a simple notion to grasp: if you want to move forward, you take a step forward; if you want to head off to your right, then you take a step in that direction; if you want a clean car, you wash it yourself or take it to the carwash; if you want some dangerous excitement in your marital life, you get a lover.

> **Effectiveness is central to success in any realm of life.**

I use these simplistic examples because I learnt a long time ago that knowledge doesn't have to be complex and heavy; keeping things simple always helps my own comprehension and communication with others. In reality, of course, the outcomes we want tend to be far less simplistic than turning left or driving a clean car. Nonetheless, the fundamental concept of *doing the right things* to achieve the outcomes we want remains the same, even when those outcomes are results as complex as outsourcing a key business process or building a successful Procurement function.

The challenge often comes because we get muddled in our thinking, not helped by the societal or environmental factors that confront us daily, whether in our private lives or in our organisational existence.

Economic activity and most organisational endeavours are measured by numbers – gross domestic product (GDP), unemployment, sales revenue, profit margins, ROI, cost savings, and so on. So it is understandable that most of us end up viewing our activities at work and measuring 'success' by numbers. Typically, these numbers are direct or indirect measures of efficiency – how much output we achieve for our input efforts.

But efficiency measures never tell us whether the outputs we achieve, or are pursuing, are the right ones. Efficiency just tells us how slick we are at getting the outputs. Effectiveness, on the other hand, forces us to consider what we *really* want in the first place. Focusing on effectiveness demands that we maintain a strong sense of appropriateness, even in the midst of an efficiency-biased environment. We really have no choice; because, in the long run, whether we are talking about Procurement functions or entire organisations, an entity's ability to consistently achieve its goals, and, thus, deliver long-term sustainable performance success, depends on the actions it takes. The landscape of corporate history is littered with abundant examples for us to learn from. I was part of some of that history in a small way while at Marconi, as the company fought desperately for survival in the early 2000s.

Hindsight, they say, is a great thing. I can see many things we did greatly in my six years with Marconi. For instance, internal communications to employees during the dark days of negotiating the debt-for-equity swap – the act that saved Marconi for a while – was excellent. We were kept informed of what was being done to salvage the business by regular update briefings, usually via the company's intranet which employees across the world could access. (The news wasn't great though; it was like being a passenger on the *Titanic* after it had struck the iceberg.)

I also recall several strategic moves that, perhaps, we really shouldn't have made. And you don't need a PhD in business to work out the first of those: dumping our interests in several other sectors to focus the entire business on telecoms. But let's not get into the minutiae of that episode; that's another story, one which has been well covered by the financial press. The bottom line is that we didn't take the right actions to safeguard the long-term future of the company. This sort of oversight is one that more than a few organisations are guilty of, at enterprise and functional levels.

Procurement and Organisational Success

Many Procurement functions are guilty of such oversight; they fail to take the right actions to strengthen functional capability and raise awareness of Procurement's aggregate value-add to the enterprise. When we think broadly about the role effective purchasing plays in the success of an organisation, it far exceeds the financial benefits delivered through good spend management. In today's industrial world, where third-party products and services provision is dominant, the suppliers we bring to the table in procuring goods and services for our organisations are, in effect, extensions of our organisations. If the suppliers are sub-standard, so will our organisation become eventually. If they are stellar performers, we will reap stellar benefits too.

In the same way, when Procurement sources supplies from distant regions, perhaps for cost benefit reasons, we inherently create greater risks in our extended supply chains – risks which inevitably affect the organisational capability of the wider enterprise. We could go on to list several other examples of Procurement's direct and indirect influence on the capability and success of organisations. How strong these influences are depends on the positioning of the Procurement function. Even if we do choose to focus purely and myopically on the impact of Procurement through spend management, the potential return on investment an organisation gets is obvious. It is a result that directly affects the bottom line, irrespective of the squabbles Procurement often gets into with budget-holders and Finance.

A key challenge for Procurement functions is always balancing the myriad of conventional factors that affect 'success' – purchase price, cost savings, non-financial benefits, supply reliability, supply risks and organisational perceptions. But there are other factors to be considered, especially when we talk about *long-term sustainable success*. Issues like alignment to the corporate agenda, development of human capital and avoiding those internal squabbles, for instance, immediately spring to mind. These are the sorts of issues which impact long-term success but may not always hinder short-term performance results if ignored.

For some Procurement functions success comes in stages. They excel in one or two dimensions initially, then consolidate and expand to tackle other areas, gradually building up the functional capability. We frequently hear of many examples of success, usually in particular aspects of supply management. The nominees and winners of the annual CIPS Supply Management Awards are good examples, as are those nominated across the pond for the Institute of Supply Management's annual ISM Awards for Excellence in Supply Management. Some are really inspiring chronicles of Procurement people finding their mojo, creating functional organisations that delight their stakeholders while keeping other enterprise benefits flowing. One residential services business successfully revamped its purchasing operations under the leadership of a new Procurement head who was hand-picked for the task. Procurement was transformed into an integrated function with improved focus and people capability, an endeavour that yielded significant financial gains and greater credibility with stakeholders right up to the CEO.

Other success stories exemplify how the pursuit of effectiveness in Procurement can result in game-changer strategies that turn the conventional view of purchasing on its head. There is probably no better public example in corporate history than Gene Richter's achievements with Procurement at IBM in the 1990s, an effort that contributed in no small way to IBM's turnaround.

Richter was brought in as Chief Procurement Officer at a time when Big Blue's standing in supply markets left a lot to be desired. The situation inside the business was not much better, with purchasing activities fragmented across multiple business units. Yet Richter recognised the actions required to deliver the necessary improvements to support the business turnaround. He re-engineered Procurement and instilled an organisational ethos that boosted stakeholder satisfaction ratings by over 100%, while delivering billions of dollars in purchasing spend value improvements. The enhanced purchasing capability helped secure IBM's position in the marketplace. The company subsequently extended the reach of its Procurement function by providing outsourced purchasing services to external clients. Today IBM is one of the premier global providers in that sector and has frequently been listed in industry rankings of top performers.

Procurement success stories are not limited to developed economies. Even in the developing world, where functional capability tends to be below Western standards, purchasing people in companies like Absa and Sappi have shown how effective approaches to supply management can yield significant benefits to the wider organisation through enhanced supply base alignment. Both companies were winners of the CIPS Pan-African Procurement Awards in 2011 along with several others. It is worth pointing out that in both cases the strategic benefits derived were more important than any related financial gains.

Of course, there are also many Procurement success stories which go unpublicised. In some cases, one- or two-man Procurement functions are delivering real value to their small business employers, making a tangible contribution to organisational success that is easily visible. But all these success stories belie a concrete truth: that most Procurement functions today are still fighting for higher recognition in their organisations, and the capability to showcase the function's true value-add – they are still searching for their Procurement mojo.

Many widely-available trade publications and surveys provide insights on the perceptions of Procurement among business leaders. One survey reported that almost forty percent of finance directors view Procurement's influence as detrimental or, at best, neutral. Other reports suggest that people outside the function often feel that dealing with Procurement is exasperating. Such perceptions constitute a damning indictment to us in the purchasing profession.

Things may have changed in the last decade or so, but progress has not been as marked as most of us would like. Still far too few people really understand and appreciate the value of effective purchasing in many organisations. Despite being the function with the most financial impact on enterprise profitability, Procurement is still not perceived as a strategic lever or an enabling function in most organisations. Its reputation is the ball and chain that slows progress. That reputation still centres on a narrow perception of Procurement as a function that exists solely for cost savings, supporting bids, drafting contracts, raising purchase orders, chasing suppliers and general policy enforcement.

We don't really need others to make assertions for us to learn. We all acquire knowledge in different ways to form our own opinions. Thus, as you read this, think about your own Procurement function and its standing in your organisation. Think too about the Procurement functions in the last two or three organisations you have worked in. And think about insights you have gleaned about other Procurement functions from your professional peers and acquaintances. Is Procurement really as effective as it could and should be in the majority of cases?

Several practitioners and commentators have identified various reasons for the suboptimal perceptions of Procurement that exist in many organisations. The list includes: Procurement functional activities are typically not aligned to business priorities or direction; business leaders do not truly understand the power of effective purchasing in building competitive advantage; business leaders are focused on other organisational priorities; Procurement leaders and practitioners lack the requisite skills, experience and motivation to sell the function's value proposition; an identity crisis in the broader supply chain management profession blurs functional distinctions and creates misunderstanding for stakeholders; ... I am sure we could find one or two other things to add to the list. But before we do, we should hark back to the earlier question about turning up to a gunfight with a knife. The moral of the question – that the onus is always on us to be appropriately prepared – applies perfectly to the predicament many Procurement functions face in their organisations. The onus is on Procurement people to take the actions necessary to get the outcomes they want.

I made an assertion earlier that effectiveness – doing the right things, or taking the right actions, to get one's desired outcome – is not a requirement which is peculiar to Procurement. In fact, effectiveness is a critical requirement not just for other functions but also the wider enterprise as a whole. In capitalist society, where we mostly worship at the altar of money (whether we like to admit it or not), controlling the flow of funds through an enterprise is important. And, when it comes down to it, only two funds really matter: the money flowing into the enterprise and the money flowing out. For most organisations, the single largest or second largest area of expenditure is third-party spend. As custodians of that spend, Procurement is undoubtedly a critical function, even for non-profit organisations. Thus, the requirement for effectiveness is even more vital for Procurement functions. If third-party spend is not managed effectively to extract optimal value, the long-term impacts on the financial health of the organisation can be dire. This is in addition to the risks posed by a suboptimal supply base that can result from ineffective supply management.

Procurement's importance to any organisation is profound when properly understood. Many of the companies that have demonstrated long-term success and retained top positions in popular rankings of corporate performance recognise the power of effective purchasing. Harnessing Procurement's true value proposition is something they have come to master, though the trap of complacency will always be close-by. Companies like Vodafone, Cisco Systems, Coca-Cola Enterprises, Apple, Samsung and several others, many of whom quietly get on with their business and shun the limelight, have reaped the benefits of economies of learning from their repeated efforts to leverage Procurement's true value-add. Organisations like these appreciate much more the direct impact Procurement has on the bottom line, though such impacts may not always be easily visible or quantifiable in some businesses. Sadly, many organisations – the laggards – do not even display a rudimentary understanding of this impact as yet.

People with enough commercial nous and business experience know that it is far easier to boost a company's profitability through effective purchasing than it is through sales growth. (Of course, the level of organisational and market maturity are always added factors.) While this is an important element of Procurement's default contribution, it also constitutes a double-edged sword; hanging the function's value proposition entirely on its financial impacts risks exacerbating the myopic view of Procurement as a 'cost savings' function. We must think beyond the numbers – issues like supply risks, supply base alignment and corporate social responsibility (CSR) can rarely be adequately encapsulated by numbers alone. These are all issues in which Procurement has a lead responsibility.

The Need for 'More and Better'

Procurement's influence on the success of the wider enterprise can not be overemphasised. Many business leaders nod sagely when this issue is discussed. But, judging by the status of Procurement in most organisations, only a minority have grasped the nettle. Yet there appears to be a general acceptance of the notion that organisations should devote effort and resources to securing top-notch purchasing and supply chain management know-how. A number of studies, covering organisations of various sizes in different industry sectors, have explored the fit between Procurement's role and the strategic development and financial or operating performance of the wider business. The overriding consensus that misalignment between Procurement's ethos and the enterprise strategic agenda creates economic and non-economic detriment is unsurprising. Those who understand Procurement's true value-add already know this. But it certainly helps when our instinctive knowledge or professional judgement (or, common sense, as some would view it) is backed up by empirical evidence.

We have ample proof that when purchasing is done effectively it becomes a vital component of sustained competitive advantage. In times gone by it was easy, and appropriate in some situations, to focus organisational and leadership attention on enhancing profitability solely through sales growth. But in today's world, where the jet engine, the internet and falling telecommunications costs have combined to create a global village, things are radically different. For instance, the continued push for better shareholder returns and higher business efficiencies, combined with competitive pressures arising from a more globalised economy, has created an outsourcing industry that has mushroomed beyond anyone's imagination. Today the global outsourcing market is estimated to be worth over US$600bn; it has increased a whopping five-fold in a decade, and a significant proportion of that market is offshore outsourcing.

Onshore and offshore outsourcing are great examples of the new world factors organisations of all sorts face today in all three sectors – public, private and charity. We are also confronted by other social, economic and geopolitical factors constantly; such as civil unrest and consequent political instability in the Middle East driving up the price of oil, or natural disasters in far-flung places wreaking havoc on our ability to ship products to customers. For purchasing people, the aggregate impacts of these factors tend to come down to increased complexity, hence risks, in our supply pipelines. The Japanese earthquake of March 2011 is a recent example, one I am sure many buyers of Japanese-supplied stock won't forget in a hurry. The devastation caused chaos for industrial companies of all sorts, from manufacturers of technology products to car producers. A natural disaster some six thousand miles from its Paris headquarters brought some of PSA Peugeot Citroën's manufacturing to a stop – talk about global village!

It is not just buyers in PSA Peugeot Citroën that might have suffered a few heart palpitations from supply challenges in recent times. Globalisation and other new world factors have created headaches (and opportunities) for many business leaders. Competitive forces in modern times have certainly made it more difficult to expand profitability simply via the old sales growth route. Consequently, boardroom discussions on enterprise financial performance are increasingly turning to different avenues, not least, better cost control and management of third-party spend. The implications for Procurement are obvious – a growing expectation, though sometimes fuzzy, to make a greater contribution to the financial wellbeing of the wider organisation.

The desire for enhanced Procurement contribution is not restricted to the boardrooms of businesses in the developed world. A growing clamour is also emanating from the developing world where Procurement effectiveness, especially in the public sector, has particular implications for social and economic development. Effective purchasing plays a vital role in socio-economic development; it contributes to trade liberalisation and growth of local enterprise through lower cost of delivering public services. Yet few third-world economies are reaping this benefit in totality.

Of course, third-world countries in Africa, Latin America and elsewhere have very unique problems which are widely publicised.

Corruption probably tops the list. A joint OECD-World Bank roundtable in 2003 highlighted an estimated 20% leakage in government budgets in some developing countries due to corruption and fraudulent purchasing practices. In Africa alone, corruption, including fraudulent purchasing, is estimated to cost the continent as much as a quarter of its GDP and artificially raise cost of goods by up to a fifth. And as recently as a couple of years ago, one African finance minister publicly lamented that purchasing activities remained a major source of leakage in national government programmes. But perhaps more poignant for purchasing professionals in the region, he also decried the fact that government structures do not recognise purchasing as a profession, a key failing that needs rectification.

When we amalgamate the varied pixels forming the image portrayed of Procurement from different quarters, the message seems clear: purchasing people must become change agents to champion enhanced Procurement effectiveness. We must strengthen the function; re-define our functional value proposition to illustrate the true benefits we bring to organisations; and we must sell that proposition by delivering relevant results, delighting our stakeholders and building greater organisational awareness – we must find our Procurement mojo.

The recent global recession and the current state of business and national economies offer a great opportunity for Procurement functions to find their mojo. The economic challenges of recent times have galvanised those boardroom discussions, turning mere exchanges into corporate mandates. It is a shame that Procurement still has no de facto seat in the boardroom, enabling more direct influence over those discussions and how the ensuing mandates are executed. In many ways, the absence of a Procurement seat at the top table indicates the stature of the function in most organisations.

Of course, in some organisations with leading purchasing practices the Procurement function already plays a key role in shaping and implementing corporate strategies. Benchmarking surveys and trade publications frequently reveal some organisational traits and approaches adopted by such Procurement pioneers. In particular, many recent studies illustrate how supply management in such organisations has changed, augmenting enterprise strategies to adapt to new world factors. In such businesses Procurement has been elevated up the corporate ranks. Some studies indicate that over fifty percent of Procurement functions in such leading organisations now report to a C-level board executive. The picture is even better in a relatively small proportion of organisations where the most senior Procurement executive sits on the executive board – at the time of writing, Siemens AG and Anheuser-Busch InBev are two examples of this tiny minority.

Undoubtedly, boardroom representation is one of the strongest indicators of any function's esteem in an organisation. Procurement *has* come a long way from the days when a move into the department was, in effect, a relegation to the backwoods of organisational existence. But even as recently as the early 1990s, Procurement was still seen as a back-office function immersed in traditional tactical purchasing activities. The more strategic supply management approaches adopted by organisations with leading purchasing practices have helped bolster Procurement's image and get the function closer to the top table. This is a welcome development, not just for mature purchasing practitioners (especially those who for years have felt like their job is akin to banging their head against a wall 8 hours a day, 5 days a week), but also for the development of the profession as a whole.

Purchasing is not yet widely perceived as a premier league profession; certainly not when compared to, say, marketing, law, investment banking or entrepreneurship. But continued efforts by leading companies to exploit the power of effective purchasing have given Procurement a more important role in the corporate theatre. The recent economic slump has been an added boost as organisations of all sorts have sought to protect profit margins. Suddenly the spotlight is on Procurement and it is shining brightly. Will our performance truly delight the audience?

It won't be a case of 'time will tell'. Rather, only those Procurement functions who find their mojo by enhancing effectiveness will indeed delight their stakeholders.

The increased popularity of Procurement in many quarters is a good stimulus to attract new talent and help develop the profession further. They say nothing succeeds like success. The more opportunities the Procurement function has to succeed, and the bigger its successes, the more bright, young talents it will attract. This is an often overlooked fact in the debates on growing Procurement talent. We must remember that in the talent war for new career entrants Procurement is competing with functions like Human Resources (HR), Finance and Marketing. These are functions that are, arguably, significantly more established and more highly regarded in many organisations. Other functional areas that are relatively new to the corporate landscape, such as Corporate Communications, are also competitors in the talent war, especially as they are often perceived to be more 'sexy'.

Making purchasing an appealing career path is part of enhancing functional effectiveness and sustaining the collective Procurement mojo. No matter how good the bench-strength and competency of your Procurement function is today, it is inevitable that at some point some of your best people will leave. Hence, it is vital to nurture a pipeline of emerging talent, just like many top-flight soccer clubs do through their youth academies. And just as any gifted young soccer player has a choice of youth academies to join, so too does any talented young professional, undergraduate or school-leaver have a choice of professional paths to embark on.

Some purchasing people might disagree with my assessment of the function's standing in most organisations today. My own Procurement team at one erstwhile employer didn't quite get my drift initially. So I encouraged them to do a simple test: to stand at our Reception or one of the elevators with a clipboard and carry out a random survey of at least twenty-five passersby, at any time on any day of the week, asking each person the following questions:

(1) Do you know where the HR department is at this company? What do they do there; what are they responsible for?
(2) Ask the same questions, but for Finance
(3) And for Marketing
(4) Then, ask the same questions for Procurement.

Rightly or wrongly, perception can sometimes be more important than reality, especially in large organisations. Trying to argue Procurement's case in a mire of organisational misconceptions is like complaining about your opponent who turned up to the gunfight with his pistol while you turned up with that knife. Raising the profile of our newly-created Procurement function at that former employer was one of our key priorities. We never did do the survey – we didn't need to; I was eventually able to get the team to understand the importance of our profile, and they 'got it'. But perhaps a similar benchmark survey, as illustrated in figure 1.1, might be an interesting experiment in your own organisation.

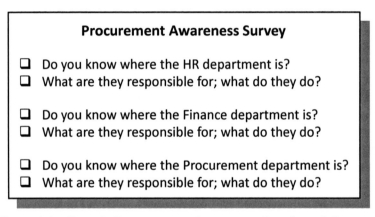

Figure 1.1 – Sample Procurement Awareness Benchmark Survey

What do you think the results would be? Will people know as much about Procurement as they should, considering its importance? Will they know as much about Procurement as they do about the other functions? And will they have a robust awareness of what purchasing is really about?

If you are really interested in enhancing your Procurement effectiveness, I would suggest sitting down with a pen and paper and noting down *your* opinions on the likely answers to these questions. What do your own opinions reveal about the effectiveness of your Procurement function?

It could be even more interesting to have a few detailed discussions with your most important consumers or internal customers – the budget-holders, whose third-party spend Procurement is accountable for managing for value. What do they *really* perceive Procurement's role to be? What benefits, or value-add, do they feel they get from Procurement? Do they feel their needs are well met? Do they feel they have a functional 'business partner' who adds something valuable to their attainment of *their own* business objectives? How do they feel overall about Procurement's service to them – disappointed, indifferent, satisfied or delighted?

Irrespective of what you or your Procurement team members think, it may be instructive to carry out this survey anyway. It could prove to be a conduit to critical insights on finding and boosting your Procurement mojo.

Countering suboptimal perceptions of Procurement is integral to enhancing the effectiveness of the function. It is a vital element of how we find the Procurement mojo, through raising awareness of the function's true value proposition. This may be less of a requirement for organisations with high calibre Procurement functions, where the value of effective supply management is fully appreciated. But such organisations are the minority. And, typically, they tend to be large multinational corporations. Yet most of us work in small and medium-sized enterprises (SMEs). Even with the added significance Procurement has garnered due to the global recession, in majority of organisations the search for the Procurement mojo remains unfulfilled.

Procurement Effectiveness is Foundational to Sustainable Success

When we start focusing on Procurement effectiveness things start to fall into place. I mentioned earlier that too many Procurement functions give overriding focus to the numbers, an understandable trait given that we operate in a numbers-driven commercial world. Even in organisations with leading purchasing practices, Procurement success still typically imbibes the amount of savings delivered. When we focus too much on the numbers we fail to leverage the power of our collective imagination and converged effort when channelled towards building sustainable capability. Think about the power of Bill Gates's vision of a PC on every desk way back in the early 1980s, and how that vision (not merely the projected sales revenue!) propelled Microsoft to a position of dominance and long-term success in its sector. Or think about the Apple team that developed the iPhone and brought it to market, a product that revolutionised the mobile phone industry; do you think they were inspired by the number of handset sales predicted or the vision of their game-changer product?

Some Procurement functions get hung up on other things – processes; tools; contracts; strategy; how much spend they have under control; the department's name; and so on. The name of the profession or the department, the functional strategy, the organisational structure, the enablers (processes, systems and tools), the cost savings we deliver... are all important to varying extents. And they require corresponding levels of our attention, along with other aspects of 'the purchasing job'. Most of these issues come with the territory, so to speak. But we must recognise that they are all subsets of the Procurement mojo – that special spark, an amalgamation of these and other subsets that creates long-term sustainable success when pursued coherently.

All told, recent evidence does indicate that more and more organisations are starting to recognise the importance of effective purchasing and its potential strategic value. But only a small proportion is able to leverage that value. No doubt, the global recession forced many organisations to accelerate the pace at which they build a comprehensive understanding of how they can gain that leverage. It is a fantastic opportunity for Procurement – Procurement functions can find their mojo at the very time others want us to; we can exploit the focus Procurement is getting under the spotlight in these times. But to do that Procurement people must imbibe a different ethos to our own perspectives on our functional role and how we go about gaining success in that role.

For starters, we must put aside our conventional beliefs of what is important in the purchasing job. We can begin by learning from our own organisational existence as a function. The issues that prevent most Procurement functions from achieving long-term sustainable success are not the technical issues we traditionally focus on. Rather, they tend to be the 'soft' issues, the very issues most of us give inadequate time and attention to. For instance, the critical challenges I mentioned earlier – functional leadership skills, staff competency and stakeholder relationships – are significantly more vital to success than factors like sourcing strategies, purchase-to-pay (P2P) processes or e-auction platforms. The overriding consensus from relevant studies demonstrates that Procurement capability and success relates directly to the calibre of leadership and people capability in the function. My experience with various organisations and discussions with peers support this. These 'human factors', more than anything else, are the underlying attributes that drive performance.

> **The issues that prevent most Procurement functions from achieving sustainable success tend to be the 'soft' issues, not the technical issues we traditionally focus on.**

Of course, 'performance' is multi-faceted. So delivering sustainable performance success requires a holistic approach, one that imbibes these critical human factors or soft issues as well as other more technical aspects like Procurement systems and tools. The key to this holistic approach is the overarching goal of enhancing Procurement effectiveness – giving prime focus to doing the right things to achieve the performance success we want. The conventional efficiency measures we focus on as indicators of performance are always reflections of the past; we have already made the input effort and witnessed the output. Focusing on effectiveness, instead, forces us to question the actions we are taking in the present, today, and how they relate to the end-goals we are pursuing.

Efficiency is the well oiled machine that enables us to achieve more output with less input, the slickness that gives us a bigger bang for our buck. Being efficient *is* important for success. But it is only half the story; the second half at that. The first half, the more important bit, is to be effective.

As indicated in figure 1.2, efficiency without effectiveness leads to failure, it's just a question of how fast or slowly failure comes.

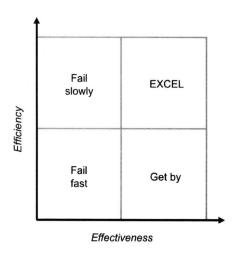

Effectiveness

Figure 1.2 – Effectiveness and Efficiency

One of the biggest challenges we sometimes face is that effectiveness is often difficult to measure. Here again, I find the approach of simplicity invaluable. To assess Procurement effectiveness you can simply question if what your Procurement function is focusing on – the key actions and initiatives you are expending effort and investment on – will deliver the outcomes you want. If developing sexy sourcing strategies, implementing a best-practice P2P process or delivering bucket-loads of savings do not yield improved functional capability or heightened recognition of Procurement's value-add in the enterprise, then you must go back to the drawing board.

Countless research studies and industry surveys have been carried out which illustrate the vital link between effectiveness and achieving performance results consistently. Time and time again we hear many eminent people and prominent business leaders concur on this. As Abraham Lincoln is said to have put it, "Things may come to those who wait, but only the things left by those who hustle."

Waiting for your Procurement mojo to materialise without doing the right things to manifest it is like waiting for a ship at the airport. Success in personal and organisational life is always preceded by the hustle for that success. My own research on management effectiveness and organisational performance, coupled with my career experiences, were enough to turn me into a convert; perhaps, because I, myself, had suffered the consequences of demotivation and failure to achieve my objectives due to my ineffectiveness early in my career.

Years later, when I started coaching and mentoring supply management teams to boost functional effectiveness at various organisations, it wasn't just to achieve the tangible goals I had been tasked with. It was also to grow the individuals. When we focus on Procurement effectiveness, and, thereby, recognise the critical importance of those soft issues like people capability, it brings clarity to the connection between fulfilling organisational goals and the growth and aspirations of the individuals in the organisation. Procurement effectiveness allows us to fulfil the hungry spirit we all have, the innate desire to be part of something worthwhile, to gain more from our work than the salary we are paid each month. It draws our attention to the added benefits to individuals in the Procurement function, the people who actually do the purchasing work.

You reading this now may be one of those individuals. Finding your Procurement mojo in the work you do is an element of sustaining the effectiveness of your Procurement function. At an individual level, remember that your Procurement mojo won't come looking for you unless you go looking for it. So think about your own effectiveness in carrying out the responsibilities of your role, and how that augments the effectiveness of your team, or not. You might need to alter your personal perspectives, thinking patterns and behavioural attitudes in several areas. You might, for instance, need to enhance your insights on and appreciation of 'stakeholders', starting to view them instead as 'customers', 'consumers' or 'investors'. Such attitudinal changes help enhance effectiveness at a personal level, which feeds functional effectiveness.

The pursuit of Procurement effectiveness forces and enables us to create a functional context in which people can flourish and grow, providing benefits that far exceed the obvious and direct financial returns to the wider enterprise. Achieving those benefits is never a done deal though. The changing nature of business and the societies we live in today means that Procurement functions can never become effective and then rest on their laurels. Organisations restructure, recessions come and go, new political and societal issues arise constantly – it is the nature of our existence today. Few businesses worried about corporate social responsibility twenty years ago, yet it is a key topic in many company annual reports today. Few Procurement functions worried about child labour or slave wages in their extended supply pipelines in times gone-by, yet these are now important issues for many of us due to the impact on corporate image, aside from our personal ethics. One of the organisations I mentioned earlier as a Procurement success story broke up its centralised purchasing some years later, negating some of the long-term benefits of the prior Procurement transformation. These are all examples of the dynamic nature of our new world, a dynamism we must contend with continually. Keeping our focus on Procurement effectiveness enables us to do this.

In some of my talks on supply management, leadership or organisations, I often share the tale of Vincent to simplify the meaning of effectiveness. In the days soon after the national lottery was first launched in the UK, Vincent had gone through a life-planning exercise in which he decided that what he wanted in life was to enjoy a millionaire lifestyle, with all the trappings that would bring. Having clarified his life goal, he decided that his route-path to achieve it would be to win the lottery. So, come Saturday evening, shortly before the lottery draw programme aired on TV, Vincent was up in his bedroom, on his knees, saying a prayer, "Please God, please God, let me win the lottery." The lottery draw TV programme came on, the presenters read out the winning lottery numbers and Vincent didn't win. The following Saturday he was up in his bedroom again, on his knees repeating his prayer, "Please God, please God, let me win the lottery. I promise to take my wife shopping, to be nicer to my kids, to give some of the money to charity..." The lottery draw programme came on TV shortly after, the winning numbers were read out, and, yet again, Vincent didn't win the lottery. But Vincent had one of the important traits we all need for success – persistence. So come the next Saturday, there he was again on his knees in his bedroom, "Please God, please God, let me..." Before he got any further in his prayer he suddenly heard a great, booming voice coming from nowhere and everywhere, "Come on man, will you stop hassling me; at least meet me halfway and buy a ticket!"

> **Procurement effectiveness is about taking the right actions to achieve the outcomes we want. You can't win the lottery without buying a lottery ticket!**

Just as you can't win the lottery without buying a ticket, so too can you not achieve sustainable success without *doing the right things* to bring about that success.

Procurement functions that are serious about 'winning their lottery', achieving the functional outcomes they thirst for – where the function is strengthened and has high regard in the wider organisation – must take the right actions to bring about those outcomes; they must find their Procurement mojo.

Enhancing Procurement Effectiveness

The search for the Procurement mojo, how we enhance Procurement effectiveness, forces us to think critically about those aforementioned outcomes. You must start by recalibrating your deeply held conventional beliefs of what performance success means to Procurement. The 'key performance indicators' (KPIs) we commonly adopt are exactly what the phrase infers: they reflect what we view as the key dimensions of Procurement performance and the measures we use to establish how well we are doing. As shocking as it sounds, some Procurement functions do not even measure their performance. And for those that do, the principal KPIs typically concern financial benefits and regulation or governance. The most common examples include cost savings or purchase price variance; Procurement ROI;

spend under management; and supplier performance. But where are the measures that indicate how well we are doing with building the skills and competency of our people, the same people who do the work? What about the measures that tell us whether or not we are succeeding in serving our internal customers robustly, delighting them in a way that feeds a positive perception of Procurement and its value-add? And which measures tell us whether or not Procurement is appropriately aligned to the corporate strategic agenda?

Many years ago I was appointed to lead a regional Procurement function at a global FTSE 250 business. The instruction from my boss, the regional Procurement VP, was to "...sort the place out." I went in and found a department suffering a complex malady of everything that could be wrong with any organisational unit – inconsistent job titles; an acute lack of focus and direction; poorly defined responsibilities; broken processes; poor team spirit; everyone running around like the proverbial headless chickens, yet operational performance was significantly below par... It was as dysfunctional as it could get, and it was clear to me that the department needed a complete turnaround. In defining some clear goals and related KPIs for the group, I found myself in a debate with my VP on the importance of measuring 'Organisational Health', using 'Staff Attrition' and 'Sickness Absence' as appropriate KPIs. He eventually agreed with me.

If you are going to revamp the culture and entrenched ways of working in a team of almost fifteen mature professionals, it goes without saying that the personnel will have to cope with a significant amount of unsettling change. Some may struggle to cope; and it may be more effective to encourage others to seek their destinies elsewhere. Whatever the case, the stress of the change will impact the health of the organisation, hence its capability and performance, just as stress impacts us as individuals and, thus, our work performance.

Recognising the vital importance of the human capital element of Procurement capability, and imbibing that recognition to our definition of performance success, is not just critical for Procurement functions going through change; it is a prerequisite for all Procurement functions. It is part of the recalibration we must go through as we search for our mojo to enhance Procurement effectiveness.

We must redefine Procurement's value proposition, starting by extending beyond cost savings and other traditional notions. If we examine Procurement functions that are effective and continue to achieve long-term success, we can amass a different set of pixels which give a more progressive picture of Procurement's true role in organisations today: to harness the power of supply markets for enterprise success and competitive advantage, in a safe, ethical and cost-efficient manner.

Enhancing Procurement effectiveness affords all Procurement functions a roadmap for achieving our true functional obligations. It enables Procurement to go about selling and delivering the value it brings to the wider enterprise with greater success. As the model in figure 1.3 illustrates, enhancing Procurement effectiveness requires focused actions in 5 key areas:

(1) Building an effective Procurement organisation
(2) Deploying enablers – processes, systems and tools – that are fit for purpose
(3) Managing the supply base robustly
(4) Applying an appropriate framework for managing performance
(5) Building the Procurement brand through positioning, stake-holder management and effective public relations (PR).

These are the five critical steps Procurement functions must take to find their mojo, building effectiveness through strengthening the function and raising awareness of its value proposition in the wider organisation.

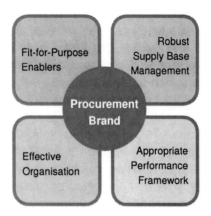

Figure 1.3 – Enhancing Procurement Effectiveness

Each of these actions entails varied challenges for different Procurement functions, depending on the current state of functional effectiveness and maturity, and the prevailing perceptions of Procurement in the wider enterprise. Some of these actions require new ways of thinking and executing for most Procurement functions. In the next few chapters we examine what each of these actions means – how each aspect fits into a coherent, holistic approach to enhancing and sustaining Procurement effectiveness, and what Procurement functions have to do in executing these actions.

Some areas require more detailed exploration as they are elements of Procurement effectiveness we traditionally give less attention than we should. Others may be easier to grasp for many purchasing people; so, as much as possible, I will avoid trying to 'teach granny to suck eggs' in those areas.

Whatever the case, having explored each of these five steps in detail, you will end with a robust insight to the Procurement mojo and how to enhance Procurement effectiveness to enable long-term sustainable success.

STEP 1: BUILD AN EFFECTIVE PROCUREMENT ORGANISATION

Organisational effectiveness is the most critical requirement for long-term sustainable success, whether we are talking about Procurement, other functional areas or the wider enterprise as a whole. It is impossible to overemphasise this point. Procurement functions, like all organisations, are about people. It is people who do the work and deliver results, not computers, strategies or processes. Those things are simply tools or enablers we employ to achieve our objectives or to get the work done efficiently.

I often try to get this critical point across to clients by explaining that if you take the strategies, processes, computers and so on out of any business but leave the people in, the business will still find a way to function; after all, businesses and non-profit organisations existed before the invention of computers, PowerPoint and whatnot. But do the reverse – take the people out and leave the computers, strategies, etc., behind – and the enterprise will come to a stop.

Of course, those enablers are also important for success. But their role is secondary to that of 'people'. Creating an effective purchasing capability requires a cohesive alignment of these and other elements, starting with organisational effectiveness in the Procurement function.

By combining the requisite core components of organisational effectiveness we are able to build a bridge to long-term sustainable success. The key is in knowing what those core components are, how they fit together and how they relate to our conventional purchasing activities.

Many of us may not know what an effective Procurement organisation looks like. But some of us will know what it *feels* like to work in one – we feel our spirits come alive, we feel a part of something meaningful, and work becomes much more than the daily eight-hour grind. Sadly, for most of us, we are more likely to recognise a Procurement organisation that is ineffective – the telltale signs are usually difficult to hide, and typically include some of the following:

- Too many people involved in every decision
- Unclear or changing priorities – Procurement reacts to the latest driver from the upper echelons
- People are not really sure what they should be doing, or they think they should be doing what someone else is doing
- Processes are fragmented, ill-defined and inefficient, with many non-value-adding activities, and working practices are disjointed
- Objectives and targets are routinely missed, if there are any clear objectives to start with
- Functional bench-strength is low, with managers who are technically savvy but lack leadership effectiveness
- There are repeated incidences of duplication of work or 'reinventing the wheel'
- Most people are able to point out problems easily, but few highlight solutions as easily
- People are not given clear direction or held accountable for their performance and behaviours
- Individuals are 'treading water' in their jobs – they are bored or, certainly, not stretched, with no effervescence in the team
- Procurement initiatives are not synchronised, and typically not aligned to key activities outside the department
- Procurement is a collection of individuals rather than a team
- People outside Procurement think purchasing is solely about purchase orders; contracts; tactical supplier liaisons; and other rudimentary functional activities.

Do any of these indicators ring true to you? Are they reflective traits of your Procurement function? How does it make *you* feel coming to work each day and spending forty hours-a-week or more in this organisational climate?

If you are a Procurement leader in charge of the whole function or a team within the function, think about how each of the individuals in your team feels if you, yourself, recognise these traits in your organisation.

Whether or not you lead a Procurement team, we all have an obligation to support our Procurement function in finding its mojo. You must do your part to address such organisational ineffectiveness because it drains value, the very thing Procurement should be delivering to the wider enterprise.

I deliberately posed the earlier probe to Procurement leaders because they have a critical role to play, not least as the bridge between senior management and the Procurement function. Understandably, some Procurement functions are ineffective because they suffer a shared ailment that plagues the whole enterprise. For instance, we have seen many organisations choose to focus on other 'priorities' or approaches rather than address their underlying organisational ineffectiveness – the list includes Operational Excellence; Total Quality Management (TQM); Lean; Value-Based Management; Six Sigma and so on. Many organisations continue to fall into the delusion that there really is a magic bullet, some sort of panacea, that will address all their challenges. They latch onto these fads expecting a fantastic boost to enterprise-wide competence, including enhancements to purchasing capability.

Procurement functions in such organisational situations inevitably get caught up in the collective and often slavish adoption of such approaches. Even when not subject to such organisational factors, many Procurement functions inappropriately focus on similar fashionable concepts or methodologies as the perceived route to success – e-procurement, strategic sourcing, spend analytics, Supplier Relationship Management (SRM) and category management are just a few examples.

Our overriding focus on such techniques and instruments are often misguided, whether at functional or enterprise level. In an article for one trade magazine, I mentioned the example of the 'Excellence' movement that followed the publication of Peters and Waterman's *In Search of Excellence*. Published in the early 1980s, it became an international bestseller and remains one of the most widely read business books. It is one of my favourites too, a book that provides many nuggets of wisdom on various dimensions of organisational success. Soon after its publication a plethora of organisations jumped on the 'Excellence' bandwagon. Poignantly, some of Peters and

Waterman's 'excellent companies' didn't stay excellent for long. IBM, for example, nearly went into extinction and was only really put back on the corporate map years later by Louis V. Gerstner, Jr. And a couple of others subsequently went into decline.

I suspect that many companies that sought 'excellence' without building underlying organisational effectiveness soon discovered that you can't draw water with a sieve. They missed the essence of the message.

> **Those that seek "procurement excellence" without building underlying organisational effectiveness will discover that you can't draw water with a sieve.**

Organisations that 'get it', those that stay attuned to the message, understand that, in reality, Operational Excellence, TQM, Lean, strategic sourcing, category management, etc., are simply tools. You or I can pick up any kitchen tool or utensil – potato masher, egg whisk, serving spoon, chopping board, etc. – but using the tool does not necessarily guarantee that our cooking will come out like Gordon Ramsay's or Nigella Lawson's. In the same way, any Procurement function can implement strategic sourcing, e-auctions, category management and so on, but that doesn't mean they will become consistent high performers over the long term. The potato masher and chopping board are required to create the meal. But the key cooking factor in the kitchen is the chef's culinary skill, an intangible blend of abilities, style and taste. In the same way, we may require enablers like category management and spend analyses to deliver purchasing value. But the key factor in achieving long-term sustainable success is organisational effectiveness – the aggregate effectiveness of the people in the Procurement organisation. It is what separates winners from losers; it is what separates those Procurement functions that remain leaders over the long term from those that are simply mediocre or laggards, or those that deliver flash-in-the-pan performance every so often.

Effective Procurement organisations consistently achieve their goals and deliver sustainable long-term performance success. It is worth remembering that 'performance' and 'success' are multifaceted. A Procurement function can be successful in some specific performance areas but not in others. Hence, to achieve success that encompasses the multiple facets of performance, we must be cognizant of Procurement's varied and often conflicting obligations – to internal and external customers; shareholders; Procurement employees; suppliers; and the wider community in which we do business. Do you recognise each of these groups as having a valid stake in what your Procurement function does? How do your functional priorities reflect your obligations across these different stakeholder groups? What are you trying to achieve for each of these distinct groups of stakeholders, if anything:

- Delighting your internal customers? Supporting internal customers to deliver value to the external customer? And what level of performance constitutes 'success' *from the customers' perspective*?
- Improving the efficiency or productivity of your Procurement operations, hence enabling the enterprise to provide healthy, sustainable returns to shareholders?
- Attracting, retaining and developing top Procurement talent?
- Managing the supply base robustly, hence ensuring alignment to the enterprise strategic agenda and minimising business risks? Growing your brand equity in supply markets?
- Making a positive contribution to the community?

> **Effective Procurement organisations consistently achieve their goals and deliver sustainable long-term performance success.**

When we talk about delivering sustainable long-term performance success, these are questions all Procurement functions must take into consideration in setting their direction. I am not suggesting that all Procurement functions embrace all of these performance considerations. Rather you should think about Procurement's true role in the enterprise, and the related obligations that accompany that responsibility. When you reflect on this deeply it becomes evident that Procurement 'performance success' is much more than the conventionally held notions of how much cost savings is delivered or how slick your purchase-to-pay process is. This added awareness is valuable, as it enables you to create cohesion as you build your effective Procurement organisation.

Figure 2.1 – The Effective Organisation

As shown in figure 2.1, effective organisations have some specific traits that are always easily visible, if you look closely enough; traits that nurture capability to deliver ongoing performance success. Each of these elements is important in itself. But it is the holistic combination of these traits in a coherent manner that creates an effective organisation. For instance, investing in developing people capability yet retaining outmoded reward systems that do not adequately recognise stellar performance is simply self-defeating. So too is sustaining a regressive culture while trying to embed clear and appropriate goals. Such inconsistencies between the different components of organisational effectiveness will never deliver an effective organisation.

Functional Leadership

The first and most vital trait of effective organisations is effective leadership. Just as an effective organisation is the most fundamental element of the Procurement mojo, so too is effective functional leadership the keystone of building an effective Procurement organisation; because a fish rots from the head down.

Leadership is the glue that binds together the other components of an effective organisation. It is the single most important factor affecting people's motivation and performance at work. Aside from the evidence from my research in this field, my discussions with numerous professionals and my own career experiences bear testament to this. I will always remember how Harry Hughes's mentoring and inspirational leadership reignited the fire of enthusiasm in my belly, enabling me to reconnect with my personal mojo. I have no doubt whatsoever that it was the most important factor in my subsequent success in improving supply management at that company. Even my immense drive and ambition, coupled with my in-depth technical knowledge, had previously been inadequate to secure lasting success in the job.

In the years to come, I would adopt the same approach in inspiring individuals and teams I was responsible for to reach beyond what seemed possible or likely. One of my fondest recollections of these experiences is Jeremy, my Purchasing and Materials Control Manager at another previous employer. Jeremy was as versed in supply management as any other middle manager I have come across. He understood the key elements inside-out and did a good job, technically. But he left a trail of damaged relationships in his wake. And I found myself expending considerable time and energy picking up the pieces to repair those stakeholder relationships. I had to address the issue. I decided to mentor Jeremy on nurturing effective business relationships, even when his prime internal customer wanted him to flood the place with inventory against his better judgement. I encouraged him to start educating his internal customers and make efforts to build a positive brand with them.

The drastic change in the feedback I subsequently got from Jeremy's stakeholders was incredible, though not surprising. Jeremy, himself, seeing how his improved relationships created 'organisational space' for him to get on with the 'task' elements of the job, came to appreciate the critical value. When I left the company, he sent me a 'thank you' email expressing what it had meant to him to learn some of those soft skills – he described it as "...a life-changing experience." It was music to my ears, because I have always believed one of my key responsibilities as a leader is to develop people. As I mentioned earlier, it is people that do the work in organisations, not computers, strategies or anything else. Hence, our ability to develop and inspire people to exceed their 'normal' levels of capability is crucial to overall organisational success.

Inspiring people in the Procurement organisation is a vital aspect of effective functional leadership. Procurement leaders must make their people feel that they are part of something special, and are making a valued contribution not just to the Procurement agenda but the wider enterprise as a whole. The chemistry between the Procurement leader and the team is critical. Hence, if you are going to be a Procurement leader you must like people. You must also be optimistic; because, be under no illusions, the journey to your Procurement mojo is an adventure with many challenges that will test your mettle. In those tough times when internal factors – like organisational politics, tyrannical stakeholders or failure to secure critical investment in Procurement – buffet the morale of individuals in the team or the whole Procurement organisation, the team will need massive doses of optimism to stay on-course, and the Procurement leader must provide this blanket of reassurance.

Sustaining the Procurement organisation with optimism and collective self-belief will be just as important when the function is facing major challenges from the external environment. Procurement's role sitting between the enterprise and supply markets means it will always be exposed to various factors outside the enterprise, probably more so than any other function. If it's not commodity prices fluctuating crazily, or natural disasters threatening supply continuity, it will be something else like unethical practices in the supply pipeline giving the enterprise bad press. The Procurement leader must steer the team through the choppy waters of such challenges.

Anyone can try to be a good leader when things are going well and get by. But Procurement leaders that are truly effective really show their grit when things get tough. Achieving this demands more than optimism. The Procurement leader must embody effective leadership attributes, including self-leadership. If you are going to be a leader you must be clear on what you stand for, otherwise why should people follow you? Self-leadership demands the inner discipline and strength to do things because they are the right things to do, even if your actions make you unpopular.

Having an effective functional leader is fundamental to the Procurement mojo. For any enterprise starting from a point of low capability on the evolutionary journey of developing Procurement effectiveness, this is my single most critical advice: start the journey by getting yourself an effective Procurement leader, first and foremost.

> **Get an effective Procurement leader, first and foremost. Leadership is the glue that holds it all together.**

People often confuse effective leadership with strong leadership. Indeed, an effective leader may well be strong. But the word 'strong' can have different connotations for each of us, especially in different contexts. A strong leader might be, for instance, an individual who demonstrates strength of personal conviction but goes about achieving his or her goals with a 'big stick', bruising egos and damaging relationships along the way. I wouldn't call that effective leadership. The most effective Procurement leaders are rarely 'purchasing geeks'. Rather, they are 'business leaders' who deploy their effective leadership abilities in the Procurement function. They concentrate on the corporate agenda, and channel Procurement capability to aid the attainment of enterprise goals while nurturing Procurement organisational effectiveness.

> **An effective Procurement leader is a 'business leader', not a 'purchasing geek'.**

The ability to focus on enterprise goals is an important point that should be a central theme of all competency development efforts for senior Procurement managers. Yet the ingredients that create the chemistry of effective leadership extend beyond this attribute. It becomes more obvious when you consider the basic responsibilities of management. Planning; organising; thinking; setting objectives; communicating; co-ordinating; motivating; measuring performance; and developing people are all part of those core responsibilities.

The building blocks of understanding effective leadership can be distilled into examining:

- What leaders or managers spend their time on
- What they focus their thoughts on
- What they do, and
- How they behave.

If you are a Procurement leader, ask yourself these questions: What do you actually spend your time on? How much of that time is spent on *thinking*, and how much on *doing*? What do you focus your thoughts on, or what thoughts do you allow to occupy your mind? What do you actually do – do you spend time chewing the fat in meetings or corridor conversations, interacting with your people, 'pressing flesh' with stakeholders, spending one-to-one time with individuals in your team, giving direction, coaching and mentoring people, writing emails or what?

In some ways, these questions are not just for those Procurement people in leadership roles. Therein also lies a great deal of learning for each of us through the self-insight gleaned from the answers. Aside from considerations of our personal effectiveness, those of us who might be grooming individuals for Procurement leadership responsibilities, or helping incumbent Procurement leaders expand their capabilities, might also imbibe these reflections to our efforts.

A synthesis of these considerations will reveal that effective leadership behaviour, or what effective leaders do, is in part the product of their thoughts. It may also be indicative of their orientation towards achieving their objectives. Grasping this concept may be more important than focusing on 'leadership skills' *per se*. Having good interpersonal skills, for instance, is irrelevant if the Procurement leader is unable to leverage those skills to nurture effective stakeholder relationships which foster the attainment of Procurement's goals and fulfilment of its functional obligations.

It would be great to simply set out a list of effective leadership skills or attributes which Procurement leaders can focus on. Despite the plethora of leadership and management books, articles, training courses and whatnots, the truth of the matter is that there is no definitive set of leadership skills that constitute effective leadership. It all depends on the context. Leadership styles vary, and trying to create a particular pigeon-hole labelled 'The Best Style' for aspiring or incumbent Procurement leaders to aim for is like trying to pick out the best vegetable for nutrition.

Procurement leaders can be effective in their jobs by being highly-self aware, and employing particular skills or approaches that will yield the optimum outcome *in each situation*. If all you want is for people to do the job and not learn a lot from doing it, then simply instruct them. If you want your people to grasp the various nuances or intricacies of the work they do and how it relates to Procurement's goals and those of the wider enterprise, then take the time to break it down and explore it as appropriate with them. It really is the old 'catching fish for people versus teaching them to catch fish' thing. You can direct your people to achieve results, or you can focus on teaching them to direct themselves effectively.

I once worked for a boss whose approach I found frustrating yet educative. The person concerned, who I will call David, had joined the business as a board director responsible for end-to-end supply chain management. David started out by hiring the supply management personnel for each of the teams – Procurement; Supplier Development; and Processes and Systems – before recruiting his senior managers, one of which was me. He brought me in to head the Procurement function and "...act as his second-in-command". The business investment in recruiting the Supply Chain organisation had been secured against a commitment of specific savings to be delivered. In this organisational context, where the need to achieve the task of savings delivery was paramount, David, quite rightly, had previously adopted a directive style of leadership. And, indeed, decent progress was made on the numbers front. But the price paid for that prize was the low morale, poor organisational development and misalignment within the different Supply Chain teams.

Worse still, as I came to discover subsequently, David struggled to adapt his style when the full Supply Chain leadership team was in place. It was a situation that caused immense dissatisfaction for me and my peers on his first-line. His micro-management and interventionist style of operating not only frustrated us, it also greatly demotivated the staff. They felt as if they were treated like unqualified and inexperienced people, incapable of using their knowledge and brain-horsepower to work things out themselves. I learnt this straight from the horse's mouth in the one-to-one sessions I held with my team members as I sought to build a more effective Procurement organisation and empower my people. Keeping the savings delivery target in sight remained a priority; after all, a commitment to the business had been made, and I had been brought in to help with meeting that commitment. But the importance of balancing our focus on cost savings with building functional capability (which would enable us continue to support business needs robustly over the long term) was crucial. It was something I continuously strove to imbibe to my modus operandi, both in managing upwards in my relationship with David and in my leadership style with my Procurement team.

Being aware of one's leadership style in any situation helps provide clarity on the effectiveness of the managerial approaches taken. For any Procurement leader, recognising the vital importance of your people and focusing appropriate levels of attention on that element will be the critical ingredient of your success. Take the time to develop your people, and help them be better than they think they can be. You must energise your people towards the vision you have created for Procurement and its position in the wider organisation, a vision that must be shared by the majority if not all.

Providing such clarity of purpose and direction must be supplemented with robust communication, not least on the expectations of performance and behaviours. But remember, listening is the most important part of communicating. Importantly, empathetic listening is also crucial in building effective relationships outside the Procurement function to aid its success.

The Procurement leader is the central figure who can, and should, create and nurture an organisational climate where people's creativity flourishes and their effectiveness, performance and growth is maximised. An effective Procurement leader exposes individuals' strengths, and leverages those attributes for individual and departmental benefits. By adopting appropriate leadership styles and engendering *esprit de corps*, Procurement leaders can ensure purchasing staff are engaged. Engagement is what sustains the psychological contract between employee and employer in any job. It is the elixir that propels individuals to give that extra ten to fifteen percent discretionary effort entirely of their own free will. If you are a Procurement leader, ask yourself this: Are your people really engaged right now?

I place great emphasis on the Procurement leader's approach to the 'people' dimension due to its predominant significance for Procurement effectiveness. But the Procurement leader's obligations extend beyond managing the Procurement team effectively. The Procurement leader has prime responsibility for ensuring all the other elements of building an effective Procurement organisation are in place and in the right mix, creating that cohesive blend, that magic charm or special spark that embodies all the right stuff to achieve sustainable success – the Procurement mojo.

Procurement Mojo: Some things to think about...

Ask yourself these questions, and take effective corrective actions if the <u>honest</u> answers reveal that you are not heading towards your Procurement mojo!

❖ What is our Procurement leader's leadership style, and is it effective?

❖ How visible and accessible is our Procurement leader, and does he/she exude and propagate positive energy?

❖ Does our Procurement leader provide clarity of purpose and direction to our purchasing people?

❖ How well does our Procurement leader inspire our purchasing people, and align human capital and other resources towards a common purpose?

❖ Does our Procurement leader invest adequate time and effort in developing our purchasing people?

❖ Does our Procurement leader 'walk the walk' and espouse positive values and personal credibility?

❖ How well does our Procurement leader champion the Procurement function and nurture effective relationships for the function's benefit?

❖ Is our Procurement leader a 'purchasing geek', or a 'business leader' with a strategic mindset, commercial nous, great people management abilities and organisationally savvy?

Functional Goals

I love the word 'goal' because of its clear connotation as regards achievement or outcome. The widespread popularity of the beautiful game of soccer means most people across all corners of the globe tend to 'get it' immediately when we use the word 'goal' to express a specific, desired outcome. Goals are a key element of an effective organisation. Thus, enhancing Procurement effectiveness includes defining appropriate goals for the Procurement function.

When I talk about goals here I am referring to both the long-term aspirations, or visionary purpose, of Procurement as well as the short- to medium-term objectives the function may be targeting. Both sets of goals are important, though many Procurement functions have little idea of their long-term future. Even worse, some have no clear immediate objectives. Not having goals for any organisation is equivalent to setting out on a journey without a destination. Or, put another way, if you swing at nothing you will hit it.

Goals are central to an effective Procurement organisation. They are the North Star around which the whole Procurement function must be aligned – the people, processes, systems, etc. If you are going to *do the right things* to achieve the outcomes you want, you must first be clear what those outcomes are. So it is paramount that the goals of the Procurement function are properly defined and articulated robustly.

> **Goals are the North Star around which the whole Procurement function must be aligned.**

Defining Procurement's goals demands sound thinking, balancing the function's core obligations, what the enterprise needs in the short term and the requirement to develop long-term capability to deliver what the enterprise will need in future. It is one of the most important tasks of the Procurement leader. It requires in-depth understanding of the status quo, inside and outside Procurement, and the desired future state of affairs.

But Procurement goals should not be developed in isolation. It is important to talk to internal customers, other stakeholders in the wider organisation and, possibly, some suppliers. By gaining a deep understanding of their needs and perceptions, and aggregating this broader set of views in combination with the enterprise's business priorities and long-term strategy, Procurement can develop robust and appropriate goals which reflect its obligations and are aligned to the corporate agenda.

The Procurement function's goals should be agreed with the Procurement leader's boss up front and properly documented. It is vital to do this as everything Procurement does subsequently can, and should, be related to the functional goals.

Procurement goals should be balanced across the needs of its various stakeholder groups, as appropriate to the business context. They must also encapsulate an appropriate level of equilibrium between internally and externally focused performance dimensions. Issues like value-for-money improvements (what we traditionally and myopically tend to refer to as 'cost savings'); organisational productivity; functional ROI; and employee satisfaction, for instance, centre on what is happening inside Procurement. But we must always remember that Procurement exists to serve various stakeholder constituents; very few Procurement functions exist in their own right as profit centres. Hence, it is just as important to focus on external factors like (internal) customer satisfaction; benchmark performance; and ethics and social responsibility in the supply pipeline.

It is also important to distinguish between short- to medium-term objectives and long-term visionary goals. The essence of a Procurement vision is probably best summed up by Stephen Covey's second habit of 'starting with the end in mind'. The vision of what you want your Procurement function to be like in the long term must be a key driver of your focus and actions in the short to medium term; it is where you should start the search for your Procurement mojo. The Procurement vision should be audacious and compelling, yet clear enough to inspire the team into a unified mass of focused effort. It should be articulated in a way that inspires people and gets their juices flowing.

Sometimes the Procurement vision is best articulated with an image; they do say a picture paints a thousand words. I was once driving the transformation of a purchasing operation for New Product Introduction (NPI). When I took over the role the whole NPI cycle of activities was inconsistent and unstructured. The Marketing guys sold product upgrades to customers before the product engineers had even dreamt of them. And the engineers themselves preferred to find new components and suppliers on the internet, rather than the company's approved vendor list. New product launches often involved Manufacturing being left with a morass of half-baked designs, untested processes and dodgy volume forecasts, if any at all were available. Marketing battled with Engineering constantly, while Engineering clashed with Manufacturing. The NPI-Purchasing function, caught in the crossfire of all this mayhem, ended up fighting with everyone else! The shoddy modus operandi carried over into how the function operated internally in co-ordinating supply management for product development and launch. It was chaotic, every bit like the Wild West.

To get the team to grasp the essence of the change journey we were embarking on, I explained to them that the new NPI-Purchasing function we needed to evolve into was a bit like the bunch of cowboys in the old American Western TV series, *Rawhide*. While everyone involved in NPI was running around like crazed cattle, we would "round 'em up" and corral the NPI supply activities into a robust and reliable series of structured programmes; we would bring sanity to the existing chaos. I hastily put together a simple two-slide illustration, shown in figure 2.2 below (page 60); I always started and ended my team meetings with these slides in the first few months of the transformation journey.

I suspect my team members initially thought I was a bit mad. They laughed loudly the first time I used the slides to outline our transformation intent. But they themselves were soon using the *Rawhide* analogy in discussions with me and with their stakeholders.

I am certainly not the only supply management executive to exploit the power of imagery to espouse a functional vision. Many of the most effective leaders I know of subscribe to the notion of using imagery and imagination to articulate what success looks like. Some talk about "building organisational muscle"; "laying the tarmac of the runway for successful takeoff"; "putting a man on the moon"; or "climbing to the top of the mountain". Imagery elicits emotions, and the right emotions engender alignment and drive desirable thoughts, attitudes and actions. Using a visionary image, alongside a roadmap for the attainment of the vision, can be a powerful tool to help the Procurement team understand the functional ethos and connect with the vision.

The NPI-Purchasing Job – *"Rollin' rollin' rollin' ... Rawhide!!!"*

...Lead NPI activities to key objective for successful product launch

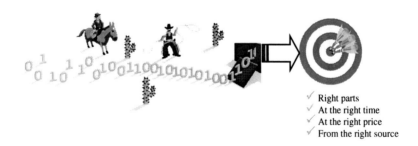

✓ Right parts
✓ At the right time
✓ At the right price
✓ From the right source

Figure 2.2 – *Rawhide:* **NPI-Purchasing Vision**

I shudder with slight embarrassment now when I look at my own rudimentary illustrations of the NPI-Purchasing vision. (Ones and zeros are probably not the best representation of the myriad of issues we were trying to manage.) I would certainly develop something more sophisticated if I had to do it today. But it was effective then. The team got it. We did become a professional and effective Procurement function with robust processes for managing the NPI pipeline, which brought discipline and structure across related stakeholder functions. The transformation yielded over fifty percent productivity increase in the function, and greatly improved our time-to-market and margin competitiveness for new products. Of course, it took a heck of a lot more than a couple of *Rawhide* slides to achieve these turnaround enhancements. But the journey began with the vision encapsulated in those slides.

There is an ancient Chinese proverb, often attributed to Lao Tzu or Confucius, which says that, "A journey of a thousand miles begins with a single step." If the search for the Procurement mojo is the collective march towards the vision outlined for Procurement, then the current year's objectives are the starting single step – the tangible physical effort that gets the ball rolling. The objectives Procurement focuses on in the short term or the current year should not only meet immediate functional and enterprise needs, they should also create stepping stones for the long-term journey.

People sometimes get muddled up in understanding the difference between objectives and responsibilities. Procurement's functional responsibilities are its raison d'être, the reason the function exists in the enterprise. While specific details may vary from organisation to organisation, broadly speaking, these functional responsibilities typically revolve around the core areas of:

(1) **Sourcing and supply** – fulfilling the organisation's requirements for supply of externally-sourced products and services
(2) **Spend management** – proactively managing third-party spend to ensure optimal value
(3) **Supply base management** – managing the supply base to ensure supply reliability, alignment to the corporate agenda and risk minimisation.

Variations reflecting specific organisational contexts include, for instance, fair trade, ethical or diversity sourcing being a key part of Procurement's obligations, if mandated by the enterprise giving priority to corporate social responsibility. Providing a purchasing service to external parties or customers and, possibly, generating income or profit may also be a key responsibility, if the organisation is an outsourced service provider and aggregates its internal and external supply needs.

Procurement functional responsibilities should not change from year to year, except when there is a radical change in the structure and business operations of the wider enterprise – this often necessitates a different set of obligations for the Procurement function. These responsibilities should be established and clarified to all within and outside Procurement to avoid ambiguity. If the search for the Procurement mojo is starting from a point of significant organisational turmoil, where people are really unclear about what Procurement is responsible for (for instance, when an enterprise-wide organisational restructure has been badly executed, or when the Procurement function is being newly established), then defining these responsibilities and providing clarity is as vital as defining the Procurement objectives. The discussions with relevant stakeholders mentioned above, especially the Procurement leader's boss, will prove useful in flushing out all the pertinent issues.

Even when Procurement's responsibilities are well known, it may do no harm to remind the organisation of those functional responsibilities at the same time as communicating the objectives Procurement is targeting. After all, those objectives should also relate to the function's responsibilities, and must be aligned to the corporate strategy.

But Procurement leaders must eschew objectives that end up being some woolly intent, difficult to nail down, hence difficult to demonstrate whether or not success has been achieved. Make your Procurement objectives as SMART as possible, i.e. they should be:

S – Specific
M – Measurable
A – Achievable
R – Relevant
T – Timed

SMART objectives are easier to articulate to both Procurement personnel and stakeholders outside the function. And they are easier to focus on and, hence, marshal resources towards in an effective manner. Let's take a look at a few indicative examples:

- **Specific** – A Procurement objective to "Reduce the number of suppliers by 10%" is much more specific than a general objective to "Rationalise the supply base". The specific objective has a much greater chance of being accomplished.

- **Measurable** – The "10%" target in the objective above is measurable. Thus progress can be tracked easily and success can be demonstrated clearly. Contrast this with the more general objective of supply base rationalisation.

- **Achievable** – "Reduce costs by 3%" or "Introduce e-auctions in 12 months" are more likely to be achieved than "Reduce costs by 30%" or "Introduce e-auctions in 2 months".

- **Relevant** – Deciding to "Introduce Supplier Performance and Relationship Management (SPRM) for the top 10 suppliers" is far more relevant for an organisation suffering recurrent and significant supply disruptions than an intent to "Introduce e-auctions".

- **Timed** – "Introduce SPRM for the top 20 suppliers by February 2013" is far more effective than simply "Introduce SPRM for the top 20 suppliers". Progress against the clock can be monitored from day one, and thus effort can be managed better.

I deliberately use simple examples to get the point across, because setting sensible objectives is key to enhancing Procurement effectiveness. Even when Procurement objectives are as complex as outsourcing a business process or sourcing for a major construction project, for instance, the same principle applies: try as much as possible to keep your Procurement objectives SMART.

> **If you are going to do the right things to achieve the outcomes you want, you must first be clear what those outcomes are: What are your Procurement goals?**

I have seen my fair share of crazy objectives pursued by supply management functions, with enormous resources wasted in the process. I once worked in a global Procurement organisation in a large multinational, where we targeted outsourcing our top two *new* products to a *new* outsourced manufacturing partner, to be made in their low-cost facility in South-east Asia, some twelve or so hours away from our main business locations in Europe; and all of this to be done in about 5 months! Sure, the significant double-digit reduction in product costs, due to the low-cost location in Asia, was a big driver for the decision. But, in the long run, we lost some of that cost advantage in the supply reliability and quality problems we subsequently suffered, and the huge travel costs we incurred sending our people over there to help address the problems. About a year or so afterwards our company was acquired, and within the first twelve months of the acquisition that outsource arrangement was cancelled. Talk about wasted effort and capital – all down to pursuing an unrealistic objective.

Setting SMART Procurement objectives doesn't mean going for easy goals. Rather your functional objectives should entail a degree of stretch for the function without aiming for dreams that will never materialise. In some senses, it is the same principle companies apply when they set business objectives or targets for each financial year. Just as those business objectives or priorities change from year to year, so too should Procurement objectives; because they must always reflect what the current enterprise needs or priorities are, at least in part.

Of course, some Procurement objectives may span more than one year. For instance, an objective to increase the proportion of supplies from low-cost countries from, say, 4% to 50% is likely to take over a year to achieve, especially for complex products. Also, it is far more effective to focus on a few critical objectives, whose attainment will have significant positive impacts on the enterprise and the Procurement function, than to go overboard with an extensive list.

The manifestation of the Procurement mojo is specific to each Procurement function as organisational contexts vary so much. Hence, what constitutes the 'right' set of objectives for one Procurement function may be inappropriate for another. Perhaps the one exception is delivery of value-for-money (VFM) improvements, or 'cost savings' as many purchasing people tend to refer to. It is understandable and appropriate that many Procurement functions are tasked with, or choose to focus on, delivering VFM improvements in addition to other objectives. After all, if Procurement has functional responsibility for managing third-party spend in the enterprise, it is sensible to expect or demand that value is being extracted from that spend. It is an opportunity to show what good purchasing can yield financially.

However, this may not always be a priority. An organisation seeking to rapidly expand into new geographical markets may place greater emphasis on establishing a reliable supply base in the new geographies – suppliers or service partners that can support the execution of the corporate intent robustly. In this situation, issues like supplier capability and supply continuity and quality may be far more important than the costs of the products or services procured; initially, that is.

Whatever objectives your Procurement function sets, it is always important to remember that the nature of the Procurement mojo demands that Procurement is effective today and will remain effective tomorrow. Thus, an intrinsic aspect of enhancing Procurement effectiveness is improving learning and agility, to ensure Procurement is adaptive to the opportunities and challenges of the future; because change is constant, and uncertainties will always be part of life.

Defining functional goals helps provide clarity of purpose for the Procurement function. And setting objectives that contribute to developing the functional capability, in tandem with others that deliver enterprise needs, is a fundamental aspect of enhancing Procurement effectiveness.

Procurement Mojo: Some things to think about...

Ask yourself these questions, and take effective corrective actions if the honest answers reveal that you are not heading towards your Procurement mojo!

❖ Does our Procurement function have clearly defined SMART objectives?

❖ How robustly do our functional goals/intent align to the corporate goals and strategic direction?

❖ How well do we understand our stakeholders' needs, and where is the voice of our 'internal customer(s)' and the external customer in the goals we have set or are pursuing?

❖ Is there a shared belief among Procurement staff in the goals of the function?

❖ Is there a functional strategy or roadmap in place to achieve our goals?

❖ Are we in Procurement all clear on our functional goals and the priority actions that will enable us achieve success?

❖ Have we communicated our goals and direction widely and effectively to our stakeholders?

People Capability

The next trait of effective organisations is 'people capability'. Organisations that are effective continuously invest significant resources (time, capital and leadership effort) on building and maintaining their people capability. The most fundamental reason for this is something I mentioned earlier: it is people that do the work, so people matter most. For any Procurement function seeking its mojo, without this component of organisational effectiveness the search will become like the pursuit of a mirage. You can never enhance Procurement effectiveness without developing your people capability, even with best-in-class processes and systems and a sound strategy. Talent that is well nurtured and harnessed sensibly is the soul of an effective organisation.

Talent acquisition and competency development are central to people capability. Your Procurement function must have the appropriate talent to achieve its goals. Taking a structured human resources development (HRD) approach can help ensure Procurement attracts, retains and develops the right talent. For starters, incumbent Procurement staff should be adequately skilled to perform their job roles. When I talk about skills here, I don't just mean the traditional technical purchasing skills required for most Procurement roles. To be truly effective, Procurement staff must have a combination of technical skills and soft skills – traits and behavioural attributes which augment intrapersonal and interpersonal abilities.

> **It is people that do the work, so people matter most.**

Conventional approaches to skills development in purchasing places too much emphasis on technical competencies like negotiation; total cost analysis; category management; strategic sourcing; and so on. Yet the prevalent evidence shows that the most effective and successful purchasing people are those with highly-developed soft skills – skills and attributes like communication; assertiveness;

influencing; results-orientation; decision-making; problem-solving; and emotional intelligence. Terry Hill's differentiation of competitive factors in manufacturing strategy is a useful analogy here. Think of technical purchasing skills as 'qualifiers' – skills that simply qualify you to play in the purchasing sandpit; whereas, soft skills are 'order-winners', the key intrapersonal and interpersonal competences that enable you to excel in the job. You can't possibly be a half-decent purchasing professional without the right technical skills. But to be effective and outclass your average peers, you must have highly developed soft skills.

Of course, no one set of skills are 'best'; it all depends on the requirements of an individual's job role. Developing and applying a formal competency model is always a good start, if done properly. And it doesn't need to be a complex, all-singing-all-dancing tool. A simple but effective competency model can be developed on a spreadsheet. Using a good competency model covering all roles in the Procurement function, and assessing incumbent staff against the defined competencies will help flush out relevant skills gaps. Robust personal development plans can subsequently be followed to help individuals close the identified gaps and grow their capabilities accordingly. See figure 2.3 for an outline illustration of this approach.

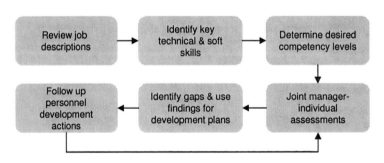

Figure 2.3 – Using a Competency Model

Developing a Procurement competency model is not as complicated as some consultants and HR managers might have you believe. In fact, if you wanted to, you could develop one on a beer mat. I wouldn't advise this though, even for a Procurement team of just two. It is far more sensible to take the time to develop a pukka competency model which suitably encapsulates the desired Procurement job competencies, and apply it robustly to support talent acquisition and development.

Figure 2.4 shows an excerpt summary of a simple competency model I used to support the turnaround of one Procurement function; the resulting competency profile from the first application is illustrated graphically in the top half.

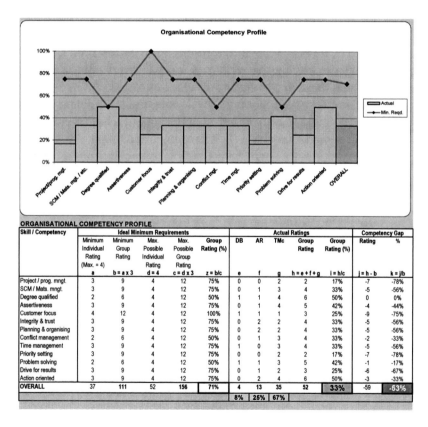

Skill / Competency	Ideal Minimum Requirements					Actual Ratings					Competency Gap	
	Minimum Individual Rating (Max. = 4)	Minimum Group Rating	Max. Possible Individual Rating	Max. Possible Group Rating	Group Rating (%)	DB	AR	TMc	Group Rating	Group Rating (%)	Rating	%
	a	$b = a \times 3$	$d = 4$	$c = d \times 3$	$z = b/c$	e	f	g	$h = e+f+g$	$i = h/c$	$j = h-b$	$k = j/b$
Project / prog. mngt.	3	9	4	12	75%	0	0	2	2	17%	-7	-78%
SCM / Mats. mngt	3	9	4	12	75%	0	1	3	4	33%	-5	-56%
Degree qualified	2	6	4	12	50%	1	1	4	6	50%	0	0%
Assertiveness	3	9	4	12	75%	0	1	4	5	42%	-4	-44%
Customer focus	4	12	4	12	100%	1	1	1	3	25%	-9	-75%
Integrity & trust	3	9	4	12	75%	0	2	2	4	33%	-5	-56%
Planning & organising	3	9	4	12	75%	0	2	2	4	33%	-5	-56%
Conflict management	2	6	4	12	50%	0	1	3	4	33%	-2	-33%
Time management	3	9	4	12	75%	1	0	3	4	33%	-5	-56%
Priority setting	3	9	4	12	75%	0	0	2	2	17%	-7	-78%
Problem solving	2	6	4	12	50%	1	1	3	5	42%	-1	-17%
Drive for results	3	9	4	12	75%	0	1	2	3	25%	-6	-67%
Action oriented	3	9	4	12	75%	0	2	4	6	50%	-3	-33%
OVERALL	**37**	**111**	**52**	**156**	**71%**	**4**	**13**	**35**	**52**	**33%**	**-59**	**-53%**
						8%	25%	67%				

Figure 2.4 – Competency Model for Procurement Programme Management

It isn't the sexiest competency model in existence, but it was extremely effective. The three individuals shown – DB, AR and TMc – all held the same job role of Purchasing Programme Manager. As the model indicates, certain behavioural competencies were far more important in the role than technical skills, especially as the turnaround I was driving centred on culture change and boosting functional effectiveness.

You might have guessed that DB and AR never made the mark after all. This can be an unavoidable consequence of up-skilling the Procurement function to enhance effectiveness – some incumbents may not turn out to be the right people for the job, even with reasonable investment in employee development; it is just not possible to fit a square peg into a round hole. Rather than trying to force things or carrying the weight of incapable individuals, it is far better to help them find their futures elsewhere.

A full competency model is an invaluable tool for building people capability. But I have also found a simple talent assessment to be effective in some situations. When carrying out a talent assessment, my predisposition to keep things simple compels me to narrow competencies down to three groups:

- **Technical skills** – relating to the specific technical competencies for an individual's job role
- **Soft skills** – relating to desired behaviours and attitudes which reflect the progressive values to be instilled in the function
- **Results** – relating to an individual's drive or orientation towards delivery of end results.

Figure 2.5 illustrates this application with an extract from the talent assessment at one supply management function I led. It is worth pointing out that the illustration only portrays the output of the assessment. A talent assessment should always be built up with supplementary notes of evidence of the assessed competencies.

Whether you choose to carry out a simple talent assessment or to deploy a full competency model, the key value is in making the effort to gauge the competency of your Procurement team.

Procurement & Supply Chain Management Talent Assessment					
Name	Function / Role	Competency Assessment			Aggregate Assmnt.	Comments
		PSCM	'Soft' Skills	Results		
BR	Procurement Mgr.	Med	Lo-Med	Lo	Lo-Med	Support & develop management capability
PB	Category Mgr.	Med	Lo	Med	Lo	Develop personal effectiveness
FP	Category Mgr.	Hi	Hi	Hi	Hi	Groom for succession planning
GS	Category Mgr.	Lo	Lo	Med	Lo	Align; replace quickly if no early improvement
RS	Category Mgr.	Hi	Hi	Hi	Hi	High potential
BD	CAPEX Proc't.	Hi	Lo	Lo	Lo	Out
MI	CAPEX Proc't.	Hi	Med	Med	Med	Develop
TC	Buyer	Lo	Hi	Lo	Lo-Med	Train properly
DF	Buyer	Lo	Lo	Lo	Lo	Replace? Manage performance & attitude
LH	Buyer	Med	Med	Med	Med	Develop?
BS	Projects	Lo	Lo	Lo	Lo	Replace quickly
DS	Supplier Dev. Mgr.	Med	Lo	Lo	Lo	Manage performance & attitude
AMcC	Supplier Dev.	Lo	Hi	Hi	Med-Hi	Develop

Legend
#. "PSCM" = Understanding of Procurement & Supply Chain Management and / or evidence of key aspects for job-role
#. "'Soft' Skills" = Competency at desired inter- and intra-personal attributes or behaviours
#. "Results" = Drive for results, i.e. focus on / orientation towards delivery of results

Figure 2.5 – Simplified Procurement Talent Assessment

Individual staff may disagree with the Procurement leader's assessment of their competencies. In some such cases, people sometimes feel they have a level of competency which exceeds the observed reality. Many of us have felt this way at one time or another, and, probably, only became aware of the disparity through the feedback we received. In other cases, people may indeed have the required skills but may not frequently demonstrate it. I often find such situations to be valuable additions to personal development plans, and I subsequently focus my effort at trying to provide adequate opportunities for the individual to do their thing, or show they can 'walk the walk' with ongoing managerial encouragement and constructive feedback.

Applying a Procurement functional competency model properly means it should be used for employee development as well as recruitment of new staff. Using a competency-based recruitment process for acquiring fresh talent is extremely valuable, in that individuals' competencies can be assessed *before* they join the

Procurement team. Of course, dishonest smooth-talkers may try to lie their way through a competency-based interview by giving false examples of situations where they demonstrated the desired skills. An experienced interviewer should be able to 'peel the onion' adequately to establish what is truthful and what is fantasy. Using a recruitment process where candidates are screened by several people to get more-rounded feedback assessment is also useful to thwart dishonest types.

The degree of subjectivity inherent in many competency models does not detract from their value as a talent management tool. As with all tools, a Procurement competency model can be used properly or badly. Even without a formal, structured competency tool it may still be possible to identify the key skills Procurement staff have strengths in and those that need development attention. Many purchasing skills development efforts centre on providing training, typically in technical competency areas. It is important to point out that while training is often cost-efficient for technical skills, it may not be the most cost-effective approach all the time. Coaching and mentoring can be far more effective to achieve desired competency development outcomes in certain skill areas. Key leadership abilities like creativity; influencing at C-level; strategic thinking; political savvy; and building trust – all critical for senior purchasing roles, especially in large or complex organisations – are usually best developed through experience underpinned with good coaching or mentoring.

For Procurement functions going through a major transformation to enhance effectiveness, my advice is to utilise the expertise of internal HR support, if it is dependable, or that of external specialists, if investment funding is available. It will be an investment that will yield bountiful returns – because, ultimately, the aggregated talent of your people is the most valuable component of your functional balance sheet.

Applying a competency model for up-skilling the Procurement function assumes that the job roles in the function are appropriate, well defined and in the right structure. Having talented individuals operating in a dysfunctional organisational structure is a recipe for frustration, frustration that can grow into negative sentiments and harm team harmony and capability. The Procurement organisational structure should be simple and straightforward, with clear ownership and lead responsibility for each key element of the portfolio of functional tasks or responsibilities. Even activities that span multiple job roles or sections should have a clear lead. Each role and incumbent individual should have well defined key accountabilities or key result areas and specified objectives.

> **The aggregated talent of your people is the most valuable component of your functional balance sheet.**

An effective organisational structure with clear roles and responsibilities, configured to support functional goals, is a key requirement for building an effective Procurement organisation. It is important not to mistake the need for an effective organisational structure as a requirement for a centralised Procurement function. It isn't a debate about centralisation versus decentralisation. Both extremes and the hybrid models in-between all have their advantages and disadvantages. While many organisations find centralised purchasing to be most effective for their context, others don't. I know several Procurement executives who head matrix or hybrid organisational structures that seem logical and operate effectively. Such operating models are typically underpinned by clarity of responsibility; individual accountability; professional values and behaviours; and reliable processes that aid the smooth flow of work activities between different job roles or functional teams.

When it comes to the specific design of the Procurement organisational structure or operating model, it is rarely a case of 'one size fits all'; cultural factors and other unique organisational considerations must also come into play. What is vital is that the adopted structure facilitates the effective and efficient execution of purchasing work, in as seamless a manner as possible.

But having the right people in the right roles is only one part of the dance. Another is to ensure good succession planning such that

Procurement capability is not dented when key individuals leave. For those of us who love the beautiful game, think about the impact Thierry Henry's departure had on Arsenal Football Club. By the club's own account, Henry wasn't even an authentic striker when he joined Arsenal in the late 1990s. With great mentoring by Arsène Wenger, Henry polished his skills to become one of the all time greats, scoring a record 228 goals or so for the club. He was The Gunners' talisman, stoking the flames of their mojo, a constant menace to opposition goalkeepers. And after he departed, Arsenal was almost unrecognisable on the pitch. Henry's absence was glaring.

Good succession planning ensures an effective Procurement function does not suffer a performance deficit from staff attrition. A decent succession planning approach should address the risk of key personnel departures, in tandem with offering career development opportunities that leverage individuals' strengths. Such an approach will continually meet the capability and development needs of the Procurement team and individual staff.

Giving Procurement staff opportunities to shine and grow is not just an altruistic endeavour. It augments Procurement's organisational capability through the positive sentiments generated, which boosts motivation, engenders progressive attitudes and nurtures the psychological contract between Procurement staff and the organisation. These are key avenues to ensure employee engagement and, ultimately, talent retention. People who are really good at what they do seldom stick around in organisations that don't bring out the best in them, whether that's through recognition, rewards or career opportunities and advancement. Expending effort to recruit or develop talent and then failing to take the right steps to retain that talent is just plain stupid. And refusing to develop your people for fear of losing them is far worse – it's like refusing to maintain a prized car because it might get stolen. An effective talent management approach always augments employee engagement. And having a high proportion of purchasing staff whose hearts and minds are aligned to Procurement's agenda is part and parcel of building an effective Procurement organisation.

Fostering employee engagement is something many of us undervalue. Yet we complain when staff have undesirable or regressive attitudes. On many occasions in my career, typically in job interviews or, latterly, discussions with prospective clients, I have been asked *how* I inspire and motivate people to align them to my intent. I always give the same answer: I don't have a pre-defined list of tactics set in stone, or a little black book titled 'How to Inspire and Motivate People' which I whip out of my pocket upon starting each new job or client assignment. Every situation is different, and each individual is unique. But one thing I hold sacrosanct is to put 'people' and their engagement at the core of my leadership efforts. I take great pains to understand how people view the world of 'work', and how that perspective impacts their attitudes, behaviours and operating styles; I expend time and energy providing clarity, direction, guidance and support for people; I hold people to account for their performance and behaviours; I try to catch people doing the right things and give them lavish praise; I invest considerable effort helping them find the best within themselves, even if the journey is bumpy and painful – I try to help them ignite the fire in their bellies while staying true to The Golden Rule.

But I'm also trying to learn all the time. Reminding myself that I'm a student at 'The University of Life', and that every experience brings opportunity for learning and growth, is one of my personal efforts to continuously enhance my own effectiveness. This learning, combined with my previous insights on management and organisational performance, always forms a key element of my approach, an approach which is encapsulated in the pages you are reading now.

I have immense faith in the human spirit. Perhaps I am too much of an optimist, but I don't believe people get up and go to work to do a bad job or to be a pain. Most people go to work to do a good job. I am certainly not alone in holding this fundamental belief. Many senior business leaders, who are far more experienced than me, also share this view. For instance, in a *Sunday Times Magazine* interview in March 2012, Fred DeLuca, co-founder of the Subway sandwich franchise business, expresses exactly the same sentiment, saying, "I do believe people show up at work wanting to do their best. It's probably bosses who screw things up more than anyone else." And he should know one or two things about building successful organisations – Subway has grown to well over 36,000 stores in 98 countries and DeLuca, himself, is said to be worth $2 billion.

> **You can never enhance Procurement effectiveness without developing your people capability, even with best-in-class processes and systems and a sound strategy.**

If your purchasing people are not giving you their best at work, or aren't fully engaged in the effort to secure your Procurement mojo by enhancing effectiveness, then the most important remedy is first to dig beneath the obvious and try to understand why. Spending quality one-to-one time with individuals, discussing their progress, growth, contribution and related issues or challenges must be a key chunk of the Procurement leader's workload. When Procurement staff have job satisfaction and are committed to making the function a success, they will 'walk the walk' willingly and proudly.

In aligning Procurement staff to the function's ethos it is important to strike the right balance between task orientation and relationship focus. Procurement people who are technically competent and deliver tangible results at the cost of damaging stakeholder relationships – the 'Taskmasters' – harm Procurement effectiveness in the long run. And those who nurture good relationships but fail to achieve their objectives – individuals who are 'Everybody's Friend' – do the same. In developing people capability the aim should always be to nurture as many 'Stars' as possible – those who are able to deliver their results and maintain effective relationships inside and outside the function.

The Procurement leader's effort with one-to-one communication should not supplant team communications. Rather it should focus on individuals' particular contexts, while also augmenting the generic communication themes across the team. It is incredible to think that some Procurement organisations don't have regular team meetings, but that's certainly the case. Imagine the LA Lakers basketball team,

Real Madrid football club or the South African Springboks rugby team not having regular team meetings to communicate and discuss issues which affect the very existence of the team, the morale of team members and the team's performance success. It's unthinkable. Yet some Procurement leaders expect their teams to gel and be successful without imbibing regular team meetings to their organisational existence.

Periodic communication, both formal and informal, not only serves to share information to support effective interactions and raise internal awareness, it also feeds a spirit of collectiveness and belonging amongst Procurement staff. These are key ingredients in the effort to build employee engagement and ensure everyone in Procurement is dancing to the same tune. When you have such alignment, and people can see how their work relates to Procurement's goals and the strategic agenda of the wider enterprise, you create magic.

Failing to invest time, effort and capital in such ongoing organisational development and expecting to find your Procurement mojo is like refusing to eat or drink and expecting to stay alive. Procurement people will treat internal customers, other stakeholders and suppliers in a way that reflects how they, themselves, are treated and how they feel about their work. Talented and engaged Procurement people who feel part of something special, something that feels magical, will always seek to recreate that magic in their interactions with others outside Procurement. Those emotions fan the flames of their personal mojos, enabling them to excel in so many ways and contribute to organisational capability. Building people capability is intrinsic to creating an effective Procurement organisation; because, as I have mentioned earlier, it is people that do the work, so people matter most.

Procurement Mojo: Some things to think about...

Ask yourself these questions, and take effective corrective actions if the honest answers reveal that you are not heading towards your Procurement mojo!

- ❖ Do we have the right aggregate talent and functional capabilities to achieve our priorities?
- ❖ Do incumbent Procurement staff have the requisite level of technical competencies and soft skills for their job roles?
- ❖ Have we aligned our people and resources around our goals and key priorities?
- ❖ Do we all understand how our personal objectives contribute to the functional goals and effectiveness of Procurement?
- ❖ Is the organisational structure clear? Is it appropriate and effective? And does it adequately align to our priorities?
- ❖ Are roles and responsibilities clearly defined and known to all?
- ❖ Do people's job roles provide adequate opportunities for learning and development?
- ❖ Do our purchasing people understand how their individual work contributes to Procurement's success and the needs of the wider enterprise?
- ❖ How do our people *really* feel about working in our Procurement function?
- ❖ Do our people feel engaged and inspired? What evidence is there?
- ❖ Are we investing adequate effort and resources in developing and sustaining our people capability?

Individual Performance and Rewards

If you have been tuning in to the message so far on how to find your Procurement mojo, then you have probably guessed that performance at the individual level is a vital component of Procurement's overall performance capability. The Procurement function is, after all, a team of individuals. Ideally, the approach to managing individual performance and rewards should be unified and harmonised right across the enterprise. But this tends to be the case only in large organisations with first-class HRD capability. Sadly, far too few organisations fit that bill, and many Procurement functions lack the professional in-house HRD support they should have.

Nonetheless, an effective Procurement leader with requisite experience can, and should, adopt a progressive approach to managing individual performance in the function. Expert HRD support would be brilliant, but managing people's performance properly is not exactly nuclear science. What is really important is that the tactics employed drive the desired capability, behaviours and results. Some pertinent key principles herein are:

- Ensure accountability. Individuals must be held to account for their responsibilities and deliverables. Everyone in Procurement is paid a salary to do a job; if they collect the pay-check, then it is reasonable to expect and demand performance delivery, all other things being equal.

- Cover 'hard' and 'soft' aspects. Ensure considerations of 'performance' reflect both hard, tangible elements such as measurable deliverables, as well as soft, intangible elements such as attitudes and behaviours.

- Carry out regular reviews and give honest, constructive feedback. Don't wait for the annual or half-yearly formal performance appraisal, if one exists; six months is a long time to wait to tell someone they are not performing or they are doing a fantastic job. Say it as it is when giving feedback, even if you have to be tactful with your words to strike the right balance between honesty and inspiration.

- Don't hold back from applying 'tough love' when it is appropriate. Research studies have shown that a leadership approach to performance that balances empathy with hard-nosed directness focused on desired outcomes achieves significantly better performance.

- Recognise and reward stellar performance, and take action to address poor performance. Address capability gaps if performance failure is due to lack of competency, linking competency development to personal development plans. Don't reward average performance; otherwise your Procurement function will also be average. Don't shy away from getting rid of people who consistently underperform after appropriate development support; otherwise your Procurement function will also underperform.

- Use effective performance management to get results for the enterprise and results for the individual – it is a valuable route to develop people and ignite their passion when done correctly.

The extent to which some of these principles can be incorporated may be influenced by parameters outside the Procurement function. But there is a great deal Procurement leaders can do even within the bounds of the organisational context. This becomes more obvious as we discuss some of these issues below.

Managing individual performance in a manner that gets the most from people and contributes to their development requires insights into the whole idea of human motivation. Get it right and you will awaken the sleeping giants in your people and reap the bountiful rewards of their collective inspiration. Get it wrong and you could waste significant organisational energy carrying 'fat' in your Procurement function – you certainly won't find your Procurement mojo, that much I can guarantee.

There are two sides to the coin of performance when it comes to individuals. One is the way we go about specifying the required levels of performance, and then monitoring and reviewing actual performance. The other is the approach taken to incentivise desired performance, reward actual performance when it is great and address poor performance. Individuals' performance is greatly influenced by their abilities, traits and perceptions of what the job demands. So even with highly developed skills and progressive behavioural traits, a misconception of the performance requirements of the job is likely to result in wasted effort and suboptimal performance.

One of the most fundamental requirements is to align individual performance to organisational goals and values. Setting objectives for individuals that link to Procurement's functional goals is vital. Individual objectives should also reflect the responsibilities of the job role; it's no use targeting a Procurement Processes and Systems Manager with rationalising the supply base if he is not responsible for sourcing or supplier selection, or has no influence on related decisions. As obvious as this sounds, there are still very many purchasing people without clear and appropriate individual objectives in many organisations.

Unless individual effort is directed at specific levers which ultimately enhance the capability and performance of Procurement, the function will not be effective. Effective personal objectives bridge the divide between 'function' and 'individual' as regards performance. The requirement for SMARTness in developing Procurement functional goals also applies to setting individual objectives – they should be specific; measurable; achievable; relevant; and timed. All the evidence indicates that people with SMART objectives perform better than those with fuzzy goals or none at all. And, as with functional goals, it is far more effective to set a few critical individual objectives than to go crazy with a catalogue of targets which will never be achieved or have any meaningful impact on the job obligations, the individual's growth or Procurement's performance.

Effective performance management at individual level should address the two key requirements of supporting organisational attainment *and* growing individuals' capabilities. We only grow when we stretch beyond what we can do already. Hence, it is just as important that individual objectives are somewhat stretching. People perform best when there is a degree of stretch in their work, enough to stimulate them and get their juices flowing. It is one of the ways we help individuals at work connect with their personal mojos – through stretching objectives. Yerkes and Dodson's work in the early 1900s is one of the enduring concepts in this area. The relationship between stretch and performance is curvilinear, and it holds true across individuals and cultures. People who are not stretched simply tread water. They plod along in a mediocre organisational existence that does nothing for their growth and stifles functional effectiveness. They are asleep on the job, and their contribution to long-term capability is minimal. The more stretching individual objectives are, the more performance increases; up to an optimum zone. Beyond that, performance suffers as stretch becomes stress, an unhealthy situation for the individual, the Procurement team and the wider enterprise.

Opinions vary on how individual objectives should be set. One school of thought postulates that objectives should be jointly developed and agreed by the manager and the individual. Another perspective is that people should be targeted with objectives that reflect what the organisation needs from the job role; think of it as setting out individual contribution to functional and enterprise requirements. There is merit in both views. What is most important is that individuals have absolute clarity on their objectives, even if that entails working out for themselves what their key focus areas must be to achieve the required outcomes. Indeed, while the Procurement leader has prime responsibility for ensuring purchasing people all have individual objectives, those with a strong desire to grow and excel should feel a sense of ownership for their own performance. This might mean setting one's own objectives and agreeing them with the manager, if the situation so demands. It is something I have done on several occasions in my corporate career. In this regard, the requirement for SMART, stretching objectives which align to Procurement's goals remain unchanged. This is a key conduit to securing desired levels of individual performance that support the Procurement agenda.

It is important to remember that 'performance' is not just about the numbers or hard, tangible results. It also relates to the behaviours exhibited in achieving those numbers. It is helpful and appropriate to clarify desired behaviours and attitudes alongside individual objectives. This may be best done in personal development plans which can be referenced in objective-setting. Whatever the case, it must be made clear what behavioural values and traits are expected, and the sort of evidence or feedback required.

> **'Performance' is not just about the numbers or hard tangible results; how we go about achieving the numbers (the behaviours and attitudes we exhibit) is as important as what we achieve.**

Earlier on, I shared the story of Jeremy, my Purchasing and Materials Control Manager at a previous employer. His initial confrontational attitude to stakeholders, including his internal customers, did no good for our supply management organisation or for Jeremy himself. Despite his technical pedigree and great efforts on the job, the negative emotions he created through his attitude and behaviour detracted from his endeavours. He became a dog with a bad name, with a notoriety that was far worse than the situation in reality. This sort of approach drains organisational energy and damages Procurement effectiveness. If supplier delivery is great, materials availability is high and VFM delivery is good, but your internal customer goes round bad-mouthing you (with some justification), then you are heading away from your Procurement mojo. As far as building long-term sustainable success goes, *how* we go about achieving the numbers – the behaviours and attitudes we exhibit – is as important as *what* we achieve – the numbers themselves.

Both the individual objectives and the desired behaviours must be properly documented and clarified to personnel in Procurement. This should be done even if the enterprise has no formal process or framework for this. A few simple typed-up A4 sheets will do, as long as both manager and employee understand the contents and keep a copy to refer to when reviewing progress.

Checking progress against specified objectives and behavioural competences must be done regularly, both formally and informally.

The manager should give ongoing tactical feedback frequently, using examples from day-to-day activities to illustrate what is working well and what isn't. It helps people stay on track on an operational basis.

Even more important is the need to carve time away from the daily grind and sit down to appraise performance formally. Some purchasing managers refrain from carrying out performance appraisals, either because this reflects the norms in the wider enterprise or because they grossly misunderstand the critical value of performance appraisals. Imagine being a professional footballer playing in football matches with no scores kept, in a league with no league table rankings; how do you know if you are 'winning' or doing well?

I have worked in organisations with varying approaches to formal performance appraisals. In some cases appraisals were an annual activity, whereas in others it was done bi-annually. In some cases formal, periodic appraisals were interwoven to the fabric of the organisation; in others appraisals were a derisory affair, if at all they were actually done. I have always held the view that individual performance needs to be formally reviewed more frequently than twice a year. I have, thus, always believed in sitting down with individuals to review performance on a quarterly basis, even if some of the appraisal sessions turn out to be a thirty-minute chat providing reassurance that all is well and the individual is heading in the right direction with their results and behavioural development. I have also always seen appraisals as a two-way affair. Hence, I always use such sessions to solicit feedback on how well individuals feel they are being managed. I have often found it to be an insightful experience, helping to grow my own leadership capabilities.

Irrespective of the frequency of performance appraisals, it is important that the review is well rounded and documented. Documented performance reviews give individuals a reference frame against which they can anchor their personal efforts. The contents of the review document should also serve as key inputs to training and development initiatives. Performance improves substantially by reviewing it and identifying successes and failures. When performance reviews are done properly and linked to personnel development, they become a key contribution to talent acquisition and development. But that is only possible when the feedback is robust.

Giving individuals constructive feedback not only drives higher performance, it also helps them reduce their "blind" behaviours – mannerisms and traits we all have but are unaware how they impact on others. This is particularly important for purchasing people who have to interact with a wide range of stakeholders, inside and outside the enterprise, due to the nature of their job roles. Joseph Luft and Harry Ingham's research work reveals how we all have a matrix of behaviours – a mix of what is known and unknown to us and to others. Understanding this mix of behaviours is a key part of increasing self-awareness. And self-awareness is one of the cornerstones of improving individual capability and performance.

An effective performance management approach should help purchasing people develop their competencies in a way that builds on identified strengths, while addressing capability and performance gaps. Poor performance must never be ignored. It is important to clarify shortcomings and probe for insights into the relevant issues – what I like to refer to as 'getting behind what you see'. The aim here should be to establish the underlying root-causes of poor performance. These might include regressive thinking patterns or attitudes, low motivation, a basic lack of skills or a misconception of desired performance. Whatever the case, appropriate improvement actions must be taken, and individuals should be properly supported and given reasonable time to close the gap.

In extreme cases it may be necessary to sack persistent poor performers. This is something you must not shy away from. If an individual has been managed effectively and given appropriate support and adequate time to improve, all to no avail, then you must take further action. If you compromise on individual performance management, your Procurement mojo will also be compromised. Failing to address poor individual performance effectively sends a message to the rest of the Procurement team, and, indeed, the wider enterprise, that substandard performance or suboptimal behaviours are acceptable in Procurement. This is not the path to your Procurement mojo.

In the same vein, it is also critical to send strong messages about exemplary performance. Reward good performance in ways that are appropriate and reinforce the desired organisational values.

Psychologists as far back as G. B. Watson in the 1920s have proved that rewards bond the relationship between desired performance and actual outcomes.

The importance of using reward structures that are appropriate can not be overemphasised. Inappropriate reward structures ultimately drive suboptimal behaviours, attitudes and performance. For instance, many organisations still base Procurement buyers' incentives and rewards purely on achieved cost savings or purchase price variance (PPV). A reward mechanism centred on cost savings will drive a performance focus centred on cost savings. Buyers' may, thus, be motivated to achieve savings or PPV targets by simply sourcing from cheaper vendors, without adequate heed to supply risks. And the business may end up suffering operational problems, and, possibly, reputational and financial damage, if the resulting supplier performance is below par. This detracts from Procurement's true value proposition in the enterprise. A reward structure that incorporates the desired VFM attainment as well as actual supply reliability performance would be far more effective.

Rewards here are not just about monetary, financial or material stuff. Of course, pay rises, bigger car allowances or corner offices are usually welcome prizes for good work. But simple rewards like recognition, public acknowledgement and praise, increased status or more autonomy can often be powerful accolades that also bolster employee motivation and engagement. A major FTSE 100 financial services company, for instance, regularly rewards top performers with paid foreign trips with their partners, in addition to contractual performance bonuses.

> **Reward good performance in ways that reinforce the desired organisational values. Inappropriate reward structures drive suboptimal behaviours, attitudes and performance.**

Effective reward mechanisms are part and parcel of a robust performance management framework. The impact this has on talent acquisition and employee motivation makes it even more critical. It may not be necessary to go as far as rewarding top performers *and* repeatedly culling the bottom poor performers at the tail-end of the organisational competency profile. But the ethos inherent in honestly letting people know the lay of the land, and helping them recognise their potential and the areas of development they need to focus on, is one that brings ample benefits. The candour required to let people know where they stand, and the mutual trust that must be part of helping them reach their best, go a long way in harnessing human capital and boosting motivation and engagement.

As I mentioned earlier, I have always held a personal tenet that no one gets up each morning and goes to work to do a bad job. So when Adrian, one of my Category Managers in a previous role, failed to attain the performance standards we had agreed, I sought to unravel the issues I suspected lay beneath his poor performance. Adrian was a first-rate dealmaker with great commercial nous. And he understood purchasing inside-out. But his success in the job was hugely hampered by a glaring lack of personal effectiveness. He was unfocused and scatty. And his motivation suffered as he, himself, grew more aware of his performance shortcomings. Investing considerable time in coaching and mentoring Adrian on his personal effectiveness proved to be worthwhile. It turned out that over the latter years of his career, Adrian had worked for a couple of 'cowboy' bosses with low standards. He had inadvertently picked up some shoddy habits from his previous roles. I started supporting him with growing his effectiveness. And his efforts paid off. He soon noticed significant benefits in interactions with his stakeholders and his own feelings of accomplishment as he got more adept. I eventually got him a professional coach to carry on the work I had started. The improvement in Adrian's abilities and success in the job was remarkable. Not only did he start to blossom, the transformation he showed reaffirmed my belief in taking appropriate actions to enhance individual capabilities and motivate people to achieve desired levels of performance.

> **An effective approach to individual performance and rewards must drive the desired capability, behaviours and performance to create alignment.**

Motivation is one of the key driving forces behind human behaviour, whether it is through rewards and incentives, fear of losing the job or any medium in-between. Whatever you choose to do, it is important to remember that people matter most. For any Procurement function to find its mojo, its people must be inspired and energised to reach for a level of capability and performance that is well beyond average.

Employing an effective approach for individual performance and rewards helps keep alight the fire we all have in our bellies. It cultivates the critical factors which aid us in tuning into our mojos, what Charles Handy calls 'E' factors. He reminds us that everyone of us is full of 'E' in its various forms. The trick is to unleash that 'E' – the excitement, enthusiasm, energy, emotion, effort and expertise – and expose our true potential and abilities to excel.

Procurement organisations that are able to unlock the performance capabilities of their people are always places of great effervescence. They fizz with the collective passion of the purchasing people, who are aligned to the functional goals through their individual objectives and collectively deliver performance outcomes that enhance Procurement effectiveness.

Procurement Mojo: Some things to think about...

Ask yourself these questions, and take effective corrective actions if the <u>honest</u> answers reveal that you are not heading towards your Procurement mojo!

- ❖ Do our people all have individual objectives, and are they aware of their performance against those objectives?
- ❖ Do those individual objectives align to the department goals and priorities, and are they appropriate for the job roles?
- ❖ Are individual objectives SMART and adequately stretching to provide opportunities for growth?
- ❖ Do we all understand how our personal objectives contribute to the functional goals and effectiveness of Procurement?
- ❖ How well do we keep score on individual performance? Is performance measured, reviewed and discussed with individuals? Do we measure what is important, or what is conventional or easy to measure?
- ❖ Do we manage performance to imbibe tangible or 'hard' aspects as well as behaviours and attitudes or 'soft' aspects?
- ❖ Are people held accountable for their performance and behaviours?
- ❖ How do we recognise and reward good performance, and how do we highlight and address poor performance?
- ❖ Do we have an equitable approach to rewards based on desired performance and behaviours?
- ❖ What messages are we sending out by the way we reward good performance and tackle poor performance?
- ❖ Does our approach to individual performance and rewards augment our Procurement effectiveness?

Culture

You might be wondering what 'culture' has to do with Procurement effectiveness. Or you might be thinking, "Aha! I knew it..." Either way, I am pleased. If you 'knew it', then it's heart-warming that you recognise the importance of culture to Procurement's success. And if you were wondering what culture has to do with the Procurement mojo, the answer is: everything. The culture in your Procurement organisation says more than any scorecard, sourcing strategy or P2P process. It reflects what your Procurement function is about.

I don't often hear purchasing people talking about culture. We tend to talk more about strategic sourcing, category management, cost savings, stakeholders and so on. Yet a progressive culture is a vital ingredient for building an effective Procurement organisation. Survey findings and trade reports continue to show that one of the greatest hurdles purchasing practitioners have to navigate is an organisational culture that neither recognises nor bolsters Procurement's strategic value. The underlying critical challenges that hinder most Procurement functions from attaining enhanced capabilities and performance success always relate to 'human factors' – issues encapsulated in the culture of the organisation. Perhaps we don't voice it often enough but recognise the importance of culture in building Procurement effectiveness.

> **The culture in your Procurement organisation says more than any scorecard, sourcing strategy or P2P process. It reflects what your Procurement function is about.**

Culture really is everything in any organisation, whether it's Procurement, Finance or the whole enterprise. In any organisation, the culture is an indefinable mix of values, attitudes, perceptions, beliefs and norms which pervasively influence people's behaviours and actions. It is a vital ingredient of sustainable performance success.

In fact, it has been said to be the cornerstone of organisational capability. Yet, unlike processes, organisational structure, etc., culture is intangible, hence difficult to 'implement'. You can't write down a set of imperatives and say to staff, "Here's our culture. Go ye forth and embody this!" Rather, culture is the ethereal embodiment of who we are collectively and what we stand for – our organisational DNA; it's 'how we do things around here'.

Some time ago, I delivered a talk on Organisational Effectiveness and Capability to the global Procurement team of a prominent multinational hospitality group, at a conference event in Spain. It was part of their journey to create an effective purchasing capability spanning over 3,000 operational facilities across six continents – an undertaking aligned to a broader business-wide transformation driven by the CEO. I wanted to get across the importance of their functional effectiveness to the wider business agenda in the company. So I played the group a video excerpt from an interview with their CEO, where he shared his views on the company's transformation. He talked about the need to focus on aligning their culture and organisation, first and foremost. He said it was fundamental to being able to do anything else they wanted to do.

The company's Procurement senior leadership obviously recognised the importance of aligning their functional approach to the enterprise priorities. More important was the recognition that the organisational culture was indeed fundamental to success. Their global purchasing team consisted of individuals from different national cultures, residing in different countries across the globe. Yet, collectively, they had to create, sustain and embody a unified, progressive culture that underpinned their functional effectiveness in supporting the company's goals. The company has gone on to achieve several significant accomplishments, including gaining a top-three slot on the premier industry rankings table.

That hospitality company is not unique in recognising the importance of culture to organisational success. Many other organisations and several research studies over the years have proved this relationship. It is a relationship that applies to whole companies as much as it does to functional organisations. Without the right culture Procurement can not achieve long-term sustainable success; because culture has an indelible impact on decision-making, working practices, motivation, job satisfaction, and, ultimately, capability and performance. 'Right' in this sense really means appropriate – to enhance effectiveness the culture in the Procurement function must be conducive to its goals. Taking appropriate actions to enhance organisational effectiveness in a cohesive manner (embedding effective functional leadership; setting clear, appropriate goals around which the team is aligned; building people capability; and adopting a sensible approach to individual performance and rewards) invariably creates an effective culture, one that augments the Procurement mojo. But the culture must be cherished by individuals in the Procurement function.

> **Culture is everything in any organisation. It is the embodiment of who we are collectively and what we stand for – our organisational DNA.**

The Procurement mojo demands a culture that espouses progressive values – values like integrity, proactivity, customer focus, results orientation and business partnership; values that ignite people's passions and drive positive attitudes and behaviours. A culture aligned to the Procurement mojo should foster a high performance ethos, empowering purchasing people to stretch beyond their comfort zones and expand their perspectives. It requires a focus on both short-term results and long-term growth and capability development, always imbibing intangible elements like delighting internal customers. Procurement staff must be willing to adapt, to create a capacity for learning and change to avoid stagnation.

Creating the right culture to enhance Procurement effectiveness comes down to each individual in Procurement. Because our personal values also impact the values we demonstrate in the workplace, reflecting what we stand for. If you allow and accept suboptimal or questionable working practices, you are aligning yourself to such practices. It becomes an illustration of your own ethics. One of my memorable experiences of this was a Quarterly Business Review meeting with our outsourced manufacturing partner at a company I once worked at. It was a forum we accorded significant importance, with attendees from both organisations right up to senior executive level. On this particular occasion, no sooner had we settled down to start the meeting than Brad, our supply manager for new products, burst through the door expressing his apologies as he found himself a seat. It wasn't just Brad's lateness that rankled; he had turned up in a crumpled casual shirt and jeans, and I could have sworn the slightly orangey stain clearly visible on the front of his shirt was from the previous night's pizza!

Even simple things like our appearance say a lot about who we are and what we are about. Of course, it says even more about the organisation we represent. Brad's manager counselled him afterwards about the importance of maintaining a professional image especially when dealing with external stakeholders. If he hadn't, that oversight in itself would have been far worse than Brad's shoddy behaviour, because it would have signalled acceptance – acceptance of substandard conduct that, ultimately, negates Procurement effectiveness. You demonstrate what you stand for in everything that you do and how you think. For purchasing people seeking the Procurement mojo, it is imperative to always 'walk the walk' by adopting progressive attitudes and effective leadership behaviours.

People often associate 'leadership' with leading or managing others. Indeed, effective functional leadership is critical for Procurement effectiveness. The Procurement leader is the chief architect of the culture in the team, through his or her leadership style. Earlier on I mentioned an old boss of mine, 'David', and how his leadership style created immense dissatisfaction in the team. The demotivation most individuals felt reflected a culture of disempowerment, lack of trust, minimal engagement with the functional agenda and very low sense of ownership. Being told what to do and how to do things constantly hampered initiative and accountability, and that was evident in people's attitude to their functional role responsibilities. Also, the adversarial approach David adopted with internal customers, perhaps unwittingly, cascaded down to the tactical interactions between supply management folks and their internal customers. It was one of the specific things I sought to change.

While the functional leadership style can create these sorts of negative cultural impacts, the attitudes and behaviours of individual purchasing people can be just as detrimental to Procurement effectiveness. Individuals in Procurement must embody exceptional standards of self-leadership – the ability to exercise effective leadership over one's self. Be aware of who you are, what you stand for, how you think and act, and why you think and act the way you do. This self-insight will help propel you towards the best in you – your personal mojo – and steer you to become an enduring contributor to Procurement effectiveness.

The value of self-leadership was something I repeatedly stressed to Michael, a Buyer in a client business, as I coached him to improve his personal effectiveness and take some responsibility for issues affecting the supply management capability in his company. The company had been suffering poor customer delivery performance for quite a long time. I was supporting them with a change programme to address the deficiencies. The culture in the supply management team reflected a collective laissez-faire attitude. It was reflective of the company's historical background, the manager's leadership style and the attitudes of individuals in the team. The initial assessment I carried out had identified inaccurate purchasing parameters in the Enterprise Resource Planning (ERP) system as one of the underlying operational issues. I had asked Michael to do an audit check of a sample of materials he was responsible for, and he found a whopping 450 parts with missing purchasing parameters. And these were parts with high usage volumes. As we sat together going over the ERP report, I highlighted how these items must be repeatedly creating production shortages, which in turn contributed to the poor customer delivery performance the company was suffering. I deliberately refrained from directly instructing him to address the issue. A couple of weeks later I asked Michael what he had done about those 450 items and the answer was, "Nothing".

Whatever the reason (low personal integrity, being sucked into the prevalent culture, the monkey failing off the tree, the cat being run over by a bus while crossing the street...), Michael's failure to take responsibility for the issue and address it was one of the fundamental contributing factors to the problems the company faced. His attitude and approach reflected the culture in the supply management team. But that same attitude and behaviour is what propagated the very same culture. Individuals are the molecules of the organisation. And the roots of a progressive or suboptimal culture are entrenched in personal attitudes and behaviours. In a sense, purchasing people need to embrace the same effective leadership ethos required of the functional leader in their modus operandi. Effective self-leadership is important to nurture personal capabilities. If you can't manage yourself effectively, how can you possibly manage any category, supplier or purchasing initiative successfully? And if you can not do that, what chance does your Procurement function have of finding its mojo?

The challenge this poses for Procurement functions seeking their mojo is two-fold. Firstly, Procurement leaders must think about the calibre of people they have in their function, and how their attitudes and behaviours support or negate Procurement effectiveness. Those who are committed to the functional goals and values, and demonstrate this in the way they think and act, are the Procurement Ambassadors. They get it. They understand what Procurement effectiveness is about and how they contribute to its attainment and sustainment at an individual level. Whereas, the Procurement Assassins kill functional effectiveness through suboptimal thinking patterns, and weaken the function with their regressive attitudes and behavioural tendencies. They often think the numbers are what matter, and don't care about functional values nor watch their behaviours.

You have probably met a few Ambassadors and Assassins in your career. But what about you – what are you, Procurement Ambassador or Procurement Assassin? That is the second part of the challenge: for us as individuals to think deeply about our own commitment to Procurement's goals and the cultural values we embody in the way we think and act. Organisations are made of people. Each person in Procurement, irrespective of their job role, is a reflection of the function and its DNA – the culture.

The onus is on purchasing people to demonstrate their ilk, and the credibility of their Procurement function, through their individual behaviours and attitudes. Appropriate thought processes and behavioural approaches have a significant impact on individuals' ability to create effective outcomes. Factors like skills, attributes and experience are also important, as they shape individual perspectives which influence our thinking patterns and behaviours. The proliferation of a 'get-on-with-it' orientation in many organisations means that many people allow little time for reflection and planning, rushing instead to take action. Those actions and their outcomes become the physical manifestations of the culture.

In effect, purchasing people, as individuals, shape the culture in Procurement. That same culture impacts people's growth and performance. And individual capabilities and success play a big part in creating and sustaining Procurement effectiveness. It is important to grasp this relationship to fully appreciate the role you play as an individual in securing your Procurement mojo. Gaining that understanding requires a paradigm shift, moving from conventional orientations to seeing and thinking differently. By creating different mental models and, thus, shifting your perspective you enable and empower yourself to feel and behave differently.

> **It is our attitudes and behaviours at an individual level that shape the culture in Procurement. So what are YOU – a Procurement Ambassador or a Procurement Assassin?**

I often use a simple card exercise with individuals and groups to illustrate the concept of shifting perspectives. If I hold a normal business card up to you and ask you what you see, you will probably describe it as "a business card", and, perhaps, read out what the card says – the name, job title, company and so on. But I, on the other side of the card, will see something different: a blank card on the reverse side. Yet we'd both be looking at the same card. Of course, if we swap positions each of us will be able to see what the other had seen. So it is with shifting perspectives – it's really about seeing things from different viewpoints. And we always have the choice of deciding which perspective to adopt.

The ability to open your mind to change your perspectives is an extremely powerful tool to aid understanding of the Procurement mojo. It has massive impacts on how you interact with colleagues in Procurement and stakeholders outside the function. It is often the critical factor in your ability to delight internal customers. It is also a key aspect of personal effectiveness. It is impossible to build Procurement effectiveness without a significant majority of the individuals in Procurement being effective. One of the easiest ways of ascertaining your own personal effectiveness is to look at how you expend your critical resources.

One of the most valuable resources for any individual is time. 'Time management' has become a ubiquitous term, often misused and abused. In truth, time management is a myth. You can not manage time. Time is what it is – a second is a second, a minute is a minute, an hour is an hour... You can not massage or influence the duration of any measure of time. What you can manage is yourself – what you do with your time. Most people in the workplace spend the bulk of their time ineffectively, on stuff that may be urgent but really not important. Think about yourself and your typical work day: are the things that take up the most of your time at work *really* things that take you towards your specific objectives and contribute to your Procurement function's effectiveness in a positively impactful way?

Stephen Covey's counsel is valuable here. It is very easy to fall into the 'urgent not important' trap, not just at work but even in our private lives. Urgent things demand our immediate focus, but most of the time we do have a choice in deciding whether or not to fulfil that demand. Whereas important things relate directly to the outcomes we seek – the tasks or actions we need to take to achieve the specific goals, objectives or results we desire. So the key question for you (yes, YOU!) is this: do you spend the bulk of your time on important things, things that relate directly to your personal objectives and your Procurement function's goals, vision and intended outcomes?

As I sit here writing this, I recall a conversation I had with Henry, the Procurement Manager in a client business, just yesterday. The company is a medium-sized manufacturer and distributor of automotive products. It has been a victim of its own success. The supply management capability has not kept up with the massive top-line growth the business has experienced. And they are now suffering multiple problems with in-feed supply reliability, internal supply chain management deficiencies and poor outbound supply performance; so much so that they are facing serious threats of loss of business from several of their major customers. I started helping the organisation address these issues about a couple of months ago. And only yesterday Henry was telling me of his efforts to prod his colleague, the Production Manager, into ensuring manufacturing operations were in line with customer required delivery dates. There's no question that this is a noble ideal. The whole internal and external supply chain should be geared to delight customers by meeting, if not exceeding, their requirements consistently. But Henry himself heads a Procurement department with no goals and no performance measures. Thus, he has no way of establishing whether his own area is properly aligned to customer requirements or the corporate goals. His people have poorly defined responsibilities, no objectives and operate with shoddy working practices, having no defined formal processes. Neither he, as a manager, nor his department are succeeding in contributing value to the business right now. Yet he feels that prodding one of his peers is good use of his time, when his own house is not in order.

If, like Henry, you waste your time and brain horsepower ineffectively, rather than focusing on the important things that will take you and your Procurement function to the outcomes you want, then you are damaging your personal effectiveness and negating your Procurement mojo to boot. It is our attitudes and behaviours at an individual level, when aggregated to the functional or organisational level, that illustrate starkly what the culture is; not what we say or write in fancy presentations, sourcing plans or websites.

In many senses, perhaps culture is the most valuable trait of the effective Procurement organisation. Yet it can't be 'implemented' or 'defined' in a conventional sense, like processes, systems or organisational structures. Rather, it is an embodiment, or reflection, of the mix of all the other traits. Create the right culture and you create the right organisational context for everything that happens in your Procurement function. The right organisational context produces satisfied and engaged purchasing people. They in turn are motivated to create value by delighting internal and external customers and other stakeholders.

Procurement Mojo: Some things to think about...

Ask yourself these questions, and take effective corrective actions if the <u>honest</u> answers reveal that you are not heading towards your Procurement mojo!

❖ What is the culture in our Procurement organisation?
❖ What does the culture say about us? And how does it support or hinder our functional effectiveness?
❖ Have we clarified our desired behaviours and values to all our purchasing people?
❖ Does our culture adequately embody the values we espouse – values that ignite people's passions and drive the behaviours for success?
❖ How do I, as an individual, contribute to the culture – am I a Procurement Ambassador or a Procurement Assassin?
❖ Do I embody effective self-leadership in my thinking and day-to-day activities?
❖ Do I spend the bulk of my time on things that are truly important rather than things that are merely urgent?
❖ What should I be doing, or doing more of, routinely to nurture a progressive culture that supports our Procurement effectiveness?

To conclude this chapter, you probably weren't expecting to read about culture, leadership, people capability and things frequently referred to as "all that pink and fluffy stuff" in a book on enhancing Procurement effectiveness. But that 'pink and fluffy stuff', coupled with other tangible elements, like processes and systems, is what true Procurement capability is about. Just ask anyone who has created a Procurement function that delivers truly sustainable, long-term performance and is highly regarded for its value-add across the wider enterprise.

Procurement effectiveness is how we enable and empower the Procurement function to demonstrate and leverage its true potential. It is the very essence of true success for any accomplished Procurement function. Building an effective Procurement organisation is the most critical requirement to enhance Procurement effectiveness. It demands seamless alignment of the core elements described above – effective functional leadership; clear and appropriate goals around which the organisation is aligned; robust people capability; an effective approach to managing individual performance and rewards; and a progressive culture that embodies the integration of these elements to support Procurement's intended outcomes. Focusing on these elements to build an effective Procurement function is the first step towards finding your Procurement mojo.

STEP 2: DEPLOY FIT-FOR-PURPOSE ENABLERS

I have expounded the critical importance of the softer elements of the Procurement mojo, the intangible stuff we often refer to as 'pink and fluffy', giving them greater emphasis than the hard, tangible stuff like processes and tools. This is deliberate. The overriding focus many purchasing people accord the hard stuff is misplaced. And this prevents most Procurement functions from unleashing their true potential. Consequently, in sharing my knowledge and experience on enhancing Procurement effectiveness, I think it is vital to flag up how more Procurement functions can find long-term sustainable success by giving due attention to critical soft levers; almost like a beacon to get lost ships back on-course for the harbour. But this in no way detracts from the value of tangible enablers – processes, systems and tools – in enhancing Procurement effectiveness.

Deploying functional enablers that are fit for purpose is a key step to secure the Procurement mojo. The fitness-for-purpose requirement is far more important than the popular quest for 'world-class' or 'best-in-class'. Best-in-class may not always be best for your Procurement function and its particular context. What is critical is that your Procurement enablers are both effective (as in, they are focused at the right things) and efficient, enabling Procurement staff and end-users to do their work with minimal hassle.

Importantly, while enablers are tangible components of Procurement effectiveness, the problems most Procurement functions face here often relate to human factors or soft issues. When you examine Procurement processes, systems or tools that are not fit for purpose, the underlying root-cause issues can usually be traced back to decisions, thinking patterns and actions by 'people'. This can be seen, for instance, in the approaches adopted by the people tasked with developing, defining or improving processes, or those responsible for implementing related systems and tools. Applying a Rolls-Royce solution to a Ford Escort problem is one of the most common problems in this area. It is a salient indicator of human factors impinging Procurement enablers. Another is the behaviour of those who deliberately choose to disregard defined processes. It is people who make enablers fit for purpose, or not.

> **Deploying enablers that are fit-for-purpose is more important than the quest for 'best-in-class'; best-in-class may not always be best for your Procurement function and its particular context.**

Many of us are familiar with the term 'enablers', often used to collectively identify defined working practices (processes) and tools (systems, models, templates, etc.). While it is a handy moniker, it can also create obfuscation in attempts to enhance effectiveness. Thus, it is important to distinguish between processes and all other enablers.

If we think of Procurement responsibilities and goals as the generic and specific 'what', respectively, then we can view functional processes as the tangible 'how' – the methods we use to achieve our goals or fulfil our responsibilities. Almost all other enablers are simply aids we employ in executing the processes. This is an important distinction in understanding the Procurement mojo; because all too often purchasing people get caught up in focusing wrongly on implementation of new systems and tools without questioning the underlying processes. It is one of the reasons many system implementation efforts fail to deliver the expected benefits.

As far as enablers go, the process is where it's at, first and foremost. No system or tool should ever be introduced for its own sake; its utilisation must always relate to supporting a process. Processes, themselves, must always be aligned to organisational responsibilities and goals. This applies to both strategic and operational Procurement processes (and those of any other functional area for that matter).

The most effective and efficient processes always imbibe a high degree of pragmatism and robustness to ensure skilful execution.

I have come across loads of Procurement processes that are cumbersome, entailing far too many non-value-adding process steps or activities. Ineffective processes like these drain value from Procurement's work and negate its contribution to the enterprise. Such processes can also have a demoralising effect on Procurement staff, on top of the waste created through reduced productivity or process efficiency. I remember my own surprise and slight irritation when I joined one company to head the supply management function; I discovered that our sourcing process required the Finance Director's approval for all contracts, even those as small as £20,000 in value, yet a Category Manager could authorise and execute purchase orders with values as high as £100,000. Pure lunacy. I guess somebody somewhere, in times earlier, obviously thought a purchase order holds less weight in a court of law than a contract. As can be expected, this procedure incensed the Category Managers, especially as the Finance Director was always too busy to get hold of and his signature added no value to most sourcing activities.

This sort of lack of common sense in business processes is not unique to purchasing operations. Organisations that suffer a dearth of 'process thinking' typically exhibit this deficiency in several areas. I was still working on fixing the supply management frivolities in the company I mentioned earlier when one of my Category Managers, Peter, walked into my office one afternoon saying, "Hey Sigi, take a look at this. I bet you didn't realise how messed up we are when you took this job!" My shock and disbelief must have shown on my face as I read the document he handed me and Peter burst into laughter. I re-read it a couple of times to confirm that I had not misread the words. But I hadn't. The instructions were quite clear and succinct: "Hi Peter, you will still need to send in an empty envelope for audit purposes."

Peter had been chasing up a claim for business expenses which was overdue for payment. Following his enquiry to the team in the Finance department that processed expenses reimbursements, he had received an email asking if he had sent in the white A4 envelope normally used to attach receipts to expenses claims. He replied, clarifying that his claim was for travel mileage only and, hence, he had no receipts. The subsequent response he got was what I now held in my hand. Peter, himself, had been so astounded by the reply email that he had printed it off to read it in hard-copy before he passed it to me.

Who in their right mind designs a process that demands an employee send an *empty envelope* to Finance in order to get expenses reimbursed?! (I can assure you that this is a true story. I was so flabbergasted I kept the email print-off and still have it to this day.)

Peter was right. I had not realised how dysfunctional the organisation was when I joined. The emailed requirement to send an empty envelope was indicative of the sort of challenges to be addressed with many of the business processes. The expenses process was not our biggest priority, but it certainly had me thinking all the same.

It's surprising how many established organisations limp along with ineffective business processes, both within Procurement and elsewhere. Sub-optimal processes have ripple effects in an organisation, creating further ineffectiveness and inefficiencies that drain resources. It is not a coincidence that robust business processes is one of the defining hallmarks of organisations that remain successful over the long term. These organisations understand the severe impacts ineffective processes can have, some of which may not be immediately apparent.

Peter's frustration, masked by a healthy sense of humour, is an example of the debilitating impacts poor processes can have on employees. This adds up with other sources of dissatisfaction at work and people eventually get fed up and demotivated. Such influences damage the psychological contract between employee and employer, and in the worse instances employees leave; especially the good ones. Those that don't, simply stay to 'turn the handle'. Demotivated staff never give their best. They end up detracting from efforts to enhance effectiveness and create lasting capability and success.

Poor employee morale and low productivity are just two by-products of ineffective business processes. More significant is the poor service quality that internal and external customers experience as a consequence. Ineffective processes will always create such undesirable business outcomes, and this applies as much to purchasing activities as to anything else in the enterprise. Consultants and software houses that peddle process management or business improvement systems are forever promulgating the need for "Process Excellence". But most business processes don't need to be 'excellent'. All that is required is understanding and application of basic process thinking, and discipline in defining and enforcing processes. Oh, yes, and a massive dose of common sense too.

Of course, process discipline is not appropriate for all situations. For example, a small entrepreneurial business ramping up growth through creativity requires a more fluid modus operandi; process discipline could stifle growth in this situation. But for mature organisations, process discipline in key business activities is a prerequisite for sustained success, especially in areas like purchasing which have a direct and significant impact on the bottom line.

Processes that enhance Procurement effectiveness must imbibe three sacrosanct principles which apply generically to all effective business processes:

(1) **Focus on organisational responsibilities and goals**. Purchasing processes must be geared *entirely* towards Procurement's functional obligations and desired outcomes.

(2) **Think of the end-user**. Purchasing processes must make life easy for the people who use or are impacted by those processes; they must enable Procurement staff and related stakeholders to perform their duties in a streamlined manner. If your processes, and any related systems or tools, are arduous, don't expect high levels of compliance.

(3) **Think of the customer**. Who is the customer for the output of the process, and how does the process reflect the voice of the customer? Purchasing processes must robustly address the needs of internal customers and, where relevant, external customers also.

For Procurement functions in search of their mojo, perhaps by embarking on a transformation initiative, remember the maxim: 'If it ain't broke, don't fix it.' Transformation programmes to enhance Procurement effectiveness can sometimes become efforts to build Rome in a day, especially in boom times when budgets are large. The lure of fixing everything, including *all* purchasing processes, often wins over pragmatism and common sense. And then a few years later, with a new Procurement leader or CPO in place, yet another transformation commences. Which begs the question: Is the organisational or business landscape so complex that Procurement functions need repeated change programmes in just a few years?

In reality, taking a good look at existing purchasing processes will probably reveal that some things work well – activities that may not be world-class but are effective and adequately align to Procurement's agenda. Efforts to enhance Procurement effectiveness should thus be focused only on those processes that really need to be fixed. Improvement effort should start with applying detailed process-mapping to such key responsibility areas, with clear identification of the desired process outcome: *What do we want as the output of this process if it works well?* Based on that, the process definition can begin, covering:

- The specific process steps – the sequence of activities that must be carried out to deliver the process output
- Organisational responsibilities – the specific job role and department responsible for each process step
- Key inputs and outputs of each step, and the related acceptable standards
- Any associated systems, tools or technology enablers to be used for each process activity.

It may also be necessary to specify a Process Leader – a single person (the job role, not the individual) who has lead responsibility for the overall process. This is particularly useful for purchasing-related processes that span multiple functional areas, or in organisations with complex lines of accountability. In such cases, this approach ensures Procurement effectiveness is not hindered by ambiguities across the wider enterprise.

> **Remember that it is people who make enablers fit-for-purpose, or not.**

Many process definition efforts fail to deliver the robust processes desired. One of the chief reasons is that the personnel involved get too carried away and start adding process steps that add no value to the defined process output. Case in point: sending an empty envelope adds no value whatsoever to the desired outcome of reimbursing an employee for his business expenses. Process definition must be ruthless to be effective. Only activities that actually add value to the defined output should form part of a process; all nice-to-have elements must be canned as they are wasteful and, thus, drain value.

A critical step in developing good processes – one often overlooked – is to *walk the process*. This means simulating the process flow as it would operate in real life. Pretend you have a real sourcing requirement to test out your draft sourcing process, or a real purchase requirement to test out your draft P2P process. And even when you think your process is pukka, don't rush to implement it or the related improvement changes; instead run a real-life pilot first. These last two steps usually flush out process flaws that would otherwise go unnoticed.

Documenting the process in a formal Process Specification is the final key element of robust process definition. Process specification documents should be communicated to people in the organisation who are impacted by the process. Process specifications should also be document-controlled, with recorded issue numbers, dates of amendments and issue authorisations. Good process management practice demands that process specification documents are stored in a central location that is easily accessible to all relevant personnel (preferably electronically, such as on an intranet website or a shared area on the enterprise network). This ensures everyone always views the same latest version.

Some important tips for successfully defining and implementing effective purchasing processes include:

- **Purchasing processes should always inherently reflect the pertinent Procurement policies and values.** And adherence to defined processes should be rigorously enforced across the organisation, augmented by appropriate leadership behaviours. This ensures operational practices are in line with Procurement's ethos.

- **Process development and improvement efforts should involve the key stakeholders impacted by the process.** The people doing the job are usually a key source of tacit knowledge that may be lost or overlooked. But the process development effort must not become a democratic activity; ultimately someone, usually the process leader, must make key decisions on the process design when there are opposing views.

- **Keep it simple and straightforward.** People find it easier to understand and follow simple processes. Most ordinary folks are turned off by process specifications that contain too much formal flow-charting jargon, fancy symbols or technical language. This can be another effect of process development personnel getting carried away with the task and forgetting the objective of the task.

- **Widely publicise the launch of a new or amended process so people are fully aware.** This is especially important for Procurement's internal customers and other stakeholders. It may even be appropriate to have several one-to-one sessions, group forums or road-shows to talk key stakeholders through the new process or major improvements made to an existing process, emphasising the benefits to *them* and the wider enterprise.

The requirement to keep things simple and straightforward is a generic imperative that applies to most business activities. Yet the nature of Procurement's role in the enterprise inherently entails a degree of bargaining with internal and external stakeholders. Thus, it can sometimes be a challenge to keep purchasing processes as simple as one would like, especially for multi-faceted endeavours like managing large outsourced supply relationships. Nonetheless, the temptation to complicate processes in any way must always be avoided.

Many Procurement functions are not properly positioned in the wider enterprise, and, thus, lack the organisational clout to fully incorporate good practices in deploying processes that enhance functional effectiveness. For instance, the favoured policy of 'No purchase order, no payment' is something that few Procurement functions are able to enforce rigorously. Repositioning the Procurement function to enable adherence to such disciplines across the enterprise is part of the Procurement mojo, and this must be a priority for the Procurement leader. A structured and holistic approach to enhancing Procurement effectiveness with the principles in this book will yield significantly better process outcomes than what prevails today for many Procurement functions.

One of the key tactics to aid success in securing the Procurement mojo is to alter the conventional perspective many purchasing people hold on functional processes. Rather than viewing Procurement processes as domains of *absolute* control, we can think of them as organisational activities encompassing the full suite of Procurement functional responsibilities, from business needs identification through to ongoing supply base management. Having already defined and clarified Procurement's raison d'être in the wider organisation, this shift of perspective enables Procurement to engage process stakeholders as the prime custodian of those organisational activities – an approach that is significantly more collaborative and less confrontational.

Those organisational activities can be sliced and diced in different ways. Some are strategic, while others are operational or tactical; some are Procurement-led but span multiple functions, while others are led by separate functions but require key inputs from Procurement; some relate to the technical purchasing task, others don't but impact Procurement in a big way.

These varying classifications, shown in figure 3.1 with examples, are useful in understanding the various organisational processes which impact Procurement effectiveness, including those not thought of or labelled as 'Procurement processes'. They also help focus attention on process development and improvement efforts.

Strategic	Operational/Tactical
❖ Strategic sourcing ❖ Supplier management	❖ Purchase order processing ❖ Supplier payments
Procurement-led	**Non-Procurement-led**
❖ Category management ❖ Spend analyses	❖ Budget planning ❖ New product/service development
Technical Purchasing-related	**Non-Technical-related**
❖ e-Sourcing ❖ PPV/VFM improvements	❖ Employee appraisals ❖ Recruitment

Figure 3.1 – Process Classifications and Examples

Basic Procurement Processes

Many Procurement functions in large organisations operate several functional processes. In some cases this reflects the greater importance accorded purchasing activities across the enterprise. Even in conventional organisational contexts, where Procurement may not yet be fully appreciated for its true value, the number of functional processes may be many and varied. But when it comes down to it, for most Procurement functions there are three basic functional processes that must be bolstered to enhance effectiveness:

(1) Sourcing
(2) Supply execution, and
(3) Supply base management.

The specific structure and content of each of these, and even the process names, vary from organisation to organisation. But the end results are the same – they all relate to the core areas of Procurement's functional responsibilities.

The essence of the sourcing process should be about identifying enterprise supply requirements and planning for the fulfilment of those needs. Procurement should work with internal customers, and other stakeholders as required, to clarify supply needs properly. An effective sourcing process should entail early Procurement involvement, such that purchasing people can provide expert advice up front and influence the development of requirements specifications. Proactive customer relationship management is always a great advantage here.

Supply execution processes should be focused on actual fulfilment of sourcing requirements. Fulfilment may involve deploying pre-established category strategies, or developing specific supply solutions where appropriate. For many organisations this is where the purchase-to-pay (P2P) procedure can augment process efficiency and productivity, or drive employees and suppliers mad with frustration. The cycle of actually buying and paying for goods and services is one of the purchasing activities most fraught with internal conflict and misunderstanding.

The P2P process is poorly understood for a number of reasons, one of which is a lack of clarity on functional responsibilities – which function should be doing what in the process. Also, different organisations adopt different practices for different types of spend. In some organisations the sourcing activity is integrated to the P2P process and is not viewed or managed as separate from supply execution. Whereas, for others sourcing is distinctly different from the P2P activity. The nature of the procured goods or services also plays a part in how organisations structure their core purchasing processes. However, the fundamentals of an effective P2P process are straightforward. Figure 3.2 outlines the basic structure of a simplified P2P process with integrated sourcing and typical feedback loops for queries; we can examine some of the relevant issues here.

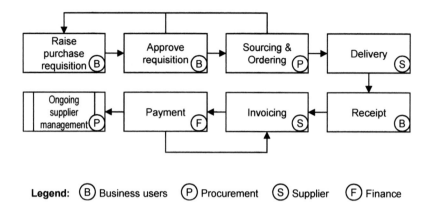

Legend: Ⓑ Business users   Ⓟ Procurement   Ⓢ Supplier   Ⓕ Finance

Figure 3.2 – Basic Purchase-to-Pay Process

An effective P2P process involves the core steps shown. It starts with a requisition raised by the person who has a supply requirement, or someone specifically nominated to raise purchase requisitions. Requisitioning is the means by which the organisation formally stipulates a need for the purchase of goods or services.

Next, the manager responsible for the cost centre (the budget-holder) must approve the requisition. This approval signifies that the person who 'owns' the budget from which the goods or services will be paid for is happy for the purchase to proceed. This is the point at which the organisation, in effect, approves the commitment of finances for the purchase. A widely accepted good practice here is the use of Delegated Financial Authorities (DFAs) to allocate appropriate levels of expenditure approval to managers or budget-holders in line with organisational hierarchies and responsibilities. It is appropriate that requisitions are created and financially approved by the internal customer departments as they are the users of the goods and services to be procured, and they typically own the relevant budgets.

Once the requisition is approved sourcing can begin. Sourcing is a critical area where Procurement can demonstrate its value-add to any organisation. Unfortunately far too many people have tried to overcomplicate this rudimentary purchasing activity. Sourcing is quite simply finding the right 'source' – right supplier, right quality and right commercial terms, including delivery lead-time and price – for the required goods or services, a key responsibility for Procurement.

An effective Procurement function should be leveraging its functional expertise to ensure the enterprise gets value-for-money from supply markets. Such expertise includes working closely with internal customers to develop a sound understanding of current *and future* requirements; aggregating requirements across the enterprise to leverage spending power; and maintaining robust supply market intelligence and awareness of competitive dynamics, to augment successful negotiation of optimal sourcing arrangements that secure desired value on purchasing spend.

Quite often, it may be appropriate for Procurement to involve internal stakeholders in the sourcing activity; for example, supplier selection for specialist services or bespoke goods. While such collaboration can be effective, ultimate responsibility for sourcing must lie with the Procurement function in most cases. Cost-effective sourcing arrangements are a core Procurement functional deliverable.

In situations where sourcing strategies are developed up front, the purchasing activity here is limited to ensuring that goods and services are procured in line with the pre-defined sourcing arrangements, e.g. getting quotes or ordering only from preferred or approved suppliers, or ordering at the pre-agreed prices.

Ordering goods and services from suppliers is best done using Purchase Orders (POs), not telephone calls, emails or verbal instructions. And issuing POs electronically is most effective, as it creates an audit trail which is available for query if problems subsequently occur. Electronic means of ordering can range from basic facsimile to Electronic Data Interchange (EDI) and supplier extranets.

As custodians of third-party spend Procurement must control the financial elements of purchase ordering. It is important to clarify that this does not necessarily mean Procurement must do the tactical activity of raising POs; a well structured, technology-enabled P2P process can enable business users or internal customers to raise their own POs (with in-built compliance governance). Procurement's key responsibility here is spend control – making sure purchase spend is in line with defined functional governance. Enforcement of this control is best done through a Delegated Purchasing Authority (DPA) mechanism, which sets out the specific levels and categories of purchasing spend which individual Procurement personnel should approve before POs are issued.

DPAs are usually set to reflect category ownership and organisational hierarchies within the Procurement function. DPAs may also include the Finance Director and CEO who must approve certain spends in addition to Procurement. Effective DPA mechanisms are structured such that most routine expenditure is approved within Procurement. Only exceptionally high levels of spend or extraordinary supply requirements need further approval beyond Procurement.

A supplier can deliver the required goods or services after a PO is received. Once the goods or services have been delivered, the recipient within the enterprise must confirm receipt of the items, usually via related transactions on the ERP system. The recipient may be a dedicated person who has been allocated responsibility for goods receipting such as a store-man.

Suppliers should send their invoices as early as possible after the goods or services have been delivered, except where the pre-agreed sourcing arrangements include specified timings for supplier invoicing, e.g. on a specific day each month. Supplier invoices must include accurate information such as the relevant PO number. Suppliers should only be paid after invoices have been accurately reconciled against pertinent purchasing information, e.g. the invoice quantity must match the received quantity. Invoice reconciliation, or approval for payment, is usually best done by the personnel who received the goods or services.

In many organisations the Accounts Payable function in Finance is responsible for paying suppliers. Payments must only be made against invoices that have been approved. Supplier payments should be done via formal, regulated transactions, such as cheques or electronic transfer payments, but never by cash. This ensures audit traceability and minimises the risk of fraud.

Ongoing supplier management is an integral part of the purchasing spectrum. Its importance to Procurement's value-add is critical enough to demand the same structured approach adopted for the P2P cycle – a defined process. Sadly, supplier management is an activity many organisations still ignore, only typically engaging existing suppliers when supply disruptions occur or at contract renewals. Managing suppliers proactively ensures an organisation's supply base is more cost-effective, aligned to the enterprise strategy and poses minimal business risk. We examine these issues in more detail in the chapter on Adopting Robust Supply Base Management.

Of course, a P2P process with integrated sourcing, as illustrated above, may not be appropriate for all contexts. In some cases, such as purchasing for capital goods, new product development or large projects, sourcing is typically a multifarious activity demanding a distinct procedure that is separate from the operational elements of the P2P process. Here the supply solution is typically bespoke and must be developed as such, prior to P2P execution. The P2P cycle, thus, typically entails the tactical tasks of requisitioning; purchase ordering; invoicing; and supplier payments. In such cases, the flow of information and transition of tasks from the sourcing phase to the operational P2P phase must be governed tightly while maintaining an intrinsic degree of seamlessness. This is best achieved when the up front sourcing procedure is robust.

Figure 3.3 illustrates a simplified version of a discrete sourcing process that subsequently inputs to an operational P2P process.

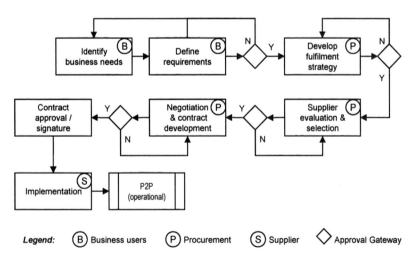

Figure 3.3 – Simplified Sourcing Process

It is worth clarifying a few important points here.

- Identifying enterprise supply needs in such situations is typically done by the business user department. Appreciating the underlying business drivers is as important for Procurement as developing a solid understanding of the requirement as early as possible. Procurement should exert appropriate influence to ensure requirements are valid and do not detract from other enterprise activities.

- Having fleshed out and examined all the pertinent issues, the requirements must be properly stipulated. This is best done using a formal Requirements Specification document, which may also incorporate supplementary information like drawings, test requirements and so on. Procurement should use relevant expertise to help the customer-department structure the requirements definition. For example, business users may be unaware of the advantages of specifying supply requirements by desired performance outputs rather than input activities. This can be extremely beneficial to the enterprise in subsequent value extraction.

- Formal approval of the requirements definition is vital, because the Requirements Specification, in effect, is what Procurement will go to market with. Procurement, the internal customer and other relevant key stakeholders must sanction the Requirements Specification formally before Procurement expends effort developing the fulfilment strategy.

- Having a solid grasp of the business needs combined with deep supply market intelligence positions Procurement strongly to develop optimal fulfilment strategies. It is important to consider a range of sourcing options, taking into account the total lifecycle value offering and inherent risks of each option. The optimum supply solution may not necessarily be that which offers the maximum financial benefits.

- Formal approval of the intended fulfilment strategy is just as vital as approving the requirements definition. The defined approach herein will be a key factor in subsequent supplier evaluations and the contract structure. The internal customer and other relevant key stakeholders must be happy with Procurement's defined approach, and signify this formally to avoid squabbles and finger-pointing later on. This is a key gateway where the enterprise indicates collective consent of the 'what' and the 'how'.

- Evaluating prospective suppliers and making a final selection is often where the seeds of subsequent supply fulfilment deficiencies are sown. Situations where sourcing is done discretely from operational P2P inherently entail a degree of captive supply, where it is often time-consuming, costly and painful to change suppliers later on. Hence, it is critical that ample effort is expended here, taking in inputs from various sources and functional areas, to properly evaluate prospective vendors and select the best-fit supplier. For some goods and services, assessing best-fit may even extend to considering the cultural alignment, leadership bench-strength and strategic direction of prospective suppliers. Some of the pertinent issues here, including risk management, are covered in the chapter on Adopting Robust Supply Base Management.

- As with other approval gateways, collective endorsement of the selected supplier must be done formally by all relevant stakeholder functions, prior to the selected supplier being notified. You can't tell a supplier they've been selected for a particular requirement and then go back and say, "Oh no, XYZ department disagrees with Procurement's decision." Indeed, as mentioned above, it is often appropriate that supplier selection is jointly decided by Procurement and the relevant stakeholder department(s).

- Contract negotiations are another activity that can often be problematic. A typical problem issue is business users demanding things which were never stipulated up front in the requirements definition or fulfilment strategy. Spending more effort with these preceding activities should free Procurement up to tackle the deal-making better. This is another activity where individual purchasing people can prove their worth by leveraging their functional expertise.

- Approving the contract structure and contents is the final endorsement by which the key parties – Procurement; the internal customer department; any other relevant key stakeholder departments; and the supplier – signify collective agreement on the 'what' and the 'how', including the commercial terms.

- For some organisations and some types of purchases or levels of spend, the designated signatory for major supply contracts may be a senior executive, such as the Finance Director or CEO.

Of course, sourcing processes that are distinct from the operational P2P cycle vary across organisations. However, the heterogeneous nature of such sourcing activities is a common trait. This unique characteristic necessitates rigorous governance to avoid enterprise risk exposure. Thus, approval gateways must be mandatory and tightly policed, but must also be simple and sensible. Only relevant functions or personnel need to approve specific gateways, not every man and his dog. Approval documents must be formal, using defined templates or pro-formas.

Sourcing initiatives that fail to meet the defined approval criteria must be rejected – people must be made to go back and re-do the work properly whenever appropriate. Progressing non-compliant sourcing initiatives through approval gateways for any number of excuses more often than not creates massive problems later on. Purchasing folks who take this cowboy approach – trying to bypass process governance steps or failing to do things properly – damage Procurement effectiveness. They must be recalibrated.

Sometimes such suboptimal practices are driven by senior executives or powerful players in the enterprise. Rather than rolling over backwards and permitting this, it is important that purchasing people educate such stakeholders on the value of process discipline – this is part and parcel of effective stakeholder management, which is covered in the chapter on Building Your Procurement Brand.

The sourcing process specification should define which function has lead responsibility for each process activity to avoid ambiguity. However, most such sourcing activities demand close collaborative working between Procurement and stakeholder functions. So Procurement may have key inputs to activities led by the internal customer department and vice-versa. Quite often, the sourcing requirement may be so large as to require a formal, multifunctional project team. When this is done properly and people leave their egos at home, it can often be magic.

Whether or not a project team is used, it is imperative that the enterprise communicates with suppliers with 'one voice'. This is best achieved when Procurement plays its true role at the centre of such enterprise endeavours, steering the 'requirements-fulfilment-supplier management' cycle with requisite process discipline.

The varied nature of purchasing in many organisations means that Procurement processes may extend beyond the basic three mentioned above. Other than those rudimentary activities which relate directly to Procurement's core functional responsibilities, other processes should be defined where appropriate, following the same core tenets of process thinking and process discipline. Some specific examples of such additional functional processes include procedures for Early Involvement; Design-for-Purchasing; Supply Risk Management; Target Cost Management; and so on.

The requirements for unique Procurement processes can be as diverse as the differing enterprise operations and product and service offerings that exist. What is common and appropriate for purchasing in the defence industry may be of limited value in the fast-moving consumer goods sector. And what makes sense for purchasing in a construction business may be inane for a financial services company. The key thing is that Procurement deploys processes that are fit for purpose and support its functional obligations in serving the enterprise. In that regard, one functional activity which often demands the deployment of structured process governance is the management and execution of value-for-money (VFM) improvements.

> **Keep it simple and straightforward.**
> **People find it easier to understand**
> **and follow simple, clear and pragmatic**
> **processes.**

I always urge purchasing people to think in terms of 'VFM improvements' rather than 'cost savings'. A cost-oriented mindset can create a perspective that focuses too much on the price paid for goods or services, or even the Total Cost of Ownership (TCO). And, of course, any reduction in those figures is a welcome contribution to the bottom line, provided quality and supply reliability are not compromised. But cost orientation offers a narrow view of Procurement's potential contribution. A more appropriate view is to apply the value equation to procured goods and services – a measure of the benefits provided against the cost or price paid. Think about it in terms of your common postage stamps – if you want to reduce costs, just buy a second-class stamp; but your letter won't get there the next day, because you have comprised on your first-class service benefit.

Adopting the 'value' perspective impacts our thinking and approach in two important ways:

(1) It forces us to think about the service or performance level we truly need. All too often we get caught up in fanciful desires for gold-plated solutions, when enterprise needs might easily be met by less stringent service levels.

(2) It compels us to *also* consider getting more for the same cost or price, if not for less, in pursuing better financial performance on purchasing spend.

VFM improvements will always be a key deliverable for Procurement, quite rightly. Yet it is an area many Procurement functions still manage poorly, often getting into squabbles with Finance on what was really delivered versus what is claimed to have been delivered. Many Finance Directors and budget-holders still view claimed purchasing savings with a sniff of suspicion, as if the whole 'Procurement savings' issue is all smoke and mirrors. VFM measurement that should be straightforward and transparent often seems shrouded in mystery and ingenuity.

But it doesn't have to be that way. A well thought-out, properly defined and sensibly implemented formal VFM management process can provide clarity. Figure 3.4 illustrates a VFM process which I introduced at one organisation with the support of my colleagues. Working collaboratively with my Finance Business Partner, our internal customers and *their* Finance Business Partners, we were able to agree a simple but effective process for identifying, tracking and banking VFM improvements.

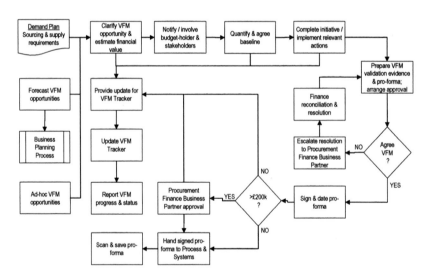

Figure 3.4 – Sample VFM Management Process

I deliberately involved these stakeholders in designing and implementing the process to ensure their buy-in. And structuring the process such that all VFM initiatives were formally signed-off by Procurement, relevant budget-holders and Finance provided clarity on each initiative. This put a stop to the inter-departmental squabbles on 'Procurement savings' that I had inherited. Additionally, working collaboratively with my Finance colleagues to develop and institutionalise the process engendered a heightened level of trust, both at a personal and functional level. The experience of 'doing it together' drew our Procurement and Finance functions much closer.

The above process is shown only for illustrative purposes. You don't have to replicate an identical process in your Procurement function as your situation may be different. What is vital is that you understand the importance of structured process governance for managing VFM improvements. Your VFM management process must fit your Procurement function's responsibilities and positioning in your organisation. It may well be that your situation demands a more complex process, possibly involving more stakeholders. On the other hand, you may be lucky enough to get away with a much simpler process. Whatever the case, it is imperative that the process governance for VFM management is effective, provides clear visibility of Procurement's achievements and enables easy validation of those achievements. That helps ensure fitness-for-purpose significantly.

Technology Enablement

Admittedly, when we implemented the VFM management process I referred to above, it relied on a basic Microsoft Excel tool as our database for tracking VFM benefits. It isn't the most sophisticated tool for a VFM management process, but it was fit for purpose. Many Procurement functions could do worse; the robustness of the VFM management process is far more important than the sexiness of the accompanying tool. The widespread availability of technology enablers for purchasing process automation makes it even easier for Procurement functions to implement good VFM management processes. For example, there are several software packages on the market now which make spend analyses and VFM benefits tracking much less cumbersome than can often be the case, providing significantly improved visibility. And there are even more IT solutions available now for e-procurement. Technology enablement is a key lever that makes a big difference to the ease of deploying sound processes and tools to enhance Procurement effectiveness.

There can be no argument on the critical value technology brings to purchasing activities, once you strip out the hype from software vendors and consultants. Automating purchasing processes and tools enables consistency; reduces transaction costs; improves visibility, especially access to real-time information for decision-making and reporting; and boosts efficiency and organisational productivity. It can also help cut maverick spend and increase spend under management through easier compliance enforcement.

Procurement functions seeking their mojo must leverage technology appropriately by automating as many purchasing enablers as is possible, practical and sensible to. This should be done in a cost-effective manner, rather than pursuing 'me too' system implementations.

Technology enablement should never be applied to broken processes or inappropriate tools. Automating a dysfunctional process simply transfers the process deficiencies onto an IT system. Root-cause problems must be fixed prior to deploying technology. Some typical technology application areas include e-sourcing; automated vendor schedules; supplier extranets; e-catalogues; contracts management databases; spend analytics; electronic knowledge repositories; and online user guides, in addition to the traditional use in MRP, MRPII, ERP and other workflow systems, email and intranets. Such technology applications can provide fantastic enterprise benefits by streamlining activities and boosting process efficiency. But they can also be a major source of frustration for end-users. This is typically the case when technology enablement is not well thought out or when the implementation approach is flawed. To avoid such pitfalls in your application of technology to your Procurement enablers, some specific key points you can imbibe include the following:

- **Secure executive-level support and the required investment for any new technology application or upgrade**. Executive support is a critical success factor for any change effort, not just technology enablement in Procurement. And when you have that, it's easier to secure the investment required. But you must also be able to demonstrate the returns on that investment, which might exceed financial benefits. Develop a solid business case that clearly articulates the balance of costs, benefits and risks.

- **Focus on the end-goal.** Right from the initial idea, through developing the specification, to configuration and implementation, stay focused on what the objective of your technology enablement is. Far too many applications end up adrift from the intended end-goals, and alienate users in the end or turn out to be a waste of resources. For instance, many organisations buy full-suite ERP systems with promises of many wonderful enterprise-wide benefits, yet fail to use the capability fully, typically limiting their actual application to MRPII, or, even worse, basic MRP, for many years hence. If you're really not going to fully leverage e-auctions, spend analytics or online catalogues in a way that enhances the effectiveness and efficiency of your purchasing operations, then don't bother. Don't do it for doing it sake. Do it because you have clarity of the benefits of the end-goal, and stay focused on that end-goal to ensure you do secure those benefits.

- **Remember end-users when developing and implementing your technology application or upgrade.** If the technology application doesn't make life easier for the users they will resent it or reject it outright, and this will detract from the actual benefits derived after implementation. Soliciting end-user inputs as part of developing the specification is a good way of getting buy-in and ensuring ease of use, both of which are key for successful end-user adoption.

- **Drive high levels of acceptance, uptake and compliance through robust communications.** This must be part of a sound change management approach that must incorporate effective programme management of the whole initiative, from concept through to post-implementation stabilisation. (See the chapter on Applying Appropriate Performance Frameworks for more details on effective governance of Procurement initiatives.)

- **Baseline the efficiency of the related process up front**. And after implementation, confirm that projected efficiency improvements have indeed been achieved through the technology enablement as expected. This validates the return on investment and also builds credibility for your Procurement function, which will make it easier to gain future investment for other purposes.

Any application of technology to purchasing activities must imbibe the same fitness-for-purpose principle that applies to all Procurement enablers. No application should ever be pursued for the sake of doing so; it must be done as part of an overall approach to deploying enablers that enhance Procurement effectiveness. Focusing on the effectiveness intent will provide the crucial guidance on selecting the most important technology applications that are appropriate for your particular Procurement function.

It is important that Procurement functions seeking their mojo adopt a broad perspective in considering processes, systems and tools that enhance Procurement effectiveness. Such enablers are not limited to those used for the technical purchasing activities. Other generic or enterprise-wide enablers can also impact Procurement capability. Some key examples include competency frameworks discussed previously; leadership development programmes; recruitment and induction processes; employee development plans; and performance management enablers. Such processes, systems and tools, though not owned or led by Procurement, can be appropriately exploited to augment the drive for Procurement effectiveness; provided those enablers, themselves, are fit for purpose in the first place.

A senior purchasing executive once told me of his experience of one company's recruitment process, something I have never forgotten. He had been recruited as VP of Supply Management and accepted the job offer, agreeing a start date a couple of months hence. Lo and behold, he turned up on his first day only to find out the organisation was as unprepared for his arrival as it could ever be – the job he had been recruited for no longer existed as a result of a reorganisation! Incredible. I know the chap and can vouch for his impeccable leadership abilities. He would have been a great asset to the organisation, and, quite probably, the critical ingredient for attaining their Procurement mojo.

Procurement functions that seriously desire to enhance effectiveness must ensure non-purchasing enablers do not derail their efforts. Such enablers can augment or hinder Procurement effectiveness just like the core purchasing processes, systems and tools. In any case, it is crucial to remember that it is people who make enablers fit for purpose, or not. Make sure that those tasked with designing, implementing and managing enablers to support your Procurement effectiveness incorporate the principles outlined above. This will be a major step towards finding your Procurement mojo.

Procurement Mojo: Some things to think about...

Ask yourself these questions, and take effective corrective actions if the <u>honest</u> answers reveal that you are not heading towards your Procurement mojo!

❖ Have we defined and implemented processes, systems and tools that enable people to be effective in their work and deliver their results efficiently?
❖ Are our processes formally documented and well communicated?
❖ Do the processes clearly articulate the process steps; responsibilities; and outputs/deliverables?
❖ Are all process steps value-adding; have we eliminated all value-draining/non-value-add activities from our processes?
❖ Do the documented processes reflect actual working practices?
❖ Are our systems, tools and other enablers truly fit for purpose?
❖ Are staff adequately competent with these enablers?
❖ Do our enablers fully leverage technology to maximise efficiency and productivity?
❖ Are there any non-Procurement-led enterprise processes which hinder our Procurement effectiveness?
❖ How well do our Procurement enablers align to our functional responsibilities and goals?

STEP 3: ADOPT ROBUST SUPPLY BASE MANAGEMENT

Enhancing Procurement effectiveness is about building effectiveness throughout the purchasing or supply management infrastructure of the enterprise. The supply base is simply an external aspect of the organisation's value chain. Robust supply base management is how we extend effectiveness to this external element of the supply management infrastructure.

Many years ago, when most large businesses were still highly vertically integrated, a lot of the goods and services sourced externally in many organisations today were provided in-house – from support services like facilities cleaning and maintenance, management of fleet vehicles, IT infrastructure and travel, to core business operations like manufacturing. While many organisations continue to carry out some of these operations internally, securing goods and services from external supply sources is now a huge part of most organisations' operations. To ensure we get as much value from the external supply base as we seek from our internal Procurement function, we must think of suppliers as an extension of our capability.

The requirement to think of suppliers differently is critical. The way we think of suppliers always manifests itself itself in how we manage them or the actions we take in our interactions with them. These thinking and behavioural practices reflect our individual and collective levels of effectiveness, and, crucially, reveal that we, as people, are the key factor in Procurement's ability to manage the supply base robustly. This applies to everyone – the senior executives or budget-holders who are typically powerful players in the enterprise, the internal consumers of the goods or services supplied and even the CEO. But mostly it applies the folks in Procurement who do the job.

Managing the supply base robustly is particularly vital for Procurement effectiveness for the very reason that it is external. We in Procurement are just as responsible for what our suppliers deliver to the enterprise – satisfaction or pain – as we are for our internal operations. No matter how streamlined the internal purchasing infrastructure is, Procurement will always be limited or augmented in its overall capability and performance by the capability and performance of the supply base. In today's world, where issues like ethics, the environment and corporate social responsibility (CSR) have high prominence, it becomes even more crucial that the supplier management approach is aligned to Procurement's goals and the corporate agenda.

> **The supply base is simply an external aspect of the enterprise value chain. Think of suppliers as an extension of Procurement capability.**

Adopting robust supply base management requires you to apply the same sacrosanct ethos of effectiveness in your dealings with suppliers – do the right things to get the outcomes you want. The impact suppliers can have on any organisation can not be overstated. In early 2012, for instance, a major outdoor clothing brand faced huge customer backlash when it was reported in the press that feathers used in its jackets were from a supplier that force-fed geese for *foie gras*. One newspaper article quoted a brochure published by the clothing company a couple of years earlier, in which the company had claimed that force-feeding for *foie gras* had been banned in its supply chain for many years. Somebody obviously forgot to execute this properly in the supply pipeline and ensure the supply base reflected these ethical sourcing claims. The cumulative financial damage the company suffered as a consequence of the revelations will probably never be known. Neither will the reputational damage ever be easily quantifiable.

The same can be said for the international supermarket giants whose beefburger products were discovered to contain horsemeat in January 2013. Yet again, the problem appears to have originated in their supply base.

Back in 2007, a prominent North American toy manufacturer suffered similar repercussions when it had to recall vast quantities of products which had been covered in lead paint. The toys were made by a contract manufacturer in the Far East, and the toy company's chief executive clarified that it was a supplier facility the company had worked with for over a decade. It just goes to show that even with long-term supply partners the need to maintain robust supply base management remains vital.

There can be no doubt that such deficiencies in a company's supply chain do immense harm to brand equity and CSR credentials, even when there are no related supply disruptions. CSR and protecting the corporate brand image are not the only justifications for robust supply base management. Managing suppliers robustly offers opportunities to leverage their expertise and capabilities for competitive advantage, if properly harnessed. But such benefits are never a one-off; they need to be optimised and sustained over time, while continuously ensuring alignment to enterprise needs and the strategic agenda. To secure these advantages, purchasing people must be able to identify the core supply base issues relevant to their organisations. Whether issues like ethical sourcing and environmental considerations are important to the enterprise or not, fundamental factors like supply capability; supply reliability; competitiveness; value for money; and 'ease of doing business' must always be central to a robust supply base management approach.

It's interesting to note how many organisations or purchasing professionals make sourcing decisions based, entirely or largely, on cost or price. The phenomenal growth of low-cost country sourcing is indicative of this drive. The opportunity to save up to forty percent of purchase price is too much of a lure for most buyers and their organisations. Low-cost country sourcing is good for global trade and world economic development, that's for sure. But purchasing people are not macro economists or social development professionals; our job is not to drive global trade and economic development but to secure value for our employers. And there's no doubt that low-cost country sourcing offers some enticing avenues to deliver that value and expand product margins. But value is not just about financial gains or savings. We must always consider broader factors than just the purchase price advantages. The challenges and risks of doing business with low-cost country suppliers can sometimes override the benefits of purchase price reductions. Risks like political instability; foreign exchange controls; threats to intellectual property protection; fraud; poor product quality; and deficient supply reliability are not always easy or inexpensive to address.

When your low-cost country supplier starts causing you supply disruptions and production shortages (which is often the case when the initial sourcing decision and ongoing supplier management is flawed), the purchase price saving will not seem worth it. And your internal customers won't be thinking, "Ah, the supplier Procurement use is delivering late or their quality is poor, but the cost is cheaper so I'm happy." Situations like this damage the Procurement mojo, because the performance of suppliers is reflective of Procurement itself and what it stands for.

The client I mentioned earlier – the automotive products manufacturer – is a good example of this point. The business moved a huge chunk of its purchases to the Far East some years ago and made considerable savings. It has continued to migrate more supply sourcing to Asia, which currently accounts for about forty-five percent of direct material purchases. I remember the sourcing manager telling me with pride of his "8% PPV" achievement when I first started working with the client. Today, poor supplier in-feed reliability on their Asia-sourced materials is creating such havoc for their operations that the company is now paying out hefty penalties and liquidated damages to customers for line stoppages due to late deliveries. Their On-time-In-full (OTIF) delivery performance has dropped to below fifty percent and customers are screaming; some are even threatening to move their business. No one has sat down to do the calculations, but it's clear that some of the savings from the low-cost country sourcing is being eroded. In fact, that sourcing strategy, or suboptimal approaches to supply base management in executing the strategy, may well end up costing the company some business revenue. Does the sourcing manager incorporate these broader considerations in his view of the world, or is his mind narrowly focused on his 'great PPV'? What do you think?

Considering the wider ramifications of how we select and manage suppliers means seeking the optimal balance between costs, benefits and risks. Before focusing on any savings or financial benefits you might secure from your supply base, it is crucial to ensure supplier capability and reliability match your organisation's needs. This should constitute the fundamental criteria upon which your sourcing decisions are made. And these criteria must be key factors in how you manage your supply base on an ongoing basis.

Of course, Procurement does not operate in a vacuum. And it may be part of the 'organisational dance' to get senior management and other key stakeholders thinking this way too. Purchasing people must not shy away from challenging organisational thinking and leanings which might detract from long-term value considerations. Part of the job is to educate the wider organisation on what makes sense for the enterprise, while balancing short-term needs with long-term capability development. As I have mentioned previously, we must never lose sight of the fact that our supply base is an extension of our organisational capability, one which Procurement has prime responsibility for.

> **The performance of suppliers is reflective of Procurement itself and what it stands for.**

Securing optimal value from the supply base is the essence of robust supply base management. It provides a unique conduit to harnessing supply market intelligence and capability for organisational benefits, which can transcend to competitive advantage. To ensure the supply base delivers value for the enterprise it is important to continually drive competitiveness. The conventional notion of a competitive supply base is another area where traditional perspectives fall short of what is required for the Procurement mojo. Purchasing people must expand their perceptions of value for money from the prevalent notion of 'cost savings' – getting the same service for less cost or price.

Firstly, it is crucially important to recognise what 'value' means to the organisation in the broadest sense, without losing sight of the key aspect of economic value. Value for money enhancements might also include getting more for the same price, or leveraging opportunities for supply innovation. It can be as simple as asking suppliers directly what they can bring to the table beyond the basic product or service being supplied.

It may sound patronising to say this, but far too many purchasing people still fail to leverage their supply base fully. This is partly due to the fact that many Procurement buyers are inadequately versed in deep knowledge of their supply markets. And the lack of underlying effectiveness in the way they operate hampers their ability to leverage what they know properly when they have decent supply market knowledge. This competency gap is one of the key deficiencies at the heart of the 'lack of talent in Procurement' that many surveys and commentators highlight. To identify and fully exploit the immense value locked in the supply base, buyers must develop a solid understanding of the supply market forces and levers, just as any good sales and marketing guy has to do at the front-end of the business. And like any good salesman, buyers must incorporate effectiveness into how they go about the job. Applying the principles explained in this book is a good start, especially the requirement to think differently.

Thinking of suppliers as a component of the Procurement function can help bring about the mindset shift that offers valuable insights to harnessing supply base potential. It demands a holistic perspective, taking into account the 'total lifecycle value-offering' of a supplier or potential supplier. In stating this, I've deliberately refrained from using 'Total Cost of Ownership' (TCO), a widely accepted term which is well understood by many experienced sourcing professionals. TCO was popularised by the IT industry as a vehicle to reveal all costs associated with IT investment decisions. Since then it has seen wide application as a tool or methodology that goes beyond initial purchase price to take account of other costs, such as operations and maintenance costs and end-of-life management costs.

TCO application is a significant step forward from traditional considerations in sourcing which tend to focus only on purchase price.

And supply base considerations which embrace TCO principles are much more likely to deliver enhanced value for the enterprise than an approach which focuses purely on purchase price. Despite this, it is worth pointing out that TCO models are still financial mechanisms – they provide a broader view of 'costs' than the conventional approach, but remain constrained to economic elements. Less tangible costs and benefits can easily be overlooked, yet some of these can be critical considerations in managing the supply base robustly. How well a supplier's technology roadmap aligns to the enterprise needs or strategic agenda is an example of non-economic factors which purchasing people should consider in value assessments for relevant supply lines. Others include a supplier's ability to deliver both commercial and operational innovations, preferably as proven by a track record.

Having a pre-defined list of such considerations is less important than the thinking that must precede it. It is crucial to take the time and effort to think through what the immediate and long-term requirements are and what value truly means to the enterprise. For some organisations, value in the supply base is illustrated by the relative positioning of their suppliers; some will be seen as 'Partners' and managed accordingly, some may be 'Preferred' vendors and others simply 'Approved' suppliers on an Approved Vendor List (AVL). Organisations that take this approach must ensure that so-called partners indeed deliver value beyond what is expected or demanded of non-partner suppliers. Oftentimes, organisations make such distinctions and then fail to continuously monitor and manage the supply base to ensure the appellations remain valid and reflective of reality. Taking an effective approach to how you manage supplier alignment to enterprise needs will reveal those suppliers that really deliver true value to the organisation; it will enable you to separate the chicken salad from the chicken shit in your supply base.

Supplier Performance and Relationship Management

Irrespective of the tactics used to identify and harness suppliers' value offerings, one fundamental tenet of robust supply base management is the need to manage supplier performance and relationships effectively. Supplier performance is always important; actual performance is the common denominator across the supply base. It can be used to distinguish those suppliers who are true value creators and those that are simply adept at sales pitches that win them business. While basic performance measures like in-feed delivery and quality may be applied to most vendors, a more holistic structure is required for suppliers that are true partners, or deemed to be critical or high-risk. With this cadre of vendors, nurturing effective relationships is as essential as managing performance. The relationship must never be segregated from the performance.

Supplier Performance and Relationship Management (SPRM) offers a structured approach to managing suppliers to optimise value leverage. True SPRM that seeks to unlock and extract supply base value optimally takes some effort to get in place initially. It must be implemented in a sensible, methodical manner. But the effort is a very worthwhile investment that always yields long-term benefits when the approach is right.

The first consideration is that SPRM can't be applied across the board with all vendors. Rather, it must be focused on the critical few. Some organisations choose to call this special cadre of vendors their 'strategic suppliers'. I am hesitant to use the term because it is often abused. All too often, far too many suppliers are categorised as 'strategic' or 'partners'. And many organisations don't actually manage their so-called "strategic suppliers" strategically. Whatever term is used, what is vital is the understanding that this group of vendors are indeed special. The critical importance of their supply offering to the enterprise's value chain is what makes them special.

So who are these suppliers, and how do we define 'strategic' or 'special' in this regard?

> **Nurturing effective relationships with suppliers is as important as managing their performance.**

While many proponents of SPRM and its subsets – Supplier Performance Management (SPM) and Supplier Relationship Management (SRM) – often offer prescriptive answers to these questions, the truth is that the definition of who these elite suppliers are will vary from organisation to organisation. There can be no singular, definitive answer because enterprise needs and strategic priorities vary so much. Remember, what the Procurement function does must always be about delivering value *aligned to enterprise needs and the strategic agenda*. For one organisation the emphasis might be on the financial or economic aspects of value such as spend optimisation or cost efficiencies, while for another it might be innovation or technological capability. Thus, purchasing people must think deeply to properly identify suppliers that are truly strategic to the enterprise. These deliberations are best done jointly with internal customers who are the consumers of the supply service. It is also imperative to sit with appropriate senior executives to gain insights on the organisation's strategic roadmap.

Some of the key considerations in subsequently assessing supplier alignment and relative positioning must include questions like:

- How critical is the supplier's product or service to the successful operation of our business or the functionality of our own product or service value offering?

- How much do we spend with them, and what proportion of our total spend does that constitute?

- How well does their technology, product or service roadmap align to ours?

- How similar or complementary are their enterprise goals or strategic direction to ours?

- What opportunities are there for collaboration for mutual long-term benefits towards our respective enterprise goals or strategic intents?

- What benefits beyond sales revenue accrue to the supplier from staying in the dance with us over the long term; and, conversely, what benefits do we get beyond the goods or services supplied?

The answers to such questions may well lead to other considerations. That's good; because achieving the goal of value extraction through SPRM starts with the quality of thinking that goes into identifying the target suppliers. Taking a structured approach to identify critical or strategic suppliers must not be a one-off activity; it should be repeated periodically – perhaps once a year – as enterprise needs and supply market dynamics can be ever changing.

An effective SPRM framework should centre on shared goals for the relationship between the buying enterprise and the supplier to ensure mutual alignment. These goals should be clearly stated and serve as the bedrock of a governance infrastructure to manage interactions. In this regard, two key elements that must be incorporated to the governance are the use of a 'mirrored structure' and involvement of senior executives.

A mirrored structure simply highlights organisational responsibilities for specific aspects of the relationship in both the buying and the supplying organisations. As shown in figure 4.1, for instance, the apex of the interaction may be the most senior executive in each organisation with functional responsibility for the supplier-customer relationship. Though this illustration is meant to serve as a simple example, it is important to stress that a good mirrored structure should cover all strategic and operational areas of the interaction. In some cases this may best be shown with an organogram.

Mirrored Structure - Acme PLC and Supplier Limited Last Updated: June 2014	Acme PLC	Supplier Ltd.
Senior Executive	VP Procurement Heather Preshe Tel: +44 (0)20 7729 8442 E-mail: heather.preshe@acme.com	Global Account Director Tom Kidman Tel: +44 (0)7886 560 153 E-mail: tkidman@supplier.com
Commercials	Sourcing Manager Darth Vader Tel: +44 (0)7745 111 343 E-mail: darth.vader@acme.com	Account Manager Nicole Cruise Tel: +44 (0)1224 745 113 E-mail: ncruise@supplier.com
Quality	Supplier Quality Manager Colin Obama Tel: +44 (0)20 7729 8446 E-mail: colin.obama@acme.com Supplier Quality Engineer Bobi Marley Tel: +44 (0)20 7729 8446 E-mail: bobi.marley@acme.com	Product Quality Managers Barack Farrell Tel: +44 (0)7956 222 224 E-mail: bfarrell@supplier.com James Bond Tel: +44 (0)7956 222 222 E-mail: jbond@supplier.com
Ordering & Shipping	Buyers Don Corleone Tel: +44 (0)20 7729 8422 E-mail: don.corleone@acme.com Brad Jolie Tel: +44 (0)20 7729 8422 E-mail: brad.jolie@acme.com	Sales Order Administrators Indiana Jones Tel: +44 (0)1224 722 222 E-mail: ijones@supplier.com Angelina Pitt Tel: +44 (0)1224 722 222 E-mail: apitt@supplier.com

Figure 4.1 – Mirrored Structure for Acme PLC and Supplier Limited

Involving appropriate senior executives in SPRM (which may extend beyond those with functional responsibility) is as important as having periodic, structured reviews. There is no one-size-fits-all prescription for the frequency of such reviews. For important suppliers who may not be classed as strategic, a bi-annual review frequency may be adequate, while an annual review may be appropriate for other less important suppliers. It all depends on the organisational context – the goods or services being purchased; the enterprise short- and long-term needs; the level of stability in the supply interaction; the health of the relationship; and so on. Whatever the context though, suppliers that are truly strategic must be eyeballed quarterly.

Quarterly Business Reviews (QBRs) with strategic suppliers should be aligned to the timing of quarterly business results in the buying enterprise. This way the QBRs serve as true supply business reviews, where the last quarters' performance and relationship issues are discussed in tandem with requirements and plans for the ensuing quarter and the longer-term future. This creates consistency and coherence, and it imbibes the fundamental tenet that Procurement activities remain aligned to the enterprise needs and strategic agenda. If the buying organisation's business results include a stated intent to establish an operational footprint in new geographical markets, for instance, the QBR may be the appropriate forum to share this formally with a strategic supplier and discuss how they might be geared to support that strategic move.

Discussions about the relationship shouldn't just be a one-sided affair. The QBR can also be an appropriate forum to solicit and discuss the supplier's view on the organisation as a customer. Some purchasing folks baulk at the notion of asking suppliers for such feedback, perhaps fearing that this might open the door to all sorts of whinges from the supplier. But it takes two to tango; a partnership is a two-way affair, and if you're really intent on developing and nurturing a true supply partnership you might find the supplier's views insightful and educative.

Whatever the structure of the SPRM process, QBRs are a critical aspect of robust supply base management. But the effectiveness of QBRs can often be hampered at the stage of developing the SPRM process. This is usually because the desired outcomes are not well thought out or the implementation approach is flawed. One of the most common mistakes made is in the erroneous interpretation of Procurement's responsibility for supply base management – this often manifests itself in the exclusion of other functional areas in designing the SPRM process. A good SPRM process must incorporate inputs from other functions that play key roles in harnessing and managing supply base value. While Procurement must retain lead responsibility for the overall process, other functions like Quality,

Engineering, Manufacturing, Field Services and Finance must be involved as appropriate.

To illustrate the importance of this, let's consider a typical manufacturing company. In such an organisation the Engineering function typically has responsibility for product design and development. Their requirements of supply partners might include innovation; involvement in design-to-cost or design-for-manufacturing efforts; and responsiveness during new product development or product re-design projects. For many product businesses, most of the cost, functionality and quality of a new product are committed at the product design phase. Thus, organisations at the top of their game understand the immense value of early supplier involvement. Such Engineering considerations are important elements of creating and sustaining the enterprise's value chain, and can be critical factors affecting its long-term success. Consequently, it is appropriate and essential that Engineering have input to supplier assessments and any discussions on future supply business.

The same principle holds true for other functions like Manufacturing, who are the internal user or consumer of the supplied materials; Quality, who are responsible for quality assurance across the enterprise's internal and external value chain; and so on. The SPRM process should specify the functions responsible for each aspect of the supply base performance and relationship management spectrum. These functions must provide input assessments of suppliers for their particular areas of responsibility.

Figures 4.2 and 4.3 illustrate excerpts from an SPRM framework I implemented at one company, a multinational business which I'll refer to here as C-MEG Corporation. The company manufactured and sold equipment to major telecoms operators around the world. Changes in the telecoms market forced these companies to increasingly seek supply partners who could deliver total 'one stop shop' solutions – partners who could provide all the required equipment for a complete telecoms network, down to the interconnecting cables; design the network; and build and commission it. In some cases, the requirements included operating and maintaining the telecoms network post-commissioning.

C-MEG Corporation's strategic intent was to position itself strongly in this emerging market space as the prime telecoms network solutions provider. Providing total telecoms solutions meant a significant ramp up in the volume of non-proprietary kit sourced externally from other OEMs – products that complemented ours to create seamless solutions packages. We needed reliable supply partnerships that would augment our strategic intent. I led the strategic development of our global OEM supply pipeline to bring this to fruition. Our approach focused initially on identifying those suppliers that we saw as critical to our strategic needs.

The SPRM structure I introduced started off with emphasis on performance assurance, quite rightly. Handing over responsibility for the design of new telecoms networks or upgrades to existing networks, as well as the project management of network installations and commissioning, was a huge risk for our telecoms operator customers. The timing and capability of these network introductions were critical inputs to these companies' business plans. In the dog-eat-dog world of telecoms services, no operator can afford to spend vast marketing budgets trumpeting the arrival of new services to consumers only to have things go awry due to poor network implementation or major equipment failures. C-MEG Corporation's role in the telecoms operators' value chain was critical. In turn, we needed exceptional levels of supply service reliability from our OEM partners. We just couldn't afford the risk of poor supplier performance hindering successful project completions and marring our reputation and positioning in this new market space.

As shown in figure 4.2, the performance elements of our SPRM process was structured to provide visibility of supplier performance from project-specific level up to an aggregated global level, for those partners we used in multiple countries. It also covered both operational performance dimensions like delivery reliability and broader elements like customer service. A key aspect of the development and implementation was involving relevant functions outside Procurement who either touched and felt the suppliers' value offerings or were functionally responsible for specific dimensions of our definition of 'performance'.

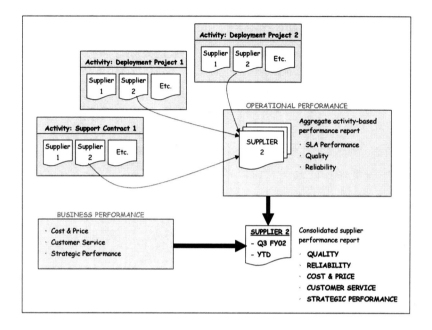

**Figure 4.2 – Performance Management Structure of C-MEG
Corporation SPRM Infrastructure**

I worked with colleagues in these other functions to develop what this definition meant – what did we truly desire from our strategic OEM supply partners to support what the business was trying to achieve? Figure 4.3 shows an excerpt of the resulting output from those deliberations. It identifies specific performance dimensions and the names of the relevant global functional leaders across the business. This structure was part and parcel of the SPRM framework, providing clarity on functional responsibility ownership and our defined key performance considerations.

Global OEM Vendor Performance Management							
Criteria	KPIs	Performance Factors	Field Services	Supplier Quality	Finance	Engineering	Procurement
			D. Arnold	J. Snarr	H. Green	P. Menzies	D. Coates
Quality	Product quality	% In-coming rejects by quantity		*			
		% Field pre-service returns (DOAs)	*	*			
	Service quality	% SLA adherence	*				
		Cycle time to repair	*				
	Quality management	Quality Management System (QMS)		*			
		Corrective actions		*			
Reliability	Delivery reliability	% On-time-In-full deliveries					*
		Deliveries with documentation errors					*
	Service reliability	Problem resolution response times					*
		Problem resolution lead times					*
Cost & Price	Cost management	Cost reduction					*
	Pricing	Market benchmark					*
		Volume discounts					*
Customer Service	Flexibility re: changes to...	Schedules					*
		Volumes					*
	Responsiveness	RFQ responsiveness					*
		Product lead-times					*
	Terms & Conditions	Warranty support					*
		Other T&Cs - Discounts, credit period, etc.					*
Strategic Performance	Financial stability	D&B assessment, et al.			*		
	Global coverage	Spread & scope of operational locations					*
	Technical capability	Product enhancements				*	
		Product lifecycle management				*	
		New products / technologies				*	

Figure 4.3 – Performance Dimensions and Functional Responsibilities for C-MEG Corporation SPRM Infrastructure (Excerpt)

Supplier performance should be captured and documented in a simple, easy-to-use and well structured scorecard. This should form a key aspect of QBR discussions. Figure 4.4 shows the cover sheet of the version I introduced at C-MEG Corporation. Each top-level performance criterion had input assessments from the relevant functional leads defined in the responsibility specifications. We sat down together at the end of each quarter to jointly review and discuss each key supplier's performance and other aspects of the relationship which were pertinent, and plan our approach, prior to the each QBR.

I have introduced SPRM frameworks in several organisations over the years. But I specifically chose the one at C-MEG Corporation for illustrative purposes for a number of reasons. Notice how the bulk of our definition of 'performance' is accounted for by Quality and Reliability, constituting nearly 80% of the total. Whereas Cost/Price accounts for only 8 percent of the performance spectrum. Why?

Because our telecoms operator customers didn't hassle C-MEG Corporation on the cost of our products and services. Their prime concern was timely project completion and network reliability. In turn, these considerations were uppermost in C-MEG Corporation's perspective on performance requirements from the supply base and the internal business operation. I'm very pleased that my Procurement colleagues and I were able to work with our stakeholders to successfully create and embed something that aligned perfectly to the business strategic agenda. That's Procurement mojo at play.

OEM Vendor Performance Scorecard

OEM: Supplier's name		**PERIOD:** MMM-MMM YY	
Code: Supplier's code		**REGION:** Business region	

CRITERIA	Max. Achievable	Actual Score	% Score
Quality	230	0	0%
Reliability	150	0	0%
Cost/Price	40	0	0%
Customer Service	60	0	0%
Strategic Performance	20	0	0%
Overall Performance:	500	0	0%
Classification:			'D' : Unacceptable!

Issue: 3   Effective: September XXXX

Figure 4.4 – Supplier Scorecard (cover sheet) for C-MEG Corporation SPRM

The above illustrations from C-MEG Corporation are only for indicative purposes. The aims and focus of each SPRM process will vary from enterprise to enterprise, though the fundamental essence remains the same. Importantly, performance is only one aspect of the SPRM framework. It is just as crucial to give emphasis to the relationship element. Both go hand in hand. Supplier relationships should not gain focus only after volume supplies begin. Managing the interaction right from the early supplier involvement phase is vital. It not only demonstrates to the supplier the importance the enterprise places on their contribution to its business, it also provides invaluable insights on the supplier's long-term intents, and how well they are likely to remain committed to growing the relationship.

Managing relationships with key suppliers effectively can deliver immense value to the enterprise. But this only happens when it is done properly. Most reliable suppliers want to deliver superior performance when they feel positive about the relationship. Hence, strong, progressive and mutually beneficial relationships tend to inadvertently lead to enhanced performance, and, frequently, supply innovation. With the greater levels of trust that ensue from a healthy relationship, suppliers are more willing to strive to secure or sustain a favourable position by efforts to please the buyer. This can extend to collaboratively exploring uncharted waters together, the place where innovation and hidden value often lie untapped.

It is always vital that purchasing people nurture constructive, collaborative relationships with key suppliers. Sound supplier relationships are the wellspring of harnessing tangible and intangible value from robust supply base management.

Risk Management

Even where the supplier relationship may not be ideal, it is still crucial to continue to manage supplier performance robustly. Actual supply performance is the most rudimentary indication of value as regards the supply base. It must also be a key criterion in awarding new or re-sourcing contracts, not just the contents of submitted bids or RFQ responses. Awarding business to a new or existing supplier without incorporating their actual performance on existing contracts is an avenue for risks. Without validated evidence of a supplier's true operational supply capability, such an approach inherently incorporates the risk of poor supply reliability. If Procurement's role is to add value to the enterprise, then this is certainly not a value-adding approach.

Avoiding such risks is not just something purchasing people should imbibe to supply business awards; rather, it should be part of a wider-ranging, structured risk management practice that forms an integral component of a holistic supply base management approach.

Structured risk management is a critical aspect of robust supply base management. Even with good supplier performance and relationships, managing risks across the supply spectrum remains vital. My interactions with purchasing professionals in different countries and the related opinions shared in industry publications reveal that most purchasing people agree on this. It is one of the key areas Procurement must expand its functional obligations to cover, beyond the traditional focus on cost savings, contracts and so on. Yet it is also one of the areas that suffer neglect by many purchasing people who hold a conventional and myopic perspective of Procurement's role. One trade survey revealed that almost a third of Procurement functions are unable to develop their risk management capabilities above the rudimentary stages of maturity. This is another damning denunciation of traditional purchasing orientations, but one with important implications for the organisations Procurement serves.

Effective risk management is crucial to safeguard business continuity. As custodians of third-party spend – the largest or second largest area of expenditure in most enterprises – it is imperative that Procurement protects the enterprise robustly. How can we gain the organisational respect and kudos we crave if we are not protecting the organisation in our sphere of responsibility?

This is particularly important for all purchasing people to ponder, especially in light of the geo-political and socio-economic challenges of today's business landscape. It becomes even more momentous when considered in addition to the myriad of supply-impacting natural disasters we have witnessed in recent times. The 2011 earthquake and tsunami in Japan, the floods in Thailand, the Icelandic volcanic eruptions and several hurricanes in North America are just a few examples. These and other similar events had significant, expensive impacts on organisations in various sectors (in addition to the devastation caused to millions of people.)

But 'risks' in the supply base do not just pertain to those factors which pose a threat to supply continuity in an obvious and direct way. There are other risks which may not directly cause supply disruptions but are related to the supply pipeline, and must, thus, be mitigated. I previously alluded to financial and reputational risks in the examples of the outdoor clothing brand, the global toy manufacturer and the supermarket multinationals. But issues like volatility in commodity prices; political instability; legislative requirements; and exchange rate fluctuations are also becoming more important risk-creating factors across many organisations' supply pipelines. The same can be said for the heightened supply risks many enterprises currently face as a result of the uncertainty created by the recent global economic downturn. This has become an issue with a double-risk effect for some organisations. On one hand, the resulting unpredictability has created such volatility in top-line performance that projecting sales turnover now almost requires a PhD in voodoo and clairvoyance; sales directors now need to retrain as shamans. On the other hand, suppliers to these enterprises are facing identical challenges, thus creating further headaches for these organisations due to the business failure risks posed, especially from smaller suppliers.

We could go on and identify a number of other risk categories in the supply base. Some are specific to particular sectors, geographies or types and sizes of organisations, while others are factors almost all enterprises are exposed to. What is important is that purchasing people in all organisations embrace risk management as a fundamental aspect of their functional responsibility as regards managing the supply base robustly. Thinking broadly, unencumbered by the shackles of conventional purchasing perspectives, what risks do you see your organisation faces across its supply base? What about your stakeholders who hold different positions, hence, perspectives, in the organisational landscape – what risks do they see? Have you asked them? And what are you doing to mitigate those risks?

> **Procurement people must embrace supply base risk management as a fundamental aspect of their functional responsibility.**

I deliberately ask that you free yourself from the myopia of traditional purchasing perspectives in considering risks in the supply base. Our conventional focus on cost savings and other rudimentary purchasing issues can oftentimes be a hindrance to Procurement effectiveness. As I sit here typing this right now, I recall a client I spent some time with recently, helping to resolve some supply management challenges. One of the improvements I introduced was a structured supply risk management process. As I explored the intent with the Purchasing Manager, and probed deeper into the current key supply base issues, we got round to discussing a significant supply failure risk: the sole supplier of a key component material in Continental Europe was facing severe financial difficulties, so much so that they had halved their factory operating hours and had borrowed from the bank for the first time in thirty-eight years of trading. Probably a classic example of supplier failure risks many buyers are familiar with. But the sad truth is that the supplier ended up in this situation, ultimately, because my client had squeezed them too hard for materials price reductions. My client was the supplier's biggest customer and the supplier could not afford to lose the business (that was the threat). They had acquiesced to the pricing my client had got from a low-cost country sourcing benchmarking exercise. For a year or so afterwards the resulting double-digit cost saving brought smiles to many faces in my client's organisation, right up to the group CEO. But is that true Procurement effectiveness? When the net effect of a traditional savings-driven action is the creation of a mammoth supply continuity risk?

Risks pertaining to supply base management can be categorised in several ways depending on the organisational context. My preference is always to keep things simple. In that regard, most types of risks here can be grouped into four broad categories as shown in figure 4.5.

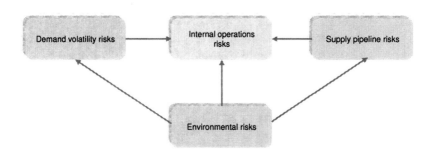

Figure 4.5 – Supply Base Management Risks

The risk categories can be summarised as follows

(1) **Demand volatility risks** – these are risks that relate to the demand which the supply chain must fulfil. Such risks include things like unexpected fluctuations in demand volumes, which can cause material shortages or excess inventory, and, thus, severely hamper efficient utilisation of third-party-spend or working capital; overreliance on an inappropriate number of customers; and financial stability of existing and potential new customers.

(2) **Internal operations risks** – these risks pertain to the internal operations of the enterprise. They include issues such as product obsolescence; intellectual property management; operations planning and fulfilment deficiencies; internal process failures; and organisational competency gaps.

(3) **Supply pipeline risks** – the conventional risks many purchasing and supply chain management professionals would easily recognise fit into this group. They include issues like single-sourcing; supplier capability and stability; supply market capacity; supply pricing changes and variability; supply contracts; and transportation disruptions.

(4) **Environmental risks** – these risks relate to issues external to the enterprise and outside its control. They include issues such as exchange rate changes; natural disasters and weather impacts; and global or regional macro-economic factors. Interestingly, risks in this category typically also affect the enterprise's customers and suppliers alike.

Grouping risks into categories as above might be educative and aid understanding for some. But in truth it adds little value to Procurement effectiveness. The true value lies in actually managing the risks robustly. This requires an effective risk management process which must include the key steps shown in figure 4.6.

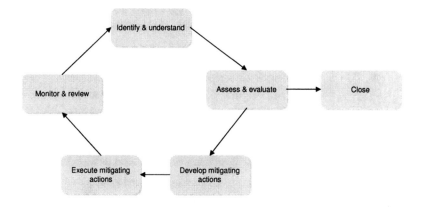

Figure 4.6 – Sample Risk Management Process

Step 1: Identify and understand
Identify the supply base-related risks pertinent to your organisation, and really get to understand these risks and the underlying key contributory factors. What are the real risk drivers – where does the risk originate from and how? Getting to understand each risk properly is important. It not only aids better awareness, it also adds value by way of the information gleaned which helps ensure subsequent decision-making is robust.

Step 2: Assess and evaluate
Assess each risk and evaluate its relative impact and priority. This is best done by considering:

- The probability of the risk materialising
- The severity of its impact if it does mataerialise
- Rating both 'probability' and 'severity' individually.

Some risk management processes use a simple 'Red-Amber-Green' or 'High-Medium-Low' system for such assessment ratings. While this may be adequate for many applications, my experience has taught me that numerical assessment ratings are usually more effective.

With numerical assessments, risk ratings might still be as simple as a '1-2-3' ratings range, with '3' being the highest rating; a '1-2-3-4-5' range; or a range of '1-to-10'.

Figure 4.7 provides an overview of three different risk severity rating systems and generic descriptions of how each system's ratings can be interpreted. And figure 4.8 provides a similar overview of different risk probability ratings.

Risk Severity Ratings			Description
1	Very Low	Green	Insignificant impact/Negligible consequences/Supply capability or operations schedule will remain mostly unchanged
2	Low		Minor impact/Minimal consequences/ Supply capability or operations schedule can absorb impairments, and requirements can still be met
3	Medium	Amber	Moderate impact/Noticeable consequences/Supply capability or operations schedule may suffer minor disruptions and may require some modifications; important requirements can still be met
4	High		Significant impact/Serious consequences/ Supply capability or operations schedule will suffer major disruptions; important requirements may not be met
5	Very High	Red	Severe impact/Catastrophic consequences/Supply capability or operations schedule will suffer complete failure; inability to meet minimum requirements

Figure 4.7 – Risk Severity Assessment Ratings

Risk Probability Ratings			Description
1	Very Low	Green	Rare/Very unlikely to occur/Do not believe event will ever occur
2	Low		Unlikely to occur/Do not expect event to occur
3	Medium	Amber	Possible/May occur
4	High		Likely/Will probably occur
5	Very High	Red	Almost certain/Certain to occur

Figure 4.8 – Risk Probability Assessment Ratings

The product of the probability and severity ratings gives a Risk Priority Number (RPN) – it is the aggregate rating of the risk, incorporating both the probability of occurrence and the severity of impact. This is one of the advantages of a numerical ratings approach, in that it is much easier to attain the risk priority, and, thus, the importance of each particular risk relative to others. For instance, if we consider the two sample risks below:

- Risk A: "Acme GmbH, our single-source supplier for glass (a key production material), is financially unstable and may go out of business":

  - Assessment of probability of occurrence results in a rating of '2'
  - Assessment of the severity of impact on the business results in a rating of '3'
  - Resulting risk priority number (RPN) = 2 x 3 = '6'

- Risk B: "XYZ Inc, the new main supplier being introduced for supply of aluminium, may lack adequate capability to assure supply continuity":

- Assessment of probability of occurrence results in a rating of '1' (This low rating may be based largely on having previously taken a robust pre-selection approach that included visiting the supplier's facilities; auditing their internal process capabilities and financial stability; talking to their reference customers; and going through a dependable sample approvals process)
- Assessment of the severity of impact on the business results in a rating of '2' (This may be because there are existing pre-approved alternative suppliers for aluminium)
- Resulting risk priority number (RPN) = 1 x 2 = '2'

A numerical assessment ratings system makes it much easier to demonstrate that Risk A should be given much more focus than Risk B. This is particularly useful for situations where the number of risks being addressed is high, or where resources (time, people, capital or budgets, senior executive attention and support, etc.) are tight and, thus, effort must be focused at the most important issues for better efficiency.

Risk assessments shouldn't be a one-time event. Subsequent (re-) assessment ratings can change, perhaps due to mitigating actions previously taken or new information coming to light which leads to better understanding of the risk.

Step 3: Develop mitigating actions
Once risks have been assessed and evaluated, actions to mitigate each risk must then been developed. It is important that the actions decided upon directly impact the identified risk as effectively as possible. Hence, mitigating actions must be geared towards:

(1) Avoiding the risk completely
(2) Reducing the probability of the risk manifesting
(3) Lessening the severity of impact
(4) A combination of two or more of the above intents.

Identifying effective mitigating actions demands a good understanding of the risk, which should have happened in previous steps. Mitigating actions must be specific – this is no place for poorly defined activities that might end up wasting resources and exposing the enterprise to hazards which could be avoided. Each action must have a clear owner, a target deadline for completion and a clear definition of the desired outcomes.

Step 4: Execute mitigating actions

Clarity of ownership, target deadlines and specified desired outcomes help drive effective execution of mitigating actions. It is vital that this is progressed properly, and as expediently as possible. It is sometimes the case that the execution of mitigating actions leads to further information on the risk; this can provide added insight, or it may be information which challenges the validity of pre-conceived notions and any assumptions previously made.

Step 5: Monitor and review

Progress with executing mitigating actions should be monitored and reviewed regularly, to provide assurance that risks are indeed being effectively mitigated. Such reviews should also include re-consideration of each risk – have there been any change of circumstances which inform new or increased understanding of the risk factors? Indeed, does the risk still exist; and if so, is the previous evaluation still valid?

Closure

Such considerations are important for continued, cyclical reassessment of identified risks. This re-evaluation must continue as part of the risk management process cycle until the mitigating actions are completed and the risks are managed to closure. Of course, it is possible that such considerations reveal information which nullifies the risk, leading to a similar end-result of closing out associated risk management efforts.

The disciplined effort required for effective risk management extends to capturing the related information in a formal risk register. The risk register should detail all identified risks; the risk assessments and priority ratings; the mitigating actions; and the status of each action, as illustrated in the sample in figure 4.9.

ABC Limited - Procurement Department							
Supply Management Risk Register							
Last Update: 19-Aug-2012							
No.	Risk	Probability (P)	Severity (S)	RPN (P x S)	Mitigating Action(s)	Resp.	Deadline	Status
1	Acme GmbH, our single-source supplier for glass, is financially unstable and may go out of business	2	3	6	Commence sourcing of 2 possible alternative suppliers, and progress at least 1 to 'Approved' status	James Bond	30-Jan-13	WIP
					Re-assess Acme's financial stability assessment since last QBR in collaboration with Finance dept.	James Bond	19-Sep-12	Not started
					Explore possible avenues for financial support to Acme with Finance Business Partner and CFO	Tony Montana	30-Jul-12	Overdue
2	Threat of industrial action by XYZ Ltd. personnel following company takeover and redundancies (affects XYZ on-site staff providing outsourced logistics services)	3	3	9	Clarify readiness of business continuity plans with XYZ senior executives and account manager	Don Corleone	30-Aug-12	WIP
					Work with HR and temp. agency to have emergency temporary labour available for rapid deployment	Don Corleone	30-Aug-12	WIP
					Review outsource arrangement with XYZ and re-source to alternative provider	Jason Bourne	19-Sep-12	On-hold
End-of-Risk Register							

Figure 4.9 – Sample Risk Register

Risk registers can be kept simple but still effective, or can be made as complex as the user or organisation desires. In the same vein, risk registers can be deployed generically across the whole spectrum of supply base management, encompassing all relevant risk issues, or they can be applied to specific subsets of the Procurement responsibility scope. For instance, the risk registers I introduced at one previous employer were specific to individual product supply programmes, though the basic structure was harmonised across all programmes. And at another company, the risk registers I instituted were specific to individual purchasing categories and strategic sourcing projects, but also based on a common template and process. Whereas, the risk registers I have implemented at several client organisations have been generic to the supply base management activity as a whole.

Different organisational and situational contexts demand different approaches. But the fundamental tenets of Procurement effectiveness remain unchanged. Organisations that adopt category or commodity management structures must imbibe supply risk management to their category strategies. The same applies to strategic sourcing projects and conventional purchasing activities. If you want to find your Procurement mojo, then supply risk management must always be part of your Procurement functional activity scope.

Whatever approach is taken with the use of risk registers in the risk management process, the need for effectiveness remains sacrosanct. This means that Procurement must own and drive the supply risk agenda across the enterprise. In doing so, it is vital that Procurement adopts a multifunctional approach that incorporates consideration of the multifarious elements of supply-related risks. For instance, the operating structures of some organisations result in personnel in other functions having much more operational interface to suppliers than Procurement staff. In such situations, such functions that touch and feel the service delivered by the supply base should have key inputs to pertinent supply base management efforts; it may be valuable to seek the views of people in such functions in identifying, understanding and assessing risks and developing mitigating actions. That notwithstanding, Procurement's accountability for third-party spend management inherently brings with it the functional responsibility for supply risk management and other aspects of robust supply base management.

Beyond SPRM and Risk Management

The most important principles of robust supply base management are encapsulated in SPRM and supply risk management. Get these two aspects right and you are more than halfway towards a sound supply base management approach. However, the notion can be extended to other aspects of managing the supply base. Taking a robust approach to issues like spend under management; supply base segmentation; and supply contracts can increase Procurement effectiveness even more, when added to the mix of the two core aspects above. Indeed, well structured supply contracts with judicious terms and conditions can often be the means of mitigating certain risks, particularly with new sourcing activities.

Good supply contracts can be very effective in encouraging and supporting suppliers to deliver more innovative solutions, which ultimately enhance competitive advantage. Gain-sharing agreements are a great example of driving better cost-efficiency in the supply pipeline, through effective contracts that incentivise suppliers for value improvements. Using output-based specifications is particularly important for the supply of services, rather than the traditional focus on input requirements specifications. In fact, even for product supplies, taking the time and effort to really think through and understand enterprise needs to facilitate a thorough specification of requirements is one of the most valuable levers for robust supply base management. Value extraction from supply markets always improves significantly with better requirements specification; consideration of a broad range of commercial and technical options; and a solid grasp of total lifecycle cost structures.

Irrespective of the products or services supplied, and the structure and terms of the supply contract, it is always more effective to specify the standards of performance desired of suppliers through defined service levels against which actual performance can be measured and assessed.

Contrary to the inclinations of some purchasing folks, Service Level Agreements (SLAs) are not meant to serve as ammunition to shoot suppliers with. SLAs should reflect the collaborative supply performance expectations of the supplier-buyer relationship, including any associated positive and negative consequences of performance over or under the defined standards. Your SLA should define what you really want – keep it reasonable; don't ask a supplier to build Rome in a day. Make sure it is defined in simple, clear language to ensure it is easily understood and the related actual performance can be validated with minimal effort. Also, it is crucial to involve internal product or service users in developing and specifying supplier SLAs.

While SLAs are not supplier-bashing instruments, suppliers who fail to meet defined performance standards must not be tolerated. Poor supplier performance is often one of the factors that give Procurement a bad name in the enterprise. Even where Procurement is highly regarded, our functional obligations demand that poor supplier performance is tackled robustly.

Underperforming vendors must be calibrated and supported to up their game. For some organisations, this can extend to seconding support personnel – sometimes referred to as 'Tiger Teams' – into the supplier's operations to help identify root-cause problems and ramp up performance capability. For others, supplier development support may entail financial assistance in various forms to assure the continued stability of the vendor. Whatever the specifics of the situation, suppliers who continue to underperform after reasonable development and improvement support should be got rid of, no matter how painful this *may seem* to be. Limping along with suppliers who consistently underperform over the long term will certainly not lead you to your Procurement mojo.

Some Procurement functions misunderstand the essence and role of contractual SLAs. They place undue an emphasis on so-called "contract management" as a means of calibrating suppliers. Undoubtedly, well structured supply contracts can be vital to secure optimal benefits from the supply base, especially for complex services or products provision or in cases of multi-party supply chains. But your contract might only be of value in a court of law without good SPRM and risk management. If you want to find your Procurement mojo, then focus on managing the supply performance, relationship and risks, not the contract. It's like a marriage – to enjoy long-term success and happiness, you focus on loving each other and making each other happy, not on managing the marriage certificate.

That is not to say contracts are not important; it is more a case of seeing things from the right perspective to secure supply base alignment in an effective way. Other considerations like corporate social responsibility; ethical sourcing; sustainable or Green procurement; local content sourcing; supplier diversity; and so on are also becoming increasingly more important in aligning the supply base to enterprise needs. In some cases, some of these requirements may be mandated by law and, thus, can't be ignored. The Black Economic Empowerment (BEE) policy instituted by the post-apartheid South African government is a good example. So too is the 'local content' requirement stipulated by many emerging market and newly industrialised countries. Purchasing professionals operating within such jurisdictions must imbibe such statutory requirements to their supply base management activities.

It is worth pointing out, however, that some non-regulatory requirements, though well-meaning, perhaps for social aims, can be fraught with unnecessary bother. Unless such considerations are statutory, it is always worth questioning the rationale vis-à-vis the costs, risks and net effects. In this regard, it might be necessary and appropriate to expand your consideration of the 'net effects' beyond the benefits that accrue to the enterprise. Impacts on the wider society may also be important to consider. Beware of sourcing or supply management considerations with added hidden costs; it does nothing for the enterprise if third-party spend is not managed efficiently. In the same vein, purchasing people must be wary of monopsony situations – where you are the only buyer of the vendor's goods or services, or your purchases constitute an inordinate proportion of the supplier's output. Such situations can often prove expensive and immensely risky in the long run, despite the seeming enormous buying power accorded.

Few purchasing professionals will fail to recognise the advantages of increasing third-party spend under Procurement's management. Indeed, 'spend under management' is often used as a measure of Procurement's influence and success across the enterprise, though several practitioners have questioned its validity. That notwithstanding, as a number of studies have shown, expanding the proportion of spend under management correlates strongly to increased VFM. The benefits to the enterprise accrue in many ways, including better spend visibility which augments increased economies of scale and reduced maverick spend; improved compliance to contracts and Procurement mandates; enhanced purchasing efficiencies; reduced risk exposure; and, inherently, smarter business decision-making.

Leveraging increased spend under management often comes by aggregating more spend with fewer suppliers. It is far more efficient to manage fewer numbers of suppliers, though supplier rationalisation always entails some risks. The rationale for pushing the majority of spend towards fewer suppliers makes economic sense. But such key suppliers can only be identified after a thorough supply base segmentation exercise. This should focus on the critical few, where SPRM and supplier development efforts are most likely to yield maximum returns.

However, focusing on the critical few does not mean ignoring the smaller vendors that are likely to be more in number. The risks associated with these small suppliers may not be proportional in impact – a small supplier can still end up creating all sorts of major problems. While many such suppliers may not be appropriate for a full SPRM deployment, a degree of structured supply management oversight may still be necessary, depending on the goods or services provided and the associated risks.

Whether you opt to apply SPRM and risk management across your entire supply base or on a category basis is of less importance than the need for effectiveness. The principles of robust supply base management outlined above apply as much to new sourcing or supplier selection activities as they do to incumbent suppliers. Robust supply base management offers opportunities to gain better supply reliability and commercial performance.

The ability to leverage supply relationships and tap into supply market intelligence, and the opportunities to collaborate with suppliers on challenges like supply chain simplification, efficiency improvements and other co-development initiatives exemplify some of the potential benefits often overlooked. For instance, at one previous employer (a business that provided varied on-site services to many thousands of consumers daily) we worked with one of our key providers of outsourced manning services to develop a new service provision model. We introduced a 'zoning' approach that enabled the blue-collar service operators to be dynamically re-deployed at different locations of the site during the working day. This resulted in significant value improvements far beyond what we could have achieved without collaborating with the supplier. It is a good example of leveraging suppliers' knowledge and industry expertise for mutual benefit, which is what healthy supply partnerships are about – collaboration for joint advantage.

Some companies truly recognise the potential good supply partnerships offer and harness this in their marketing efforts. For instance, one multinational supermarket chain is currently running TV advertisements in the UK that feature their fish suppliers. They are exploiting the authenticity and product quality inherent in the fish supplier's heritage, by marketing the artisanal attributes intrinsic in the production and supply of smoked haddock by generations of the same family. This avenue of exploiting suppliers' quality and capabilities in organisations' marketing efforts shows how value extraction from the supply base extends beyond the goods and services purchased.

Working with suppliers on development efforts is a conduit to extracting value from robust supply base management. But supplier development should only be applied where necessary and appropriate; don't waste your efforts with suppliers you really should be getting rid of. This is a trap many purchasing people often fall into for all sorts of reasons. Usually the thinking patterns underpinning their actions are flawed. Importantly, it demonstrates how people's thinking and actions critically impact the ability to manage the supply base robustly.

Robust supply base management is a core element of enhancing Procurement effectiveness; because, as I have stated previously, suppliers are, in effect, an extension of the enterprise. Today, many organisations expend great effort in evaluating make-or-buy options for fulfilment of varied supply requirements. When these supplies are produced internally most organisations invest a significant amount of effort in ensuring their internal operations are effective, efficient and aligned to strategic intents. When the producing operations are externally-owned it becomes even more critical to expend effort in ensuring alignment, reliability and cost-efficiency. Purchasing professionals can create new paradigms by viewing the supply base as the external operations of the supply chain infrastructure. It becomes much easier, then, to comprehend the value of robust supply base management and how it contributes to the Procurement mojo.

Procurement Mojo: Some things to think about...

Ask yourself these questions, and take effective corrective actions if the <u>honest</u> answers reveal that you are not heading towards your Procurement mojo!

❖ Do we have a structured supply base management agenda, and how well does it align to our corporate strategy and enterprise needs?

❖ Do we adequately incorporate actual or demonstrated supplier capability and reliability to our sourcing decisions?

❖ Are we in Procurement deeply versed in knowledge of our supply markets, with solid understanding of market forces and levers?

❖ Do we routinely manage supplier performance and relationships in a structured and cohesive way?

❖ Do we deploy comprehensive risk management across our supply base or supply management activities?

❖ Is our supply base management effort appropriately focused on those vendors that are truly critical or strategic to our enterprise?

❖ How well do the business/technology roadmaps of our key suppliers align to ours?

❖ How well do we identify and leverage intelligence and industry expertise in our supply markets to enhance value, reliability and innovation?

STEP 4: APPLY APPROPRIATE PERFORMANCE FRAMEWORKS

Enhancing Procurement effectiveness requires a complementary approach to managing performance across all key dimensions of purchasing capability. Effective organisations always have performance management regimes that augment the effectiveness ethos. The same principle applies to the attainment of Procurement effectiveness – you must embed an appropriate framework for performance management that drives effectiveness. An appropriate performance framework must be structured and rigorously applied. It is the only way the ensuing strong, positive impacts on morale and productivity can be truly harnessed.

Performance frameworks to enhance Procurement effectiveness must span four key levels:

(1) Individuals in the Procurement function
(2) Specific programmes or initiatives pursued by Procurement
(3) Suppliers into the enterprise, and
(4) The aggregate functional performance.

The first three of these are the key contributing dimensions that create (or hinder) functional performance. Realising stellar performance from your Procurement function is only achievable when you have the same standards of exceptional performance...

- ...From a majority of individuals in the department;
- Across key functional initiatives or programmes; and
- From the majority of suppliers.

If you fail to manage performance effectively at those three levels, then your Procurement functional performance will be below par. Many of the issues pertinent to Procurement functional performance boil down to people. It is people who do the work of purchasing, whether that's mundane activities like raising purchase orders or more demanding tasks like managing suppliers or Procurement initiatives. Like most individuals, supplier companies don't deliberately set out to perform badly. In the same vein, Procurement initiatives are not living and breathing entities that 'decide' by themselves to fail or be problematic. It's always the people involved in the task that create or hamper success – in the way they think, the decisions they make and how they act. It's important to keep this in mind to get a good grasp of the interdependencies between the four levels of Procurement performance listed above.

We have discussed performance related to individuals and suppliers in the chapters on Effective Procurement Organisations and Robust Supply Base Management, respectively. Here, we will explore performance related to Procurement programmes or initiatives, and how performance management across all three levels drives aggregate functional performance.

> **Performance frameworks must span individual staff; suppliers; Procurement programmes; and aggregate functional performance.**

It is worth reiterating that managing the performance of individuals in the Procurement function effectively is part and parcel of building an effective Procurement organisation. Remember that it's people who do the work, so people matter most. Also, individual 'performance' is not just about the numbers or hard tangible results, it's also about the competencies exhibited in achieving those numbers. How we go about achieving the numbers – the values, behaviours and attitudes we exhibit – is as important as the numbers themselves. An effective approach to individual performance must drive accountability; provide avenues for capability growth; address performance gaps; and reward stellar performance appropriately to create alignment.

Likewise, managing supplier performance effectively is critical to robust supply base management. Remember that the supply base is simply an external component of the enterprise capability. Being external makes it more important that we manage the supply base in an effective manner. Focus on managing the supply performance, relationship and risks, not the contract.

The approach for managing the performance of Procurement staff and the performance of suppliers must be aligned to an overarching performance management framework that also incorporates taking a similar approach to the performance of Procurement programmes. This creates alignment and cohesion.

Performance Management of Procurement Programmes

The requirement for effectiveness in managing the performance of suppliers and individual staff also applies to programmes run by Procurement. These might be complex, large-scale initiatives, such as outsourcing projects; transition to low-cost country sourcing; implementation of shared services infrastructure; establishing an e-sourcing platform; or the introduction of CSR considerations to the supply base. Or they might be less complex sourcing and supplier selection initiatives. Whatever the case, Procurement initiatives *which do not have a predefined process* must be managed with the same discipline a structured process accords. But unlike a process, which relates to repeated tasks or activities, the structure required here is that of project governance.

To ensure effectiveness, Procurement initiatives should imbibe the orderliness inherent in good project management practices. The underlying disciplines project management affords can be summarised as planning; co-ordinating; and control of organisational activities and resources, from conception through to completion, to ensure the objectives of an initiative are achieved. Those objectives encompass performance considerations covering the same factors a well defined process should deliver – the attainment of performance outcomes that match or exceed desired standards of quality, time, cost and function.

Many Procurement-led initiatives are managed with significantly less rigour than they should be. This often leads to programmes failing to deliver the expected benefits, budget overruns, late completions or severe risks materialising, and frustration. None of these outcomes bode well for Procurement effectiveness, especially when we consider the bad image such results propagate for the function. Procurement functions seeking their mojo can significantly improve their programme outcomes by deploying some of the basic techniques of project management to all relevant functional initiatives.

Applying project governance to Procurement's non-process-driven initiatives doesn't mean you should train all your purchasing people to become project managers. Rather, a few simple practices can make a huge difference to the performance success of such initiatives; figure 5.1 illustrates a simplified project management structure that can be applied to many Procurement initiatives.

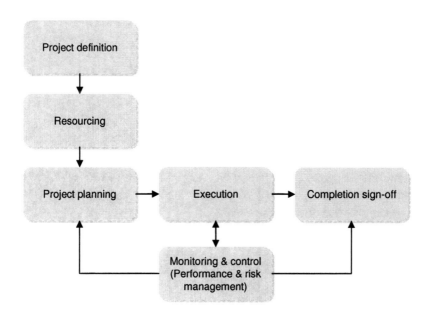

Figure 5.1 – Simple Project Management Structure

Most successful projects or programmes share a number of differentiating characteristics, amongst which are:

- A clearly defined goal
- A competent project lead
- Adequate resource allocation, including a competent project team
- Clear definition of critical success factors
- A robust plan with key milestones and scheduled progress reviews
- Effective control or governance mechanisms, including risk management, and
- A sound communications approach.

Many of these factors are self-explanatory and can be easily incorporated to most purchasing initiatives. In fact, I feel reasonably confident that if you look at the Procurement-led initiatives which have been successful in your own organisation or elsewhere, you will probably be able to identify the existence of these factors quite easily.

Defining the goal or objective of any initiative or project is one of the first things that should happen. I am not talking here about a conceptual objective that is really more of a vision. What I am referring to is defining the desired SMART outcomes of the initiative, an exercise which should be done as part of the overall project definition. Defining SMART project objectives is a way of specifying what success looks like. It will provide focus as the initiative progresses, and give a benchmark against which performance can be measured – did the initiative deliver x, y, and z which we spelled out at the beginning as the key desired outcomes?

As well as spelling out the objectives of the initiative, the project definition should also specify the scope of the initiative and the intended high-level approach or strategy. This information should be contained in a formal project definition document which must also stipulate the project core team and project leader.

Assigning an appropriate person from Procurement to lead the initiative may not be as simple as it seems. There is often the temptation, or tendency, to base such appointments, temporary though they may be, on the wrong considerations. Such appointments should not be based on who is free or who has the least workload; or, indeed, solely on who is the most competent purchasing person. Rather, project leadership appointments should be based on responsibility *and* capability, i.e. whose job role is responsible for this initiative, *and* do they have the competency and capacity to deliver it *successfully*?

The latter question is vital, because success or failure may already be predetermined right at this point. For instance, the Procurement Process & Systems Manager's job role may be functionally responsible for managing an e-sourcing platform once it is up and running, but he or she may lack the requisite project management capability to successfully lead and deliver the implementation of such a large and complex infrastructure. It may, thus, be necessary to bring in external resource in the short term to lead the project full-time. Or the requirement for project leadership competency may be fulfilled from elsewhere in the enterprise. The skills or capability requirements to manage Procurement processes and systems on an ongoing basis are distinctly different from those required to successfully define, implement and stabilise new large-scale, complex systems. Think about it in terms of a hotel industry manager who is great at managing or running five-star hotels versus one who is adept at *building* five-star hotels – two different challenges requiring different capabilities.

Such programmes may also be good opportunities to develop the competence of someone else in the Procurement team; it may be possible to second them to lead the initiative with some rescheduling of workload. If an individual without the full level of competency is assigned to lead such initiatives, it is important that they at least have an above-average degree of capability, and that they are properly mentored or guided by an experienced project champion or sponsor.

> **Procurement initiatives which do not have a predefined process must be managed with project governance.**

Poor project leadership is one of the most common reasons for suboptimal outcomes with many Procurement initiatives. Just as effective functional leadership is critically important to achieve Procurement organisational effectiveness, so too is effective project leadership vital to deliver Procurement programmes successfully. But the project leader also needs to be adequately supported with the right resources – competent, right-minded project team members, including those seconded from other support functions; sufficient finances; adequate physical infrastructure; and so on. Too often I have witnessed supply management functions try to deliver large, complex initiatives with grossly inadequate resources – the results are almost always predictable, a bit like going to sea in a sieve: nigh on impossible.

Resourcing Procurement programmes properly is not just about appointing competent project leads and team members. Very often, large Procurement initiatives which demand the structured, disciplined approach of project governance tend to involve outputs or project deliverables which impact multiple stakeholder groups. Or they tend to entail processes, systems, supply arrangements or other infrastructure with a massive impact on Procurement's capability and success. Such initiatives need the guidance of a steering group, which must include, if not headed by, the Procurement leader.

People often misunderstand the role of steering groups in project governance. The clue is in the name – the group helps steer the project team towards the end-goal in the most effective and efficient manner. The steering group's role includes:

- Aligning the project activities to other relevant developments in the wider enterprise
- Helping the project team stay on track to the defined objectives, or advising when a change of approach is required to ensure success
- Guiding or mentoring the project team to be more effective in getting things done, and
- Helping the project to secure the right profile and organisational space in the wider enterprise.

The very nature of the steering group's role means that its members must be experienced executives or senior managers with enough battle-scars to provide added wisdom to the project activities. In some large, corporate organisations where organisational politics is an inescapable reality, having the right senior executives on the steering group can make or break a project.

Project planning is one of the most important tasks of the project leader and the team. As the saying goes, "If you fail to plan, then you plan to fail." It really is that simple. Project plans do not always need to be all-singing, all-dancing affairs developed on the latest super-duper software. The larger and more complex an initiative is, the greater the requirement for a more professional project plan, such as one developed on Microsoft Project showing task interdependencies, resources and so on. But, sometimes, a reasonably robust plan can be put together on a spreadsheet. Figure 5.2 illustrates excerpts from a simple project plan we used at one organisation for a Procurement initiative to transition suppliers from thirty days payment terms to sixty days.

60-Days Payment Terms Project - High-Level Plan

No.	Action / Task / Milestone / Deliverable	Target Deadline	Status	FEB	MAR	APR	MAY	JUN
1	Develop & define project structure and governance	14-Feb						
2	Establish 'As-is' situation - suppliers, existing T&Cs, etc.	28-Feb						
3	Establish detailed benefits forecast and reporting metrics	28-Feb						
	DELIVERABLES - 'As-is' Summary and Reporting Metrics	28-Feb		◆				
4	Segment suppliers - spend / benefits, category, complexity & risks	15-Mar						
5	Develop & agree approach for each supplier; involve stakeholders	22-Mar						
6	Understand legal process with suppliers under contract	31-Mar						
	DELIVERABLES - Feasibility Summary & Cost-Benefits-Risk Assmt.	31-Mar			◆			
7	Develop supplier comms. approach & draft std. correspondence	31-Mar						
8	Produce Q&A document for Cat. Mgrs. & Business Support Centre	31-Mar						
	DELIVERABLES - Q&A Document and Standard Supplier Letter	31-Mar			◆			
9	Issue formal letter to suppliers	15-Apr						
10	Manage supplier queries via Cat. Mgrs. & Business Support Centre	end-Jun						
11	Update reviews with key stakeholders	end-Jun						
12	Monthly performance report	22-Jun						
13	Monthly project reviews	N/A		◇	◇	◇	◇	◇
	DELIVERABLES - Post-implementation & Benefits Summary	22-Jun						◆

Figure 5.2 – Simple Project Plan for Procurement Initiative

The sexiness of your project plan is less important than its effectiveness. The critical value is in the formality of the plan and the thinking that goes into the planning itself. The requirement for sound thinking here is yet another indicator of the importance of 'people' – project plans don't create themselves; it is people who create good or bad project plans. Crucially, for the sort of initiatives Procurement functions typically run, a good project plan must show the project milestones and planned project reviews.

Project progress reviews are a key tool to monitor and control an initiative to ensure it stays on track. The first progress review is the Kick-off Meeting or Project Launch Meeting. This session should also serve as a forum to reiterate the project objectives; project structure; team members and their respective responsibilities on the project; the overall intended approach; and other pertinent matters, to ensure effective execution. Subsequent progress reviews are also appropriate avenues to give feedback, just like performance appraisals for individuals – think of it as 'project appraisals'. The same requirement for candour and forthrightness also applies. If your project team is not doing the business, you must tell them so, and then support them with getting the initiative back on track. And if they are, you must also let them know and give praise accordingly. Progress reviews afford the opportunity to sit down and examine status, pertinent risks and related mitigating efforts, as well as other major issues which may impact the initiative, including soft issues like team dynamics and support from other functions.

The final progress review should include a validation assessment of the initiative, to confirm that the pre-defined programme objectives have indeed been achieved. It should also cover a review of 'lessons learned' – key organisational learning points which Procurement has garnered from the experience. These can be extremely valuable insights which, unfortunately, typically get forgotten.

Effective progress reviews play a vital role in monitoring and controlling the performance of any initiative. But this may not always be apparent; this is usually the case when progress reviews become long drawn-out affairs discussing unnecessary minutiae like how the Israelites crossed the Red Sea, or when individuals use review forums for posturing or power plays. Such dysfunctional behaviours must be kiboshed as quickly as possibly. Some organisations try to pre-empt such frivolities by using Project Charters as part of their project governance tools, wherein desired working practices and interpersonal behaviours are spelled out up front. Even without a documented project charter, behavioural expectations can be clarified up front in the kick-off meeting.

There are several other governance or control mechanisms that should be applied to Procurement programmes to enhance effectiveness. One of the most critical of these is risk management, as discussed in detail in the previous chapter (see 'Risk Management', page 146). Any Procurement initiative that is unique, large or complex enough to require a dedicated project lead and a project plan must also have a project risk register. Like the project plan, the risk register could be a simple MS Word or Excel document. The value is more in the thinking that goes into it and the actions that follow – thinking about the potential risks inherent in the initiative; developing appropriate mitigating actions to prevent those risks materialising or lessening their impacts; and following through on the identified actions. The approach for risk management on projects is similar to that adopted for supply base management; the same fundamental principles apply.

The formality of robust project documentation – at a minimum, a project definition document; a project plan; and a risk register – is an essential element of the rigour required to ensure effective governance and performance management of Procurement initiatives. It also sends subliminal messages about the professionalism of the purchasing people involved and the Procurement function itself. The impacts this has on perceptions of the function in the wider enterprise can not be overemphasised.

Procurement initiatives frequently involve or impact stakeholders outside the department. Hence, the need for robust communications as part of an overarching project management approach is crucial. Even with a technically competent project leader, a good plan, adequate resources and so on, such initiatives can, and do frequently, still fail simply due to poor communications. An effective communication strategy must be baked into the fabric of the project approach right from the start. It is worth remembering that in today's organisation it is no longer adequate to do a good job, it's just as important to be *perceived* to do a good job. Good communication is an effective way of managing perceptions. But more than that, it is also a sensible way of building awareness and buy-in for any Procurement initiative.

For Procurement functions seeking the recognition they crave within their wider organisations, delivering functional initiatives successfully is one of the conduits to enhancing effectiveness. Some of the points above on deploying project management disciplines may seem obvious, but I have seen enough poorly-managed Procurement initiatives to know how vital this is. One such learning experience for me was in a previous role heading a supply management function. I stepped in to champion a large facilities management (FM) outsourcing initiative being led by one of my peers, Stanley, who was responsible for "Strategic Projects". While Stanley had functional responsibility for shaping the initiative and its overall delivery, he had to work with two of my Category Managers who had sourcing and supply responsibility for different aspects of FM services provision. I got actively involved to curtail the build up of frustration and discord amongst the team, stemming largely from Stanley's ineffective project leadership. One of the first things I did was to pull the project team together for a progress review. I nearly fell off my chair when I discovered that this complex outsourcing initiative (worth £7.2m p.a. spend and affecting two separate category areas, several internal business units and multiple suppliers) had no project plan and no risk register.

Another more recent experience was in a client business I supported with supply management capability enhancements. One of my specific tasks was to join the steering committee of the ongoing ERP implementation project; I acted as the MD's point-man to drive the project appropriately and align project activities to the broader transformation initiative I was leading. In my first review with the team I found out that the project plan had been abandoned months earlier and there was no risk register; project meetings had become talking shops with limited progress being made, no clear route-path and a lot of dissonance and frustration. For any product manufacturing business today, an ERP implementation is one of the most challenging initiatives to undertake, especially when it's a multi-site business. It is an endeavour that demands the most rigorous project management disciplines. And you would think that the supply management professional leading such an initiative would recognise the need for such robust governance. So would I.

In contrast to the experiences described above, I have also witnessed many examples of effective project governance applied in supply management functions. For instance, I was running the Procurement function at one company when it was sold off.

Obviously, the divestment affected all areas of the business, and we had been working hard preparing for our separation from our erstwhile parent group for many months. Rather than manage the supply management aspects of the divestment as part of the business-as-usual activities, we aggregated these tasks into a project and appointed a dedicated project manager to lead the initiative. He worked hand in hand with our purchasing people but had overall accountability for the programme of work related to the divestment, with steerage from the supply leadership team. We adopted many of the project management disciplines I have described above – a solid project plan, risk register, project reviews, etc. Although it was a demanding time for all of us, it was a very effective approach and had a major impact on the successful completion of the programme, without hampering our business-as-usual performance.

Failing to apply project management disciplines to relevant Procurement initiatives is like planning to run a marathon without the discipline of an up front training regime. Aside from the significantly increased risk of failure, such laissez-faire attitudes to purchasing initiatives say something about Procurement to the rest of the enterprise. It also creates a build-up of negative sentiment which hinders Procurement performance success, as illustrated in figure 5.3.

Clear Definition	Competent Team	Adequate Resources	Robust Approach	
✓	✓	✓	✓	**Performance Success**
?	✓	✓	✓	Confusion
✓	?	✓	✓	Anxiety
✓	✓	?	✓	Frustration
✓	✓	✓	?	Dissonance

Figure 5.3 – Applying Project Governance for Performance Success

As I have stated previously, effectiveness is about doing the right things to get the outcomes you desire. Any Procurement function wanting to achieve sustained performance success must be cognizant of the fact that its success is impacted by the success of its major initiatives. Adopting the disciplined approach project governance accords significantly increases the chances of delivering such programmes successfully, and, thus, contributes to Procurement effectiveness.

Procurement Functional Performance

Measuring functional performance appears to be a widely accepted practice among Procurement functions. But we should not be hasty with applauding that observation. For starters, take a look at the performance measures your own Procurement function uses; now ask yourself how well those measures reflect the underlying effectiveness of the department and its efforts at building long-term capability. Do they give any indication of the efforts and outcomes achieved vis-à-vis internal customer satisfaction, for instance; or growing people capability? Do they reflect a reasonable balance between short-term and long-term focus? If you had to design and establish your dream Procurement function, would these be your choice of performance measures to tell you how 'perfect' your dream Procurement function was?

Even when you have good performance measures, this doesn't automatically equate to having an appropriate performance framework. People often mistake 'performance measurement' for 'performance management' – two separate things. There is a hidden fallacy in the common interpretation of the notion that 'what gets measured gets done'. Measuring performance, *per se*, will not give you performance success. Managing performance will. But you can't manage performance without measuring it. Success comes from the appropriateness of the performance measures, what we do about what the measures tell us and how we go about our ensuing actions.

Performance management at functional level actually starts before the measurement. It commences with the functional goals that are defined initially. If those goals are inappropriate or lack

SMARTness, then performance measurement is worthless. If the goals are not disaggregated into performance objectives at the three key levels of individuals in the Procurement function; Procurement programmes; and suppliers, then performance measurement is pointless. Functional performance is the outcome of performance at those three levels, supported by the effectiveness and efficiency of Procurement enablers. To manage the performance of Procurement effectively, you must manage performance at those three levels robustly and synergistically.

Great Procurement functional performance only comes from great performance at individual, programme and supplier levels. Think of these three areas as the engine rooms of Procurement performance. By far the most significant aspect of delivering your functional performance is through the actions you take to drive desired performance in those three areas. Most of the issues we have covered previously embody this tenet; for example, breaking down Procurement functional goals into performance objectives for individuals in the function; specifying performance standards required from suppliers; defining performance objectives of specific Procurement programmes; holding suppliers and purchasing folks to account; taking decisive action to address poor performance; and so on.

> **Great Procurement functional performance only comes from great performance in the three 'engine rooms' – individuals, programmes and suppliers.**

At a functional level, other aspects of performance management are really integral components of these key elements. Performance flows to the functional level by managing those underlying elements at individual, programme and supplier levels effectively. As I have explained earlier, managing performance rigorously in each of these three areas is important in its own right. But each 'performance engine' also has complementary impacts on the others, as illustrated in The Procurement Performance Paradigm in figure 5.4. For example, a poorly performing supplier will drain time, effort and energy from the buyer responsible, and detract from his successful attainment of his category or personal objectives. And a poorly performing buyer will never be able to manage a Procurement programme to successful completion. So it is important to synchronise performance efforts across these three areas, and monitor the aggregate outcome of the ensuing performance outflow at functional level. This is how you ensure your efforts at the three levels are indeed aligned and synergistic.

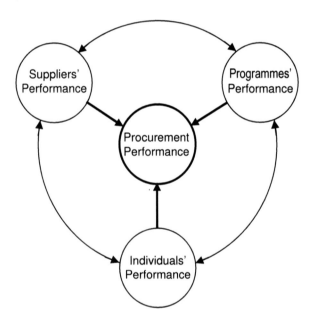

Figure 5.4 – The Procurement Performance Paradigm

In essence, performance measurement at the functional level quantifies the management effort and operational endeavours at the individual; supplier; and programme levels.

Performance measures should always reflect actual performance relative to the vision, goals or targets pursued. Hence, the earlier points on Procurement goals also apply here – the need to reflect the function's responsibilities and incorporate enterprise priorities; the importance of balancing short- and long-term focus, and operational and strategic perspectives; the necessity of covering the interests of multiple stakeholder groups, including Procurement staff; and so on. Of course, these requirements should have already been addressed when setting functional objectives.

The link between objectives and performance measurement is crucial, whether at individual, supplier, programme or functional level. It is pointless setting goals against which you can't measure progress or success. It is also pointless setting goals against which you *can* track performance, but then failing to do so effectively. Effective performance measurement requires the establishment of appropriate key performance indicators (KPIs), and then disaggregating them through all levels of performance attainment.

The term 'KPI' is probably one of the most grossly overused words in organisations today. Everything that can be measured is now a KPI, whether or not the measurement is indeed a *key* one. Your KPIs are meant to provide information on how well you are doing in the most critical dimensions of performance. Hence, it is important to use KPIs that illustrate the effectiveness, efficiency and organisational health of the Procurement function and its foremost activities. Focus on the few performance indicators that are indeed key – those that indicate the critical elements of Procurement performance, capability and growth. These will vary from Procurement function to Procurement function, as the key focus of each Procurement function will depend on its key activities and goals, which must always relate to enterprise strategic priorities.

Remembering why we measure performance should aid the selection of effective KPIs. While, in general, some performance measures exist for external reporting or compliance reasons, effective KPIs should be about enabling the Procurement function to learn and develop; to control and monitor progress in the critical areas of performance capability; and to aid effective decision-making. The requirement for balance demands that performance measures provide a view of Procurement's status and progress from several perspectives. Taking a balanced approach ensures the Procurement function doesn't miss vital feedback in all the key dimensions of its organisational existence. Effective KPIs should help Procurement ascertain and understand the answers to key performance questions like:

- How well are we doing as regards contribution to enterprise shareholder value?
- How do our internal customers see us, and how well are we meeting their needs?
- How robust and efficient are our internal and external infrastructure, including our supply base?
- What aspects of our organisational existence must we improve in?
- How can we continue to grow our capabilities and improve our value-add to the enterprise, its customers and our employees?

I stress the need for balance because many Procurement functions still focus their performance measurements at a narrowly-defined set of performance or capability dimensions. These typically revolve around traditional financial measures such as cost savings and materials or purchase price variance (MPV or PPV). An overriding focus on purely financial or short-term performance will definitely not lead you to your Procurement mojo.

There can be no definitive one-size-fits-all set of measures. However, understanding the essence of the Procurement mojo indicates that effective performance measurement must imbibe considerations in non-financial areas such as people capability and internal customer satisfaction. Thus, a more balanced approach for Procurement performance measurement might cover the key dimensions and KPIs shown in figure 5.5.

Dimension	Sample KPI's
Employees	Management team bench-strength Aggregate employee competency Staff attrition/turnover Employee engagement
Customer	Customer engagement Customer satisfaction rating Demand plan fulfilment
Financial	Cost-to-Procure VFM/cost savings/PPV Procurement ROI
Operations	Spend under management Percentage suppliers with 80% of spend Supply risks Aggregate supplier performance

Figure 5.5 – Sample Procurement Performance Measures

Procurement functions that opt to measure PPV performance must beware of the dangers of PPV impacts from factors Procurement can not influence; for example, commodity price increases against which hedging might be impossible. Also, it is important to measure what truly matters, rather than what is easily measurable. Taking this line of thought reveals the need to measure hard performance elements, such as PPV, as well as soft elements like internal customer perceptions.

In truth, hard financial measures will always be part of Procurement's performance indicators, because the function's core responsibilities entail financial management – managing third-party spend. Any such hard measures should be correlated to Procurement ROI and any key enterprise financial measures. There are two fundamental reasons for purchasing people to grasp here. First, for every dollar invested in

Procurement (for additional headcount or investment in technology or other resources, for instance) the enterprise has other investment options, not least other functional areas vying for investments of all sorts. The onus is on Procurement to demonstrate the returns the enterprise makes on investing that dollar in the function – that's what the Procurement ROI metric shows, although it only indicates the financial returns; other benefits like increased employee competency can be difficult to quantify in financial terms.

Secondly, money is the language of business, and each enterprise speaks a particular dialect of that language. By correlating Procurement's performance achievements to enterprise financial measures, the Procurement function can better integrate its activities and results in the core of enterprise financial considerations. This helps to improve Procurement's standing and augments its functional effectiveness. To ensure this approach is fruitful, it is vital that Procurement's financial results are clearly quantifiable and proven. Collaborating with the Finance function and adopting structured processes which incorporate Finance approval for VFM activities is essential.

Procurement's functional performance should be captured and documented in a simple, easy-to-use and well structured scorecard. The terms 'scorecard' and 'dashboard' often get people excited for all manner of reasons (or they have the opposite effect on those who are jaded or frazzled). There is nothing wrong with the excitement *per se*; excitement is often a sign that our juices are flowing and our passions are ignited – this is great for the Procurement mojo. The problems come when people get too preoccupied with the dashboard or scorecard itself, or how sexy or jazzy it is, and completely lose sight of its intended purpose and value. As you chase your Procurement mojo and reach the point of deploying a formal Procurement performance scorecard, try to avoid falling into this trap. Instead, keep your mind focused on the role of the scorecard in your overall approach to managing performance – it is simply a tool, not an end-goal in itself. Figure 5.6 illustrates a simple Procurement scorecard with the first three months of the calendar year shown for illustrative purposes.

Dimension	2012 Objectives	KPI	Target	Actual Performance		
				Jan	Feb	Mar
Employees	Improve overall capability and engagement of staff	% aggregate competency rating vs. ideal profile	85% by Sept.			
		Organisational health - % sickness absence man-days	≤ 1%			
Customers	Develop closer working relationships with business units, and improve forward visibility of requirements	% customer satisfaction rating from quarterly survey	95% by Sept.			
		Proportion of formal joint category demand plans in place	100% by June			
Financial	Deliver value-for-money and internal efficiency improvements	Total Finance-validated VFM	£4m by June; £6m by Dec.			
		Functional ROI	600% by Dec.			
Operations	Embed risk management in supply programmes	% risks with no mitigating actions or actions over 1 month overdue	0% by Mar.			
	Improve supply reliability	Aggregate supplier performance (delivery & quality)	85% by June; 95% by Dec.			

Figure 5.6 – Sample Procurement Performance Scorecard

A formal scorecard or dashboard simply provides an integrated view of performance in several dimensions. However, the scorecard and its contents can be leveraged to good effect in many ways. One example is boosting the perception and image of Procurement in the enterprise, by publicising performance accomplishments through the scorecard, perhaps on the corporate intranet. Even where the intended target audience is only Procurement employees, a good scorecard can prove very effective as a concise communication medium.

For any scorecard to be meaningful it must be kept up to date with the latest performance data. The reported performance must also reflect achievements relevant to pre-defined objectives. Those objectives, in turn, must be relevant to the Procurement function's raison d'être and its alignment to the enterprise strategic priorities. To ensure the performance scorecard serves its wider purpose, the reported data must be the basis of driving improvements across the key areas of Procurement's performance focus. Scorecards can also be good conduits for highlighting commendable achievements at any level of the performance spectrum. At individual level, this must be aligned to the rewards structure to propagate increased employee engagement.

Recognising the various ways in which your Procurement scorecard should be exploited is useful to avoid the pitfall of getting hung up on the scorecard itself rather than what it tells you. The value is in leveraging the scorecard to manage performance effectively, not just measuring and reporting data. This means you must be prepared to tackle performance failings directly, whether at individual, supplier or programme level.

It goes without saying that suboptimal performance at any of the aforementioned levels detracts from Procurement's performance success, and, ultimately, from Procurement effectiveness. For improvement efforts to be effective, it is imperative that performance measures are disaggregated to identify the underlying root-causes of any performance gaps. Attention can then be appropriately focused at the seeds of performance failure, the same seeds that yield success under the right conditions.

When such success is achieved, it is important to celebrate the accomplishment rather than take it for granted. Celebrating success in symbolic ways is something high performing teams bake into their organisational fabric. It helps to boost team spirit and a collective self-belief, both of which can be critical factors in sustaining and enhancing further performance success.

But what does 'success' really mean?

The primary measure of Procurement's success must be performance achieved against functional objectives. However, it is also vital to benchmark your Procurement function's performance against others'. These might be peer group functions in the wider enterprise, in the particular industry or world-class performance standards.

Benchmarking can be a valuable mechanism to drive performance growth and capability development when used properly. It provides an invaluable source of business intelligence which serves multiple purposes. Primarily, benchmarking enables a comparative assessment of existing capabilities and performance against external standards, in an objective or fact-based manner. Such assessments can help identify key areas requiring urgent or critical enhancement, and may form the basis for continuous improvement programmes or radical transformations, where appropriate; it is often the case that organisations are more willing to undertake large-scale change programmes to enhance Procurement capability when confronted with objective evidence that the current-state infrastructure is starkly inadequate.

I have used this approach a number of times to convince senior executives of the need to overhaul supply management functions. Figure 5.7 shows an extract from one such situation, illustrating a clear gap between the existing Procurement performance capability and best-in-class benchmarks. This served as a key aspect of my 'sales campaign' to promote the transformation that was indeed a dire need.

Section:	Cost/head	Practice Mngt.	OPEX Proc't.	SMD	Str. Projs.	CAPEX Proc't. (TBC)	Lean	Total FTEs	Cost
"Head of" level - perm.	£110,760		1	1				2	£221,520
Interims - ASM level	£133,200	2	4		1		1	8	£1,065,600
Perm. ASM level	£78,720		2	3				5	£393,600
Perm. Band 3 level	£57,000		1	2				3	£171,000
Procurement Hub	£13,000	1						1	£13,000
Total FTEs & Costs		3	8	6	1	0	1	19	£1,864,720

Benchmarks	'As-is'	Best-in-Class	Average	Laggard	Procurement Transformation Target
Spend	£140,000,000				
VFM delivery	£6,970,082				
Cost-to-Procure	1.33%	≤0.31% - 0.63%	0.82% - 0.91%	>1%	0.6% - 0.7% max.
Functional ROI	373.8%	≥600% - 700%	300% - 700%	100% - 300%	600% min.

Figure 5.7 – Sample Benchmark Comparison Summary

Exploiting benchmarking to educate stakeholders or secure executive approval isn't just limited to quantitative aspects, as in the example above. Figure 5.8 illustrates a summary of another benchmarking exercise I carried out at a different organisation, which I refer to here as ARC. The names of ARC's top competitors are shown with similar abbreviations. I used this summary of qualitative benchmarking as a key element of my 'pitch' to the executive board. It was a powerful means of communicating our position, and supplemented other evidence of a critical need for a group-wide transformation to improve our functional capability. I suspect the glaring lack of a functional strategy this summary exposed helped drive home the message.

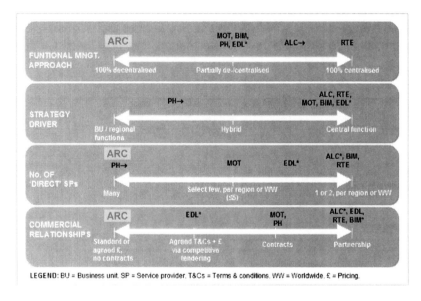

LEGEND: BU = Business unit. SP = Service provider. T&Cs = Terms & conditions. WW = Worldwide. £ = Pricing.

Figure 5.8 – Sample Qualitative Benchmarking Summary

Benchmarking against competitors or best-practice standards can be particularly insightful for folks within the Procurement function. Like most employees, many purchasing people are pulled in different directions by the demands of every-day business-as-usual tasks. Even when they are doing a good job, they seldom have or create adequate time to sit down and reflect on their personal effectiveness in the job, and how theirs and their Procurement function's performance compares to objective, external benchmarks. Yet, many such benchmarks are widely available; figure 5.9 indicates some common best-in-class Procurement benchmarks covering both quantitative and qualitative indicators.

Performance Metric/ Capability Dimension	Sample Indicative Best-in-Class Benchmarks
Quantitative Benchmarks	
❖ Spend Per Buyer	US$22.3m – US$24m
❖ Cost-to-Procure	0.3% – 0.6%
❖ Functional ROI	≥ 600%, ≥ 700%
❖ Cost Savings Rate	≥ 3.4%, ≥ 5%
❖ Spend under management	≥ 70%, ≥ 80%, ≥ 90%
Qualitative Benchmarks	
❖ Organisational Effectiveness	Clearly-defined roles and responsibilities with individual performance targets High level of technical and 'soft' competencies Effective and visible functional leadership
❖ Enablers	Defined, documented and relevant processes Full process awareness and compliance Integrated MIS/ERP with high end-to-end supply chain visibility High system familiarisation and competency among employees

Figure 5.9 – Some Common Best-in-Class Procurement Benchmarks

It is important to clarify that the quantitative benchmark indicators are not definitive, neither is the list exhaustive. The indicators shown are some of the most common, widely referred to by most purchasing practitioners and commentators at the time of writing. There are no absolutely definitive world-class quantitative benchmarks, no matter how authoritative some benchmarking surveys or industry reports might sound. Such benchmarking surveys typically yield slightly different results; for instance, some surveys indicate '3.4% or more' as the best-in-class cost savings rate and others indicate '5% or more', just as some indicate '90% or more' as the best-in-class level for spend under management and others indicate '70% or more'.

The truth is that functional, enterprise and industry contexts differ so much that searching for a single set of definitive quantitative benchmarks is like searching for the proverbial philosopher's stone. Recognising this is important; you should accept such quantitative benchmarks as simply indicative yardsticks for comparative assessments, and get on with the important task of building your capability and getting closer to your Procurement mojo. After all, the numbers only indicate the hard, tangible elements of performance capability. As you must have gathered by now, focusing on such efficiency-oriented metrics without underlying effectiveness will not lead you to your Procurement mojo.

Procurement performance benchmarks, scorecards and KPIs are all key elements of effective performance measurement. But it is important to remember that performance *measurement* is only one aspect of securing the desired performance capability of the Procurement function, one that supports the drive for enhanced Procurement effectiveness. The other key aspect is how you *manage* performance across the three performance engines that create successful Procurement performance – individuals in the Procurement function; programmes or initiatives undertaken by Procurement; and suppliers into the enterprise.

We have explored how effective performance management in these three domains feeds the Procurement mojo. Understanding how these facets combine to support the drive for enhanced Procurement effectiveness is the very essence of understanding the importance of appropriate performance frameworks. This involves the fundamental issues we have discussed, such as having clarity of vision; setting SMART goals that align to the enterprise strategic agenda and Procurement's functional responsibilities; monitoring progress towards those goals; making necessary adjustments in approach to ensure successful attainment of those goals; providing the requisite resources and support to enable people to succeed; ensuring alignment across the various aspects of Procurement's organisational existence; and measuring and reporting actual performance against the defined objectives.

As you run through these issues in your own mind, remember the most fundamental point: all these issues boil down to people – it is people who create performance, good or bad. To ensure you get the requisite levels of performance in Procurement, you must ensure people are appropriately calibrated and engaged in your three Procurement performance engines. And this must be done in a way that creates synergy – through an appropriate performance framework.

Applying an appropriate performance framework is about taking a holistic approach that brings together the effective management of the core levers of Procurement performance capability. Achieving this creates a critical link between enterprise priorities and Procurement activities, and is fundamental to enhancing Procurement effectiveness.

Procurement Mojo: Some things to think about...

Ask yourself these questions, and take effective corrective actions if the <u>honest</u> answers reveal that you are not heading towards your Procurement mojo!

❖ Have we defined performance objectives for individuals, suppliers and our Procurement programmes that align to enhanced functional effectiveness?

❖ How well do we keep score? Do we measure what is important, or what is conventional or easy-to-measure?

❖ Are our approaches for performance management of individuals, suppliers and Procurement programmes aligned, consistent and coherent?

❖ Do we report, review and communicate our actual aggregate functional performance with a structured, formal scorecard?

❖ Are our KPIs appropriate and indicative of the things that really matter to drive enhanced Procurement effectiveness?

❖ Do we tackle underperformance robustly and identify necessary improvement actions to stay on-course for our Procurement mojo?

❖ How well do we follow through on defined improvement actions?

❖ How does our actual performance compare to our stated goals and to best-in-class benchmark standards?

STEP 5: BUILD YOUR PROCUREMENT BRAND

In an article submission to a trade magazine back in January 2012, I asserted that many Procurement functions are still either tactical in their approach, or seen to be so, because they inadvertently choose to be. It wasn't a flippant comment. Achieving Procurement effectiveness demands that the Procurement function adopts a strategic approach to the manifestation of its desired organisational existence, wherein it is interwoven to the fabric of the wider enterprise as an integrated function. Many purchasing professionals get this. Yet most Procurement functions still struggle to gain a strategic platform in the enterprise. Several studies have shown that many Procurement functions are trapped in an organisational existence that sees them expend over fifty percent of time and effort on tactical activities.

Before you ponder this point in a generic sense too deeply, examine your own Procurement function and your own activities – what proportion of your functional and individual energy goes on endeavours that are truly strategic? Look at the organisational environment and ask yourself other pertinent questions:

- What is happening in the wider enterprise?
- Where does Procurement sit or report into in the organisational structure?
- How is Procurement positioned in the organisational dynamics?
- Does Procurement's organisational positioning augment or hinder its functional effectiveness?
- How can Procurement become as embedded in the organisational fabric as HR or Finance?
- Which key individuals does Procurement leverage as informal champions?
- How does Procurement really add value to internal clients?
- What is the general perception of Procurement's 'brand' across the enterprise?

The issue of Procurement's tactical or strategic focus and its relative positioning in the enterprise is one that often elicits highly emotional views from purchasing professionals. But, as I mentioned earlier, there's no point turning up for a gunfight with a knife; you'd be much better off coming prepared, by arming yourself appropriately to start with. In the same vein, purchasing people need to be adequately armed to navigate the organisational landscape to secure the functional success they crave. Don't whinge about the lack of respect or kudos Procurement suffers; it's far more effective to tackle the issue directly to attain your Procurement mojo.

Purchasing people can learn a lot from the marketing efforts of successful consumer product brands. The most successful consumer product companies expend great efforts and resources to develop a deep understanding of their marketplace and their customers. They leverage this insight to create positive perceptions and positions for their brands, and develop enduring customer loyalty. To enhance and sustain Procurement effectiveness, purchasing people must develop organisational savvy and create a strong brand positioning for Procurement. This has nothing to do with the traditional technical skills many purchasing people focus on – category management; strategic sourcing; e-auctions; etc. Rather, it's more to do with a range of soft skills that underpin organisational success – abilities like understanding and tapping into the corporate buzz; managing stakeholder perceptions through public relations (PR) and effective communications; and ethical self-promotion to advocate the Procurement brand.

> **Purchasing folks can learn a lot from successful consumer product brands; they must develop organisational savvy and create a strong brand positioning for Procurement.**

In explaining the principles of building your Procurement brand, it is critical to understand that the previous four steps we have discussed (building an effective organisation; deploying fit for purpose enablers; adopting robust supply base management; and applying an appropriate performance framework) are part and parcel of fostering a credible functional brand. Everything you do rightly in those four areas directly enhances your Procurement effectiveness and, ultimately, promotes your Procurement brand.

You might be wondering what issues like marketing, brand promotion and PR have to do with Procurement effectiveness. The answer is: everything. The global economic downturn has done a lot for Procurement's profile as organisations of all sorts have been forced to cut internal costs and third-party spend. This has created a platform for many Procurement functions to deliver results directly impacting the bottom line and raise their profile in the enterprise. But it has also propagated the misguided notion that purchasing is largely about delivering cost savings. Some Procurement functions have been able to build on that platform and extend their organisational influence into more strategic activities. But they remain the minority; most Procurement functions are stuck in sub-optimal organisational positions.

Numerous surveys, trade reports and news stories repeatedly indicate that one of the largest barriers holding Procurement functions back is the misconceptions held in organisations about Procurement's role – what it can and should do to support the enterprise. This is interesting, considering the shift in Procurement's relative position in organisational structures over the years. Back in the mid-1990s one survey of large companies found that the most senior Procurement person reported to the top dog in the enterprise – the President, CEO or MD – in only sixteen percent of cases. A more recent survey in 2010 indicated that about a quarter of Procurement functions report directly to the man at the top. In many ways this significant shift is unsurprising. It reflects the growing awareness among many large companies of the value Procurement can bring. But the overriding perceptions of 'value' continue to be largely around financial or economic contribution, which grossly belittles the aggregate value-add of effective purchasing in any enterprise. Shifting this perception is only possible by repositioning the Procurement function.

Repositioning Procurement

The positioning of any function in the enterprise organisational structure is important; it indicates the status of the function, as does the job title of the most senior functional person. A Chief Procurement Officer or Procurement Director reporting directly to a board executive does a lot more for Procurement's standing than a Group Procurement Manager reporting to, say, an Operations or Manufacturing Director. Better still is a Procurement leader who sits on the executive or operating board, as is the case with the couple of examples I mentioned earlier.

There is no ideal structural or reporting position for Procurement though; it all depends on the context. Not all organisations need a Procurement leader at board level. What is important is that Procurement is positioned in the organisational structure where it will be most effective in delivering its functional obligations. If purchased goods and services are critical constituents of the enterprise value chain, for instance, then Procurement should be positioned such that key purchasing-related issues get adequately high consideration in enterprise strategic decision-making.

However, the concept of repositioning Procurement that I refer to goes beyond reporting lines in organisational structures. It extends to Procurement's positioning in the perceptions of stakeholders and its embedment in enterprise-wide activities and relevant processes, such that effective purchasing becomes an integral aspect of the organisational DNA.

Embedding effective purchasing into the fabric of the enterprise demands that Procurement is wholly integrated into the organisation. Figure 6.1 illustrates a model of integrated Procurement I initially presented at one organisation some years ago. I have subsequently used it in several client businesses. The list of critical functional activities shown is not exhaustive. And these activities will vary in importance and magnitude depending on the specific organisational context. Of greater significance is the requirement for Procurement functions to develop and maintain top-notch competency in those technical areas that are most critical to the attainment of functional goals. Activities like spend management, SPRM and stakeholder management are core levers in Procurement's ability to fulfil its responsibility in any enterprise.

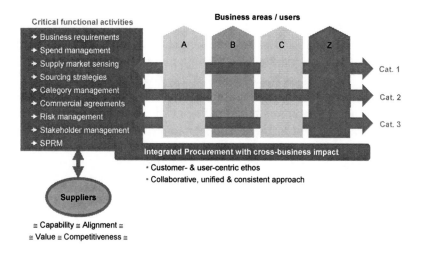

Figure 6.1 – Integrated Procurement Model

Expertise in the technical tasks of purchasing must be accompanied by organisational dexterity in liaising with internal customers or business areas. This is an issue many Procurement functions continue to struggle with. Success with integrating Procurement requires purchasing personnel to shift their prime focus from inward deal-making or savings orientation to customer fulfilment. Buyers should become the bridge between their internal customers and value delivery from suppliers. Without this mindset shift your Procurement mojo will remain an illusion. The technical activities referred to are vital, but it's *how* they are embedded in the enterprise that determines the level of success attained.

Adopting an integrated Procurement model demands consistency across business areas in the way Procurement operates. For instance, sourcing strategies may differ between different categories of spend, but *how* each strategy is developed and executed (incorporating inputs from internal customers) must follow a harmonised process. Applying a consistent and uniform approach across different business areas, combined with collaborative engagement with internal customers, helps entrench Procurement's position in the enterprise. It is a requisite gambit that goes hand in hand with the mindset shift to a customer- or user-centric ethos. It requires robust understanding of the organisational landscape and the related dynamics, including the myriad of political manoeuvres that are part of the modern day work theatre. If your Procurement leader and key purchasing people are not adept at navigating the organisational terrain, you will not be successful in embedding Procurement into the fabric of the enterprise.

Positioning Procurement appropriately is not about becoming a political animal without morals and the ability to deliver real results that support enterprise needs. Rather, it's about developing insights to organisational dynamics and using that understanding to further Procurement's agenda. If you bear this in mind all the time, it becomes easier to develop into a valued business partner to your internal customers.

Procurement provides a service. Thus, every day we rely on individuals in the function who liaise directly with various people across the organisation to deliver that service. The quality of these purchasing people and the chemistry they have with their stakeholders is vitally important. In such human interactions, 'quality' is an intangible attribute that is often based on perceptions. And interpersonal chemistry is an even more ethereal feature. Yet, more than the purchasing processes and systems, Procurement's positioning in the enterprise is deeply dependent on these factors. If every individual in Procurement embraces the business partner philosophy with customer-centricity at its core, it goes a long way to securing Procurement's position in the fabric of the enterprise.

Procurement folks must partner with the organisation, not least by getting close to the people that matter most. Get in bed with your key stakeholders and you will gain rich insights on how you can be meaningful to them, and what levers you can exploit to sell and deliver purchasing value more successfully. Some Procurement functions address this need by adopting a formal business partner organisational structure, where every internal business group has a lead Procurement person. Some go further by co-locating their purchasing people with internal customer departments. Both approaches can be helpful in positioning Procurement effectively. In one Procurement transformation I led earlier in my corporate career, I inherited a torrid internal customer relationship – the Procurement function had a poor reputation, despite the hard work being put in by the staff. As part of my repositioning effort, I relocated the team to sit in the internal customer area, having mooted the idea with my opposite number who ran the client-department. It was a resounding success. It helped to break down barriers and drive closer, collaborative working relationships at both individual and functional levels. It provided a conduit to maximise our involvement in the day-to-day activities of the client-department. But by far the more valuable tactic was the mindset shift I drove among my people. This was accompanied by revamping our processes to make them more structured and robust, and easier for stakeholders to 'do business' with us.

Imbibing customer-centricity to functional processes is an invaluable aid to positioning Procurement effectively in the fabric of enterprise activities. For instance, with many Procurement functions constantly wrangling with Finance and budget-holders about savings delivered, it's always shrewd to develop and deploy a robust process for VFM initiatives and related activities. An area often overlooked by many Procurement functions is the annual budget planning process. This activity isn't led by Procurement in most organisations. But Procurement can take steps to bake its inputs into the formal enterprise process. Many budget-holders are territorial about their operations and budgets; some can even be of a parochial disposition. But in my experience, most will welcome Procurement involvement if it will generate positive impacts with minimal pain. However, they must be convinced of the value in the first place. Positioning Procurement effectively is about creating the positive brand perceptions that establish that conviction.

> **Positioning Procurement effectively is about creating positive brand perceptions.**

Customer-centricity and constant awareness of the Procurement brand positioning help drive attitudes and behaviours in purchasing people that can leverage stakeholder interactions to nurture positive perceptions. This was well exemplified in a pleasing article I read in one trade magazine recently. It was written by a marketing director who indeed described himself as one of those stakeholders who saw Procurement involvement as an administrative obstacle he would rather circumvent. But what was particularly gratifying to read was how his subsequent dealings with his Procurement department created customer delight, through the behavioural approach of the category manager who engaged him. In describing their interaction, the marketing guy extolled the virtues of the category manager and how his operating style completely overturned his prior perceptions of Procurement. He described how he ended up *feeling* that their individual aims were actually aligned.

It is important to draw attention to a couple of key points from this article and other similar evidence:

(1) The critical factors that create internal customer satisfaction and help position Procurement positively are the progressive attitudes and behaviours of purchasing people, not primarily their technical expertise.

(2) Procurement's true positioning in the enterprise is largely determined by the perceptions of stakeholders, not necessarily the enterprise organisational structure. The more stakeholders *feel* that Procurement is meaningful to their organisational activities and existence, the better Procurement's brand position.

As a purchasing person, you must never forget that *every* interaction you have with your stakeholders is an opportunity to create a delightful customer experience and nurture effective relationships, thus, building Procurement's brand identity. This makes it much easier to sell and deliver the Procurement brand proposition, especially in key enterprise activities like budget planning which have a cross-business impact.

> **The more stakeholders feel that Procurement is meaningful to their organisational existence, the better Procurement's brand position.**

With the right relationships, purchasing people can exploit their knowledge of spend information, supply markets, supplier dynamics and VFM opportunities to support both the budget planning process and ongoing budget management. This knowledge can also be exploited constructively in early involvement interactions for sourcing requirements. Most purchasing folks, and even others in the wider enterprise, know that early Procurement involvement yields significantly better results. Aside from the obvious forward planning advantage, it affords Procurement the opportunity to influence requirements specifications, which is proven to lead to greater value attainment. It also allows achievement of more optimised sourcing solutions and better identification and management of risks.

Sadly, these are benefits many Procurement functions still miss out on. For instance, one study of Procurement functions a couple years ago found that less than half of the top-quartile performers touched or influenced enterprise spend at the planning or budgeting phase, before requirements specifications are defined. For the general survey population (non-top performers) it was even more disappointing – only about a quarter influenced spend at planning or budgeting stage. This is a challenge many purchasing people face routinely, one that I first experienced many years ago in transforming the NPI-Purchasing function I mentioned earlier. I turned the client-department's complaints about "poor purchasing support" into an avenue to sell a structured, formal Early Involvement Process, by illustrating how early engagement on new product developments enabled us to support NPI programmes better and make life easier for everyone. The process took time to bed in as people adjusted to the new way of working. Once it was stabilised, it became another medium that greatly improved our inter-functional relationships and reduced our time-to-market for new product launches.

Implementing robust formal processes related to stakeholder interactions, coupled with regular internal customer briefings or update reviews, can provide effective avenues to boost Procurement's brand positioning. But this might be inadequate, particularly when Procurement yet lacks the appropriate mandate and prominence across the enterprise. It's often necessary to complement this with astute lobbying, especially with the right senior executives. As part of the brand positioning effort, Procurement must find appropriate 'hooks' into the enterprise strategic agenda or the key issues bogging senior executives. In identifying what these issues are, think broadly; they might include seemingly inappropriate things, like factors that affect executives' bonuses. Develop a solid understanding of these issues, and use that awareness to advance a service proposition that supports executives' priorities. Successful Procurement positioning is about integration. Integration means more influence over all third-party spend. Purchasing people must learn to accept that Procurement may not always have an automatic right to own or manage enterprise spend. You may feel this is inappropriate or unfair, but that is the reality of organisational existence in many enterprises. Even where Procurement has a formal mandate, it may still need to earn the right to step into new areas of expenditure to improve its value proposition to the enterprise. The onus is on individual purchasing folks: make your involvement in internal customer organisations meaningful *from their perspective*. Effective stakeholder management is the conduit to achieving this.

Managing Stakeholders – Communication and Customer Relationship Management

The ability to view things from stakeholders' perspectives is invaluable. Stop for a minute and put yourself in your stakeholders' shoes; view your Procurement function from the outside – what do you perceive? A strong functional brand inciting positive connotations, or something else?

Seeing things from stakeholders' points of view is a prerequisite for effective stakeholder management. Most purchasing people agree that there's a definite misconception of Procurement and its value-add potential to the enterprise. A trade magazine news piece in early 2012 publicised survey findings that nearly a quarter of senior leaders in Fortune 1000 businesses were uncertain of Procurement's role in their companies, and less than ten percent regarded the function as a very strategic unit. If this is the view of senior executives – the most influential stakeholders – then purchasing people must not be chagrined that Procurement has to fight for its rightful place in the enterprise. What you must do is direct more effort and energy at changing that view by managing stakeholders better.

Your View of 'Stakeholders'

There is no universal panacea to the challenge of managing stakeholders. But there are some effective principles or approaches which aid this, including those highlighted above. It is impossible and inappropriate to separate the issues of 'stakeholder management' and 'communication', as both are complementary elements of creating a positive image and brand reputation for Procurement. I mention this because of the vital importance of communicating the Procurement agenda *to people inside the function*, which I covered earlier. We often think of 'stakeholders' as people outside Procurement. But the prime stakeholders are those inside Procurement. If your Procurement function is largely populated by Procurement Assassins, you have more work to do with building an effective Procurement organisation than with managing external stakeholders. If you have abundant numbers of Procurement Ambassadors, then you're nearly halfway to enhancing your Procurement effectiveness.

The chapter on Building an Effective Procurement Organisation covers the key principles for managing internal stakeholders effectively. Managing stakeholders outside Procurement requires approaches based on the same principles of effectiveness. Some purchasing people hold such negative sentiments about external stakeholders you'd think they were the enemy. They are not. Your attitude is, if you're one such purchasing person. Whether or not you view stakeholders as enemies, the service-oriented nature of Procurement's role demands that all purchasing people embrace the paradigm shift I mentioned earlier. Putting yourself in stakeholders' shoes is a good start to manifesting the highly tuned mindset for this. Seeing things from someone else's perspective is one of the key aspects of emotional intelligence, a vital requirement for successful intra- and interpersonal relationships.

The word 'stakeholder' inherently indicates a fundamental tenet: that stakeholders are important because they have a stake in what you do. In which case, doesn't it make sense to get to really understand these folks?

I often find it helpful to remind purchasing people that stakeholders in the enterprise are working for the same organisational outcomes as Procurement: ultimately, a strong balance sheet and a healthy P&L for the business, at the very least. By making the effort to walk a mile in their shoes, you can gain a much deeper understanding of stakeholders' drivers and motivations. This is where you will discover golden nuggets of wisdom that will prove priceless in shaping your stakeholder relationships.

> **Get in bed with your stakeholders to gain rich insights on their drivers and motivations, and how you can be more meaningful to them.**

We often group stakeholders collectively in our deliberations. Yet they are each individuals. Individual human behaviour is idiosyncratic, influenced by a complex mix of personal, psychological and environmental factors, many of which are not always obvious. Personal factors include things like gender, age, education, marital status, dependents and abilities. Psychological factors include personality types and traits, attitudes and values, while environmental factors relate to social and cultural norms, political dispositions, financial or economic circumstances and the scripts we pick up from our life experiences. Awareness of the factors that compel human behaviour is an important addition to the arsenal of knowledge required to engage stakeholders successfully – because effective stakeholder management intrinsically entails shaping *their* perceptions of Procurement.

The insights you will gain by delving into your stakeholders' perceptions, motivations and interests will enable you tailor your engagement and communication at an individual level to create concurrence. Think about your most difficult stakeholders for a minute; what do you actually know about them? How many kids do they have, and how old are they? What are their personal interests? What sports team do they support? Where did they go on their last vacation? Make the effort to really get to know your stakeholder as a person, a fellow human being like you. You'll be astounded how a little effort to create connections at a personal or individual level will help create massive improvements in engagement and alignment. Everyone knows that people are different. Yet we often fail to apply that knowledge in our interactions with individual stakeholders. I certainly do. I constantly have to keep reminding myself to apply all I have learnt to my various interactions and communications.

Shaping Stakeholders' Perceptions

Interactions with stakeholders, wherein we shape their perceptions, typically involve some form of persuasion, whether we do it deliberately or not. And persuasion is a fundamental constituent of interpersonal dynamics. As James Borg points out, Aristotle's teachings on communication and persuasion from over two millennia ago still hold true today. "The fool tells me his reasons, the wise man persuades me with my own," the ancient Greek philosopher said. He explained that people are social animals by nature, and we are habitually invoked to persuade others or win them over for various reasons. He identified three different kinds of proof persuasive people use:

(1) *Ethos* is about the ethical dimensions of the speaker – your character, integrity, credibility, trustworthiness, sincerity and reputation are all key factors which impact your persuasiveness. Aristotle's assertion that, "We believe good men more fully and more readily than others" has stood the

test of scientific research. But, remember, it is the perception of the target audience that counts; if your stakeholder perceives you as credible and sincere, you're much more likely to be able to win them over. You can influence that perception by connecting with them at a personal level.

(2) *Pathos* pertains to the emotions stirred up in the target audience. Persuasion and alignment may come about through the listener, when the communication arouses their emotions. Inspiration, happiness, anger, hope, fear, pity, guilt and so on are all emotions we each feel, including your individual stakeholders. By appealing to stakeholders' emotions you can be a lot more persuasive than otherwise. To do this successfully you must have empathy – you must be able to see things from their perspective, hence understand their feelings.

(3) *Logos* relates to the substance of the communication – the actual words or language used and the logic of the message. Quotations, analogies, facts, stories, data or statistics are great examples of different ways of tapping into your stakeholders' reasoning so that your communication makes sense to them. Avoid traditional purchasing jargon that often makes many stakeholders' eyes glaze over.

The ability to blend all three types of proof is a critical aptitude for persuasive communication. If you understand the motivations behind individual stakeholders' attitudes and behaviours, and you can communicate persuasively, you will find your capacity to win them over greatly increased. Jay Conger's work in this area offers invaluable wisdom for us all. Look around you and identify people who you consider to be effective operators, those who are really skilled at influencing others, and you'll see some common traits in how they operate. Effective operators are always persuasive communicators. They leverage their persuasive abilities by applying insights on human psychology which reflect universal principles. We can all learn to adopt these approaches, including the following:

- Open your mind, expand your thinking and grasp a fundamental truth: that people's attitudes, behaviours and decisions are not driven entirely by logic or reason. Emotions are always part of the mix, usually beneath the surface. You can leverage this by establishing an emotional connection with your stakeholders. Don't be fooled into thinking effective communication is simply about putting forward a logical argument. It isn't. Logic matters, but it's only one aspect of effective persuasion. How you present your case is as important as the underlying logic therein. So stay attuned to your stakeholders at an emotional level so you can moderate the tone and intensity of your argument accordingly.

- Always remember that credibility matters. But your opinion is less important than your stakeholders' perception of your credibility. You establish greater credibility – perceived and actual – through sensible opinions, shrewdness, proficiency, tactfulness and harmonic relationships. By making the effort to listen to your stakeholders' and take on board their opinions, you are demonstrating empathy and enhancing your credibility. The more stakeholders trust you to understand their view and consider their best interests, the more likely they are to align to you. Rather than trying to state your position with a hard sell, confined by your own perspective, try to find common ground. Try to sell your agenda in a manner that highlights the mutual benefits; you will elicit a more positive perception and greater engagement.

- Build your position and communicate your ideas by using appropriate language and evidence. Analogies, anecdotes and examples are effective ways of supplementing data to bring your ideas alive and strengthen your case. But remember that your stakeholders' opinions are important, so be prepared to give and take. Optimal outcomes are often achieved through compromise. Demonstrating flexibility can sometimes be an effective route to appeal to stakeholders persuasively.

Aristotle enlightens us that persuasion is one of the key forces at the heart of human interactions. Purchasing people can greatly enhance the effectiveness of their stakeholder management efforts by mastering this skill. Of course, it isn't always easy to develop and hone such abilities. And ability often grows with usage. Or, put another way, we learn best by doing, or at least trying. Thankfully, the modern-day workplace provides ample opportunities for you to try out your persuasive abilities. As well as tuning in to the corporate buzz and organisational dynamics, the work environment compels us to contend with all sorts of characters. Our stakeholders are individuals with different personalities, some more agreeable than others. The greater the range of personalities you can deal with effectively, the better your chances of successful stakeholder engagements.

> **Effective stakeholder management intrinsically entails shaping their perceptions of Procurement.**

Despite the uniqueness of each individual, we share the same basic 'human-ness' – we share many of the same personal, psychological and environmental factors that shape our attitudes, behaviours and sense of self. For instance, some of us are of the same gender, age and marital status; some of us have similar educational backgrounds and similar career paths, and live in the same society with common social and cultural norms; and most of us are driven by our impulses, values, logic or intuition. These similarities have allowed psychologists over the years to develop basic personality types which we each fit into. Today there are different typologies for personality types, from the four basic types introduced by Hippocrates aeons ago to the more popular Myers-Briggs classification. Being able to gauge individual stakeholders' personalities allows you to tailor your interaction style accordingly. For instance, based on their dominant personality type:

- Some people dislike chewing the fat; they prefer you to get to the point quickly, in a logical and impersonal manner.

- Some people dislike structure, process and routine; they prefer to explore ideas and analyse options with resourcefulness and ingenuity.

- Some dislike directness and abruptness; they prefer to connect on a personal level with a lot of camaraderie.

- Some dislike theories, hypotheses and intuitive assertions; they prefer hard, concrete facts which are specific and verifiable.

The more you can adapt your communication style to an individual stakeholder's personality, the more they'll develop an affinity for you and your ideas.

Stakeholders might not be enemies, but they're certainly not all angels. Many people in today's workplace hold misguided notions of 'success' and what constitutes appropriate behaviours; perhaps, driven by ambition, pressure, stress or some other unseen forces. Sometimes our discord with stakeholders is simply rooted in divergence of views, stemming from differences in personality, how we see the world or our inability to communicate persuasively. Whatever the case, it is always useful to understand whether individual stakeholders are *Supporters* – they 'get it', and do not need much persuasion; but in some cases it may be necessary to corral their enthusiasm so they work in synchrony with Procurement's agenda, rather than go off at a tangent. Others might be *Crowd-pleasers* – those who say the right things in meetings and in front of senior executives but go off and do something that breaches Procurement policies. Some of this type of stakeholders can be transformed into Supporters by robust relationship-building and quick, tangible results. The final type of external stakeholders, the *Detractor*s, will always try to fight against Procurement's agenda. Detractors need the most relationship-building effort, but some may never be won over and may need the 'big stick' approach.

Taking the time to categorise your stakeholders up front can be one of the key elements of preparation for initial engagement and ongoing management. Make the effort to analyse, assess and map your stakeholders, and use the results to plan your engagement strategy.

I first learnt about stakeholder mapping when running large-scale business process re-engineering initiatives many years ago. I found it to be a valuable activity that forced me to think about the individuals I was engaging with, and plan the most effective ways of keeping them on-side. I wish my undergraduate studies had included this topic; perhaps it would have saved me the anguish and frustration I suffered in some of my jobs in the early part of my career. Since I learnt about stakeholder mapping I have used it in every new role, and I still use it to this day on client engagements in various guises; figure 6.2 illustrates an excerpt from a supply management change initiative I led at one client organisation.

Stakeholder	Role / Function	Criticality	Interest / Stake	Assessment		Approach
Simon Hoult	CEO	1	Sponsor; 'beef-up PSCM capability'	+ve	Champion	Keep close; keep informed - weekly / fortnightly update reviews + open honest comms on all issues; leverage
Dave Rayner	Finance Director	1	VFM - wants cost reduction	?	Supporter?	Keep involved; share progress & issues via regular formal 1-2-1 presentations / reviews
Darren Beswick	Operations Director	2	'No shortages / late deliveries'	Neutral?	?	Keep involved; regular formal updates
Phil Evans	Supply Chain Manager	2	Keen for effective PSCM	+ve	Supporter	Keep close; regular informal updates; solicit opinion / inputs
Jerry Timmins	Supply Planning	3	S&OP role / involvement	-ve	Detractor?	Reinforce change ethos / calibrate & align; regular corridor conversations
David Plato	Engineering Director	3	Not too bothered?	+ve	Supporter?	Cultivate & nurture support; regular 1-2-1s & corridor conversations
Glyn Reece	Sales & Marketing Director	2	Protect influence / turf?	-ve?	Crowd-pleaser?	Cultivate & nurture alleged support; build relationship; frequent formal & informal updates; stroke ego & keep sweet

Figure 6.2 – Sample Stakeholder Mapping (Excerpt)

It's worth clarifying a few points here:

- In mapping stakeholders as such, my assessment of their 'Criticality' pertains to the influence they can have on the success of my agenda. (Remember, influence or power does not necessarily stem from job titles or roles.)

- 'Interest/Stake' relates to my subjective assessment of their agenda – what they really want, irrespective of what they may say they want.

- My decided 'Approach' is my judgement of the optimal manner of engagement, based on my assessments; the personalities of the individuals; and the organisational dynamics.

- Of course, some people are just difficult or impossible to read and I've often found myself using a question mark in such cases. These are the situations where I really wish I could use my African voodoo in the workplace!

You don't necessarily have to follow an identical structure in assessing and mapping your stakeholders. What's important is that you make the effort to analyse individual stakeholders such that you can distinguish between:

- Those who have a high stake or interest in your purchasing activities or programmes, and have the organisational authority or influence to help you succeed or negate your success. These are the key players you *must* leverage or keep sweet to progress your Procurement agenda to real success.

- Those who may not have a key stake in your activities but still have the power to make or break the success of your agenda. Build effective relationships with these stakeholders and try to leverage their organisational influence to champion your cause.

- Those who have a high stake in your purchasing activities but may lack the organisational power to champion your agenda or hamper your success. Keep them involved as appropriate, and, certainly, maintain robust communication with them to ensure they are on-side. They can become valuable Supporters, especially when you hit difficult times.

- Those who are not impacted by your activities and have little or no organisational influence. Don't waste too much effort here. But that's not to say you should ignore them completely; you just need to invest more of your stakeholder management effort where you will get the greatest returns, and it isn't with this group.

Top-notch stakeholder management is a vital component of building your Procurement brand and enhancing functional effectiveness. The investment you make here, in terms of time, effort and brain horsepower, will pay back enormously. Even where the outcomes are not ideal, it is still very worthwhile. When your stakeholder management efforts don't yield the outcomes you desire, you must examine your approach to see where you need to make adjustments, if at all; sometimes it's simply a case of staying persistent. In such situations it is worth remembering that Procurement stakeholders are really no different from the general population in a sense – they are people, not computers, trees or flowers. And people don't always embrace change readily. Some will be early adopters, keenly supporting the changes the Procurement agenda entails; others will only be persuaded to embrace the change by evidence and results; while the balance may need to be told, not sold to – of this lot, a small proportion will probably always rail against Procurement. As the French say, *c'est la vie.*

Influencing Stakeholders and Creating Alignment

Although using the 'big stick' approach with those that resist the Procurement agenda is sometimes necessary, it must always be a last resort; because stakeholder alignment based on coercion is rarely successful in the long term. Even where you make stakeholders toe the line, perhaps, by leveraging executive support or a formal Procurement mandate, it is still worthwhile making efforts to massage bruised egos and build positive relationships. This is part of having a well rounded perspective of stakeholders, a perspective that should allow clarity of thinking in distinguishing between the often differing needs of different stakeholder groups, including budget-holders; requisitioners; suppliers (yes, of course, they too are stakeholders); the board or senior executive team; shareholders; regulators, if applicable; and Procurement staff.

There might be others in your own list of stakeholder groups. They each have unique or special interests which should be catered for *as practically as possible.* The lure of trying to keep everyone happy is an ever-present risk; you must be able to identify who your *key* stakeholders are and give them priority focus.

Thinking of stakeholders as 'customers' is a nifty trick that can do wonders for your mindset. If you were running your own business and these stakeholders were your customers, how would you handle them, knowing they are the source of your daily bread? Most of us would probably take different approaches focused more on satisfying or exceeding customer expectations. You can apply the same ethos to Procurement stakeholders; after all, every user or consumer of third-party-sourced goods and services across the enterprise *is* a customer of Procurement, directly or indirectly. Procurement functions seeking their mojo can, thus, make great strides by incorporating some tenets of Customer Relationship Management (CRM) to their approaches for managing stakeholders.

> **If you were running your own business and your stakeholders were your customers, how would you handle them, knowing they are the source of your daily bread?**

One of the key ways of imbibing CRM to Procurement efforts is to make customer management part of the Procurement job, especially for job roles that directly face onto the enterprise. You can achieve this in various ways, for instance, by:

- Incorporating stakeholder alignment into purchasing job descriptions and stressing the importance to job-holders
- Imbibing internal customer satisfaction to Procurement functional goals and performance measures
- Including internal customer satisfaction in personnel objectives, and ensuring that Procurement staff give this as much attention as traditional objectives like sourcing and VFM delivery
- Calibrating purchasing people to place emphasis on internal customer engagement in their day-to-day activities.

As part of my efforts to achieve this in one Procurement function I led, I continuously encouraged my purchasing managers to go out and spend 20 percent of their time with internal customers each week. At first their reactions were unenthusiastic; they cited the plethora of tasks they had to undertake daily, seeing regular face-to-face customer interactions as "extra work". But I knew the value and insisted on it. My staff soon got to appreciate that these interactions were not only about pressing flesh, they became semi-formal forums for valuable discussions – finding out what the client-departments were up to and updating them on pertinent Procurement activities and functional capabilities. I also did the same thing with my opposite numbers. It was a fantastic way of bridging the divide between our Procurement function and our key stakeholders.

Spending time with internal customers may not change the relationship dynamics instantly, because attitudes don't change overnight. But if you give it a try and remain persistent, you will undoubtedly find immense value for your personal brand and your Procurement mojo. Such interactions are a great way to tap into stakeholders' worlds. Whether you make them formal meetings or keep them informal, these forums shouldn't just occur when Procurement is running specific sourcing programmes or other initiatives, they should be part of Procurement's modus operandi, providing opportunities to listen to stakeholders, understand their pains and concerns and decipher their motivations, agendas, needs and expectations.

Treating stakeholders' expectations and concerns with priority is crucial. It shows them that Procurement values their opinions and desires. Additionally, it is a key medium for aligning Procurement's agenda to the issues of importance to stakeholders, thus making Procurement more meaningful in their world.

You can also make Procurement more meaningful to stakeholders by studying their business operations to glean insights beyond what individual stakeholders say. Try to gain first-hand experience of how the goods and services procured are utilised, and how they pertain to the value-chain and objectives of the stakeholder function. This often provides rich information which enables more effective alignment between Procurement and client-departments. When you truly understand where stakeholders are coming from, it's easier to adapt your approach such that your efforts to sell the Procurement agenda have a greater chance of success.

Ultimately, effective stakeholder management is about building relationships that boost Procurement's position and effectiveness. And there are always two sides to the coin – as well as understanding stakeholders, purchasing people must also embed Procurement's value proposition in stakeholders' consciousness and operations. As I'm sure you've gathered, this takes concerted effort. It might seem like a lot of effort that detracts from your 'real job' of sourcing, category management, savings delivery and so on. It isn't. Rather, it is one of the cornerstones of attaining sustainable success in the purchasing job. Being effective at the job demands that you invest the effort required to manage stakeholders robustly, and involve them in relevant Procurement activities and decisions. Being efficient means that you expend the greatest effort in the most appropriate direction – develop deep relationships with the most critical stakeholders. But who are your most critical stakeholders?

The answer to the question varies from organisation to organisation, depending on the context – the nature of the enterprise's business; the organisational structure; the standing or eminence of the Procurement function, and whether or not it has a formal mandate; the Procurement leader's chutzpah; the strategic direction or immediate priorities of the enterprise; or the culture, political dynamics and power plays in the organisation. Of course, there might be other factors that determine who *your* critical stakeholders are. Whatever the case, experience suggests that for most Procurement functions the cadre of critical stakeholders includes the Finance function and budget-holders.

Finance is responsible for the financial stewardship of the enterprise. Since third-party spend is typically a huge chunk of enterprise finances, it makes absolute sense that Procurement is in league with Finance. The policies and operations of both functions should be in sync, given the shared aims of enterprise financial viability and risk minimisation. Sadly, this isn't often the case. The internet and trade publications are awash with stories, blog entries and articles telling us so. And judging from my experience and discussions with purchasing professionals in various sectors and geographies, it appears that the relationship between Procurement and Finance is certainly not the seamless partnership it should be. This is often due to misalignment and misunderstanding.

Finance folks, in general, are no different from other stakeholders who misunderstand Procurement's true value potential to the enterprise. In fact, many CFOs and Finance Directors still view purchasing as an enterprise activity centred on the most rudimentary elements of the Procurement value proposition – finding suppliers, managing purchase orders and delivering cost savings. I'm sure this isn't news to many purchasing professionals. What might be news is that the fault lies with us as purchasing people. Yes, the onus is on purchasing people to change the situation. When you take responsibility for the status of your organisational existence, you create a positive psychological shift – shifting from being a victim of the organisational status quo to becoming a shaper of the platform you seek. Talk to anyone who has overcome great challenges to create lasting success in any dimension of life and you'll hear the same message: making an effort to take control of the situation greatly increases your chances of creating the outcomes you want.

If your Procurement function's relationship with Finance or the CFO is lamentable, bemoaning the situation does nothing for Procurement. Absolutely nothing. Taking action to alter the situation, on the hand, starts to change the game. The principles expounded in this book illustrate several approaches to help you achieve this.

Achieving alignment with Finance requires joined-up thinking and close collaboration, in addition to developing good stakeholder insights as outlined above. For instance, if we consider the world from a Finance perspective, most CFOs are primarily interested in dollars; that's what keeps them awake at night – enterprise profitability, balance sheet position and cash. Their success motivators and their bonuses are also likely linked to these factors. By taking the time to understand this and spelling out how Procurement can help address *their* challenges, you start to turn the CFO into a Procurement fan. If you examine some of the financial measures CFOs focus on, for example, there are many opportunities to tailor the Procurement message in terms that align with the CFO's thinking. Figure 6.3 shows a simplified illustration of this concept using a few examples.

CFO's Interests	Potential Procurement Influence
Sales turnover	Augment revenue growth by providing customers with enhanced, dependable service and better value, e.g. through supply innovations, delivery reliability and shorter lead-times for new product introductions
Cost of sales	Use Design-for-Purchasing and Value Analysis/Value Engineering to increase standardisation and optimisation; leverage Target Cost Management, better sourcing, SPRM and VFM programmes to reduce total cost of ownership
Operating expenses (OPEX)	Exploit technology, business process outsourcing, Lean-based processes, SPRM, category management, purchasing hubs or functional clusters to reduce cost-to-procure
Working capital	Optimise inventory holding and stock turns; and improve supplier payment terms

Figure 6.3 – Aligning to the CFO's Thinking

Most CFOs and Finance folks won't get excited about Procurement's "sourcing strategies", "category management", "SPRM" or "e-auctions"; they probably don't care two hoots. Engage them in a way that incorporates their priorities, using language they understand, and you will engender better alignment. A good example is Procurement's value-for-money (VFM) improvement efforts – Finance is usually interested in opportunities to reduce costs or increase value, especially when it is quantifiable and credible. So work collaboratively with your Finance function to deploy structured planning and governance protocols that provide transparency of projected and delivered VFM benefits, and ensure these results are incorporated to the relevant financial management mechanisms in your organisation.

When you can engage Finance in a way that creates meaning in their world, you deliver on your promise and you continue to manage the relationship effectively, you will transform your CFO from a mere fan to a Procurement cheerleader. It's a disposition Beth Enslow advocates widely, which savvy Procurement leaders inherently adopt.

While financial benefits must never be the sole raison d'être of Procurement, any laudable results delivered here must be leveraged to earn the trust and support of Finance. The same applies for budget-holders; Procurement must exploit key results accomplished and effective relationship management to position itself as a credible business partner.

HR is another stakeholder function I always consider to be critical. HR may be a critical stakeholder for your Procurement function because the related spend category is significant. In such cases, the functional relationship with HR should be cultivated with the same diligence as other key client-functions. But the greater requirement for stakeholder alignment with HR comes from the imperative to build an effective Procurement organisation. Acquiring the requisite talent and sustaining the people capability to reach your Procurement mojo demands effective HR support. In this regard, Procurement is HR's internal customer. To elicit CRM-oriented attitudes and support from the HR function, Procurement must ensure that HR understands its organisational development agenda, how that agenda aligns to its functional goals and how those goals support the enterprise strategic priorities. Without robust HR support, you're unlikely to achieve an optimal Procurement organisational capability.

Of course, many small businesses have no HR department. The Procurement leader in such a situation may, thus, feel adrift on this theme. But that doesn't have to be the case. Building an effective Procurement organisation may not be a walk in the park, but it's not nuclear physics either. Even without internal HR support, in today's internet age it's easy to find good material and reliable information on developing people capability. This book already provides you with ample guidance on how to go about this. And, remember, the most critical person is the Procurement leader – leadership is the glue that holds the components of an effective Procurement organisation together. So if you are a Procurement leader in an organisation without formal HR support, focus on honing your own leadership abilities; that will lead you to seek out any additional HR-related material you need. Then tailor your deployment of the knowledge you acquire to the Procurement agenda you are driving. Having HR support does not necessarily mean having an internal HR resource.

Whether it's HR, Finance or other stakeholder functions, the need to communicate with stakeholders in terms they understand is vital. Avoid boring or irking them with Procurement jargon; don't use purchasing buzzwords or technical lingo they might not understand. Telling HR you want to improve your 'strategic sourcing' may be meaningless to them. Talk in terms of the specific competences and personal attributes you desire in your people. In the same vein, if 'cost savings' is not a priority for Finance, stop yapping on about it; you might instead talk about 'value creation' or 'funding growth'. And for market-facing business units, you might cloak your communication in issues like 'competitive advantage', 'supply assurance' and 'customer acquisition'.

As a South Korean I'm pretty sure Ban Ki-moon, the current United Nations (UN) Secretary General is fluent in the Korean language. But he doesn't use it at the UN; instead he communicates in the official languages of the UN – languages his constituent stakeholders understand (or receive formal translations from). In the same way, purchasing people must communicate with stakeholders using appropriate language to create resonance. It fosters better engagement. And it makes it much easier to educate people outside Procurement and calibrate their activities to the Procurement agenda.

Educating users and budget-holders is crucial to secure alignment and buy-in. This isn't just about tangible enterprise activities, but also about influencing stakeholders' emotions. Some months ago, I was chatting about purchasing with a senior business unit manager in a large financial products company. He complained that some new edict introduced across his company meant he couldn't go out and buy simple stationery items that cost peanuts, yet he was keeping in his office thousands of pounds worth of product vouchers for routine customer sales. He couldn't see the logic – he *felt* as if he wasn't trusted with spending a few pounds for stationery but was trusted with customer products worth thousands. My impulsive reaction was to try to explain the benefits of corporate-wide sourcing deals and how maverick buying creates leakage in purchasing value. But I held my tongue. For a moment I thought about things from his perspective instead. And it was clear that the Procurement function in his company had failed in communication on both the *pathos* and *logos* fronts. I asked if there had been any prior communication or publicity to explain the changes in stationery buying protocols, and he replied, "No".

Examples like this do nothing positive for the Procurement brand. If you don't make the effort to communicate purchasing activities or governance robustly, you are not building awareness and you risk alienating your stakeholder community. This risk becomes even more significant with non-Procurement staff who routinely interact with suppliers in their job roles. These folks must be appropriately educated on the implications of commercially-sensitive issues to avoid unpleasant outcomes.

Procurement's communication approach should not only address such issues, it must also sell the functional value proposition; by demonstrating how the Procurement agenda supports the objectives of internal customers and aligns to the enterprise strategy and key priorities. Efforts to drive such awareness must convey Procurement's functional capabilities, and facilitate inputs or involvement of stakeholders as appropriate. By sharing information and soliciting stakeholder opinions, you reduce the organisational resistance to Procurement's agenda.

Procurement PR

The tactics outlined above on persuasive communication and influencing stakeholders to create alignment are both vital ingredients to devise and execute an effective communications game-plan.

Publicising Procurement successes widely is another. It's a tactic that forms a key part of effective public relations (PR) to maintain a positive brand image for Procurement. If you are pondering what PR has to do with Procurement, hark back to my comments about learning from successful consumer product brands. PR is one of the things they do best to build reputable brand positions. It is also what you must do for your Procurement brand; primarily, within the wider enterprise. Think broadly of key avenues to maintain a high profile and consistent visibility for your Procurement function.

PR is about reputation management – crafting an appropriate message for target audiences and delivering the message with flair. Think about Procurement's PR effort as a sustained endeavour to protect the function's brand reputation, with the key aims of:

(1) Boosting awareness and understanding of Procurement
(2) Influencing stakeholders' opinions, feelings and attitudes, and, hence, their behaviours
(3) Maintaining goodwill and support for Procurement across the enterprise.

This notion must be imbibed into *how* Procurement pursues its goals, and all routine functional activities and stakeholder interactions. As a purchasing person, everything you do and say, and what stakeholders think, feel and say about you, impacts Procurement's brand reputation.

That brand reputation is central to Procurement's successful positioning in the enterprise. The brand may be enlivened by the creation of a brand logo, and even a slogan. Your Procurement brand logo or slogan don't have to be jazzy or complicated. I always use a simple, defined emboldened text with a fixed font, size and colour for a logo. But I always make it standard practice that the logo appears on all formal documents, irrespective of who the readers are. While I have seen many applications of internal functional slogans, I have seldom used one. When I have, it has also been something simple.

Simple or jazzy, the adoption of a defined graphical identity does no harm to the Procurement brand. If anything, a consistent brand logo helps disseminate the Procurement brand identity across the enterprise. And that helps the PR effort immensely.

In the marketing field, effective PR is about influencing and managing perceptions – implementing a positive change, or sustaining a favourable position, in the target audience's feelings and opinions about a product, service or organisation. The same principle applies to Procurement PR – it should be focused on positioning Procurement in stakeholders' consciousness such that their awareness, understanding and emotions about the function are favourable. For purchasing people, this translates to a requirement to ensure the Procurement brand connects with stakeholders by being meaningful to them. Make sure purchasing activities discussed with stakeholders are:

- **Important** – Pertinent to their world and helps address their most critical problems
- **Sustainable** – Will resonate with them well into the future
- **Credible** – Your claims can be substantiated.

> **Procurement PR should be focussed on positioning Procurement in stakeholders' consciousness such that their perceptions of the function are favourable.**

PR efforts to enhance Procurement's brand image are part of the overall drive to position the function in the fabric of the enterprise and promote the Procurement agenda. PR approaches should focus on propagating a structured flow of information that always positions Procurement in a positive light. This can be done by exploiting different media, including:

- Features, stories and news items on the corporate intranet website

- Updates on the Procurement intranet website
- Stakeholder testimonials, comments and interviews with Procurement personnel in the company magazine or similar internal publications
- A dedicated Procurement newsletter
- Periodic email updates
- Roadshows
- Periodic presentations or update briefings with the executive team
- Publicity slots at corporate events
- Supplier days (This is an excellent medium for positioning the Procurement agenda with this specific group of external stakeholders. But it can also be a good opportunity for internal stakeholders to hear more of the Procurement message if you invite targeted individuals, such as senior executives and key personnel from other functions.)

I often encourage purchasing people to apply a combination of different media as appropriate to the particular situation. For instance, consideration must be given to the nature of the communications message, the timing, the organisational norms, and so on. One particular medium that is often very worthwhile is a Procurement intranet website. Not only does it serve the PR purposes discussed, it offers a number of additional advantages which few other media provide:

(1) In today's internet age, majority of organisations utilise intranet websites for internal communications. This offers a ready platform to tap into; all that is required is the creation of a dedicated section for Procurement.

(2) Related to the above point, an intranet website is accessible by most employees across the enterprise, even if they are located at different sites or in different geographies.

(3) A Procurement intranet site can be wholly controlled by Procurement, supported by the IT function as appropriate.

This offers an opportunity without boundaries as regards site contents, structure, frequency of updates and so on. The site can be updated with whatever you deem relevant as often as you like.

(4) A Procurement intranet site can be used both as a communications medium and an information repository. As well as publicising appropriate Procurement news for PR purposes, you can also use sections of the site for listing and storing information on functional governance and operations. Examples include the Procurement policy; process specifications; functional templates and pro-formas; the performance scorecard; and the Procurement team structure and areas of responsibility.

When considering the development and ongoing maintenance of your Procurement website, remember to focus on the end-users. Structure your intranet website around the needs, or likely needs, of the people who will refer to it. Some of the content might be for Procurement staff; for example, templates and pro-forma documents. Other content will be for stakeholders outside Procurement. So it's important that the website makes it easy for such stakeholders to find the information they require. By making your Procurement intranet site user-friendly and easy on the eye, and ensuring the content is relevant and up to date, you increase the chances of stakeholders referring to it more often. And the more traffic you have on your Procurement website, the more effective it is as a communications medium.

As valuable as a Procurement website might be, it is unlikely to be adequate for PR purposes on its own. Hence, PR efforts must incorporate other media. Perhaps a few examples of relevant PR efforts will help to illustrate how some of these media can be exploited effectively:

PR Effort: Positioning and brand awareness for a newly-created function

At a large, multinational company where I once worked, I led a change programme to create an integrated group-wide supply management function with responsibility for freight purchasing across multiple business units, spanning some thirteen or so countries. Prior to this, each business unit did its own thing. Unsurprisingly, there were one or two Detractors and Crowd-pleasers in several geographies who resented the integration. So projecting the new global function as a successful and effective contributor to the business was important.

As part of my PR efforts, I published news features on the corporate intranet homepage, with translated versions on regional intranet sites, publicising every major success we achieved. For example, when we delivered significant efficiency savings in our Central Europe operations, I crafted a news story that included complimentary comments from the regional Operations VP and a few words from my team members who delivered the result, with their photos attached.

PR Effort: Stakeholder alignment and publicity for purchasing governance

As part of the transformation of the NPI-Purchasing function I mentioned earlier, we revamped our process governance to help improve functional effectiveness. While introducing two new critical processes – Design-for-Purchasing and Target Cost Management – I ran a series of roadshows across several sites, to spread the word in the community of Product Development and Engineering stakeholders. I made sure the presentation material and my own words were focused around the benefits these new governance mechanisms would bring to these folks. I also allowed ample time to take questions and address any concerns at each roadshow event. Once I had secured acceptance and buy-in, I publicised the launch of the new processes on the intranet, ensuring the communications message was slanted towards the benefits to our stakeholder functions and the business as a whole.

PR Effort: Embedding Procurement and driving understanding

At another large organisation, I was leading a change programme to embed a new Procurement function in one business unit. We were also preparing for the divestment of our business from the group company. As part of those preparations, we held a leadership conference for all senior managers in the business. The key themes included the EBITDA challenge we faced and how it related to the success of the divestment. A few people were handpicked to give brief talks on their experiences in the business and activities in their functional areas to support the divestment programme. I used the opportunity to flog our Procurement agenda, focusing my talk on two things:

(1) Our commitment to serve internal customers better and help them achieve their functional objectives and budget challenges

(2) How effective purchasing directly impacted the profitability of any business, and how Procurement was supporting the achievement of our EBITDA target to secure a maximum sale price in the divestment.

I knew that linking my message to the number one business priority (the divestment) was pure gold. My discernment was confirmed by the enthusiastic commendation from the CEO afterwards. That talk stamped our Procurement brand on the collective consciousness of the organisation far more than anything else we did in those hectic months before the divestment.

And here is an example that details the actual news story I crafted for publication on the corporate intranet website at a global multinational client business:

PR Effort: Highlighting Procurement contribution and boosting awareness and engagement

---

Procurement Savings Programme Hits £2m Milestone!

Since the <u>launch</u> of our group-wide "_VFM Improvement Programme_" by the Global Procurement function earlier in the year, our regional Procurement teams have been making great strides towards our direct materials cost savings target.

With direct materials forming over fifty percent of our cost of sales, the savings delivered by our regional Procurement teams are making a significant contribution to our group business profitability this year. At the end of June, our Procurement teams had delivered a whopping £2.2m of total savings, with 97% already ratified by the Finance functions in each region!

The savings delivered by our Procurement teams in North America and Middle East & Africa in particular are very impressive, with both teams achieving over 50% of their regional targets already.

Nikki Brewer (below left), our Procurement Manager for Middle East & Africa, commented, "The team has been very supportive in embracing our VFM improvement challenge. We still have many other improvements to make to our processes, but our results to-date on the VFM programme demonstrate the collective determination of the Procurement team and our stakeholders."

And Nigel Martin (above right), Procurement Manager in North America, added, "It's been really useful to analyse our direct materials spend to identify potential value improvement opportunities. Driving those savings to fruition with clear visibility of our contribution to the business profitability is proving very motivational to me and my stakeholders whose support is invaluable."

In a recent review of the programme, Derek Abraham, group CFO, reiterated the importance of the VFM Programme as part of our continuing efforts to improve our financial performance, and praised the Global Procurement team for their achievements.

For more information on the Procurement "VFM Improvement Programme" and other functional updates, visit the Global Procurement website.

This last example is particularly useful in illustrating many of the principles I have explained in this book. I'm not a great fan of tying Procurement's value-add purely to financial benefits. But effectiveness is about doing the right things; in this case, leveraging Procurement's financial accomplishments to boost awareness and esteem. The business was going through a massive financial turnaround, driven through several avenues including redundancies. I had accepted the challenge of delivering significant value improvements in our direct materials spend, largely through immediate low-hanging fruit opportunities and group-wide strategic sourcing. This organisational context was a key factor in shaping the content and delivery of our Procurement PR messages:

- Aside from the generic PR objectives of the intranet publication, notice how the story centres on Procurement's contribution to the corporate key priority of business profitability – the subliminal message is: "We are supporting the business with its key goal".

- You might also have noticed that the story doesn't mention "strategic sourcing" – because the target audience weren't versed in purchasing jargon, but they fully understood the business drive to reduce costs.

- Plugging in the CFO's feedback reflected my efforts to turn him into a Procurement cheerleader. I had sought his agreement to include his comments when I gave him a functional update presentation a few weeks earlier. To the wider audience in the company, his feedback indicated that Procurement was deemed important at the top table.

- The underlined words in the story were hyperlinks to other online content on our functional activities, e.g. we had previously published an intranet story when we initially launched the VFM programme; and we had a section of our Procurement intranet site dedicated to the VFM programme which summarised our key activities and the results achieved. The hyperlinks were an easy way of encouraging readers to see what we were doing by a simple mouse-click.

- But, of course, those results were achieved by people. So giving my Procurement managers visibility at a corporate level (by naming them, displaying their photographs and including their comments) was a great way to boost motivation and engagement in the regional teams. This was crucial as the financial pressures and redundancy programme sapped morale in the organisation.

- Publicly acknowledging that our stakeholders were supporting our efforts was a fantastic means of nurturing the relationships with those who were already Supporters and encouraging those who weren't yet.

To be effective, Procurement's PR efforts must be proactive and targeted. While structured approaches like news stories and presentations are central to the PR drive, informal media like corridor conversations are also great opportunities to promote the Procurement brand. Irrespective of the amount of emphasis you place on structured media or informal interactions, it is worth keeping in mind that your efforts to reposition your Procurement brand must be backed up with solid functional competency and results; otherwise you create dissonance – a mismatch between your brand promise and what Procurement actually delivers. This is one of the major causes of stakeholder dissatisfaction, and it damages Procurement's reputation. It's much harder to win back a stakeholder who has been disappointed than to win one who has not been engaged. Such disappointment must be avoided at all costs, not least by incorporating a few guidelines:

- Successful positioning demands good self-awareness. Undertake an honest appraisal of the strengths, weaknesses, opportunities and threats of your Procurement function. Be very candid – ask yourself, your team members and a select few internal customers and peer-group functions. Combine the findings with benchmarking intelligence, and use the insights gleaned in crafting your Procurement message.

- Tailor the style, content and timings of your communications to your status and progress on your journey to your Procurement mojo. Ensure continuous alignment between internal capability and the value proposition propagated – deliver on your commitments.

- Focus on high-value activities, with less human capital expended on transactional or mundane stuff. And publicise Procurement's achievements on issues of strategic importance to the enterprise, highlighting the related impacts and benefits.

- Always be honest with stakeholders. You are better off telling a stakeholder you're unable to reveal specific details than relaying misleading or deceptive information. Honesty and sincerity are the bedrock of your personal integrity and the credibility of your Procurement brand promise.

Selling a Procurement brand proposition that does not match the delivery capability is like selling a sports car to a punter only for him to discover it's been built with a scooter engine. You can avoid the embarrassment and reputational damage this brings by embracing the guidelines above.

Building a credible Procurement brand is right at the core of enhancing Procurement effectiveness – the brand promise and the actual brand performance reflect the underlying level of functional effectiveness. It requires broad-minded thinking and recognition of the salient factors affecting Procurement's prominence in the enterprise. Investing the effort to position Procurement favourably, manage stakeholders effectively and leverage astute communications is an essential step to assure Procurement's stature. It is an investment that also yields bountiful returns in helping to shape the Procurement agenda to enterprise needs. The combination of this effort with the other steps outlined previously will unwrap the magic enshrouded in your Procurement mojo.

Procurement Mojo: Some things to think about...

Ask yourself these questions, and take effective corrective actions if the <u>honest</u> answers reveal that you are not heading towards your Procurement mojo!

* ❖ Is our Procurement function positioned to provide clear leadership of purchasing activities and relevant contributions to enterprise priorities?
* ❖ Is our purchasing approach seamless and integrated across our internal customer operations?
* ❖ How well aligned is our Procurement function with Finance? Are our purchasing governance protocols effectively integrated with enterprise financial management activities?
* ❖ How effective is our communication – to the Procurement team, to internal customers, to other stakeholders and to senior executives?
* ❖ How effectively do we manage internal customer expectations and relationships?
* ❖ Is our Procurement value proposition to stakeholders clear and compelling, and does it align appropriately to their organisational goals and priorities?
* ❖ Do we measure/monitor our service to internal customers, and how satisfied do they feel about our service delivery performance?
* ❖ Do we leverage effective PR to propagate a high profile and consistent visibility for Procurement?
* ❖ What is the brand awareness of our Procurement function across the enterprise, and how favourable are the perceptions of Procurement held by stakeholders?

EPILOGUE

There is an adage that says, "If you swing at nothing, you will hit it." I love the simplicity of this statement and how it gets one thinking. It illustrates a basic tenet of effectiveness in the pursuit of success, whatever 'success' means to us. Success comes from being clear on our desired outcome, first and foremost, and then channelling our efforts towards that outcome. The success most Procurement functions desire is encapsulated in:

- The internal capability to deliver on their functional obligations
- The 'organisational space' to get on with delivering those obligations, and
- Recognition of the Procurement function's value-add across the wider organisation.

Achieving this success demands functional effectiveness – doing the right things to get those outcomes. The right things are not always the most popular or widely accepted actions. Some of the steps to enhance Procurement effectiveness may not be those many purchasing people would recognise as essential priorities. Yet if you examine instances of lasting Procurement success, you will find the embodiment of the principles outlined in this book.

Today, 'best-practice' purchasing is sometimes expounded as a set of technical competences, processes and tools – spend analytics; strategic sourcing; category management; P2P process; and e-procurement, to name a few. But deploying best practices in the technical purchasing domain will not necessarily deliver *long-term sustainable* success. The effectiveness of those practices and how well they are aligned with the non-technical dimensions of success is far more important. In fact, what best-practice purchasing is really about is Procurement playing its true role in the enterprise – safely and ethically harnessing the power of supply markets to support enterprise goals. It is more about leveraging organisational dynamics and managing relationships than the technical purchasing activity itself.

Having great technical purchasing competency is no longer what distinguishes Procurement functions that are truly successful from those that are mediocre or run-of-the-mill. How we build and nurture that competency and leverage it in the enterprise is crucial to success. Enhancing Procurement effectiveness is what creates sustainable success. Procurement functions that continue to rely on, or focus on, technical competency alone will increasingly find organisational life frustrating. As well as being technically adept, we must be able to influence the environment Procurement operates in. Hence, we must be competent at the requisite strategies to enable that.

When I give talks or coach purchasing teams and professionals on strategies to achieve Procurement effectiveness, I sometimes hear the response, "I know what you mean, Sigi, but you know it's not easy..." It might not be easy; it takes a determined mindset to excel, and concerted and persistent efforts at *doing the right things*. But it's only ever as difficult as riding a bicycle was before you learnt to ride one.

Procurement effectiveness is much more than the traditional focus on technical capabilities. It is also more than the myopic focus on delivering cost savings. Cost is important but value is king. Cost savings will always be a *de facto* element of Procurement's role. But the true essence of Procurement's role in the enterprise is to continuously deliver value from third-party spend. This means Procurement must deliver today's results and build capability to deliver tomorrow's by aligning to the enterprise agenda. The only route to achieving this is through Procurement effectiveness, starting with the creation of an effective Procurement organisation.

An effective Procurement organisation is the bedrock of the Procurement mojo. Coupled with the other effectiveness-enhancing steps, it provides the foundations for sustainable Procurement success. If after reading this far you still have any doubts, I invite you to do two things:

(1) Try it. Try incorporating the principles and guidelines conveyed in this book and see what results you achieve. After all, they do say experience is the best teacher.

(2) Do some real benchmarking. Talk to people who have created or been part of real Procurement success. Find out not just what they did but *how* they did it. Gaining knowledge of others' experience is another way to learn.

You don't have to look too far to find others who appreciate the vital importance of Procurement effectiveness. Writing in a leading trade magazine, one senior Procurement leader advocates many of the approaches expounded in the fundamental tenets of Procurement effectiveness. His comments on aligning Procurement's goals to corporate priorities; managing individuals' performance; personnel development; effective stakeholder engagement; and communicating to the business all reflect the basic premise of Procurement effectiveness. In an interview with a different trade publication, another senior executive who has headed Procurement functions at a number of global Fortune 500 companies proffered a categorical acknowledgement of the significance of people capability. She highlighted that supply management is a people-centric activity, and that highly engaged staff are the basis of achieving great success. Further advocacy comes from the CPO of one of the world's leading technology and consulting firms, with over a hundred billion dollars revenue, circa fifty billion dollars annual spend and about half-a-million employees. His affirms that people are the lifeblood of any Procurement function, and, hence, the performance success of the function is unequivocally dependent on its human capital.

It is pleasing to note such comments by experienced Procurement executives. They provide evidence of the growing awareness that underlying effectiveness is a prerequisite for true Procurement success. Yet it is also a fundamental truth that Procurement functions that are truly successful are in the minority. Many trade surveys, industry reports and blog comments repeatedly confirm that a lot of Procurement functions are neither positioned nor perform in a strategic capacity in their organisations. Consequently, they are not acknowledged as a bona fide business partner function that truly supports enterprise strategic goals; they live out an organisational existence of endless battles to influence the broader enterprise meaningfully.

Procurement functions that are struggling to become more meaningful and gain kudos in the enterprise must uncover their mojo – to enjoy functional success, you must enhance your Procurement effectiveness. The principles and approaches presented in this book will help you achieve this.

In explaining those approaches, I have deliberately tried to avoid being overly prescriptive. This is largely due to the slightly elusive nature of effectiveness – it isn't something tangible or measurable, and it relates as much to *what* you do as to *how* you do it. The specifics of the journey to the Procurement mojo may vary from situation to situation. However, the underlying precepts of Procurement effectiveness apply universally. Adopting these tenets requires a paradigm shift in the conventional notions of 'good purchasing' held by some purchasing folks and those outside Procurement alike. At a functional level, it demands a shift of focus that places greater emphasis on issues such as:

- Developing a Procurement value proposition that imbibes an attractive ROI for the enterprise, where the 'return' exceeds financial benefits
- Aligning Procurement goals and key activities to the corporate agenda
- Recognising the criticality of people capability, and the importance of soft skills and progressive attitudes and behaviours relative to technical ability
- Becoming more organisationally savvy
- Entrenching customer- or user-centricity in the ethos of all that Procurement does, and
- Developing and protecting the Procurement brand.

The Procurement function is made up of individuals. Thus, the paradigm shift is only possible at functional level if purchasing people are able to shift focus at an individual level, building competency in areas such as:

- Effective self-leadership
- Strategic thinking
- Managing successful change

- Emotional intelligence
- Persuasive communication and influencing others
- Effective intra- and interpersonal engagement, and
- 'Walking the walk' by living the values of effectiveness.

As I stated earlier, to secure your Procurement mojo you must take the steps outlined in this book. There really is no shortcut. I have met many purchasing people who crave their Procurement mojo but shy away from the dedicated effort it takes to get it. Yes, everybody wants to go to heaven but nobody wants to die. You will not secure your Procurement mojo without embracing the principles of Procurement effectiveness.

How you go about executing these principles will depend on the status quo of your Procurement function – your 'as-is' situation. For some functions, it will mean a radical transformation programme. For others, it may be that certain elements of Procurement effectiveness already exist, hence tackling the specific areas which reveal effectiveness gaps one-by-one is more appropriate. Either way, it is imperative that you question what your Procurement function focuses on and how you operate – the objectives, key activities and areas consuming high investment in finances and human capital; will these give you the key outcomes of strengthening the function and raising awareness of its value-add in the enterprise?

Whatever your 'as-is' situation, remember that it is people that matter most – because it's people that create performance, good or bad; not computers, strategies, processes or fancy presentations. As noted earlier, if you take all those things out of any enterprise but leave the people in, the enterprise will still find a way to function. But do the reverse – take the people out and leave the computers, strategies, etc., behind – and the enterprise will grind to a halt. People matter most because they do the work. Build an effective Procurement organisation, starting with effective functional leadership, and the rest will be easier than otherwise.

Enhancing Procurement effectiveness requires taking the five steps presented in this book. Each step on its own is valuable but will not deliver the outcomes you desire. Like notes from a symphony, the steps must be harmonised in a holistic approach to unleash the magic of your Procurement mojo. Those Procurement functions that have found their mojo enjoy sustainable success and prominence in their organisations far beyond what their average peer functions attain; because winners always win big – winners always get a hugely disproportionate share of the rewards. It's a phenomenon called Zipf's Law, and it applies as much to best-selling movies as it does to top-selling ice cream flavours. It's evident in the massive difference between the majority of Procurement functions today and the tiny minority that attain high levels of employee satisfaction, organisational esteem and long-term performance success.

The Procurement functions that enjoy lasting success and kudos are those that embody the principles of Procurement effectiveness presented here. Your Procurement function can join the list of success stories by embracing these principles too.

###

"When you're climbing a ladder, make sure it's leaning against the right wall."
– Anon.

Thank You!

Many thanks for spending your most valuable assets – your time and your intellect – on this book. I hope it serves its purpose by expanding your understanding and inspiring you to take the right actions to achieve what you really want. If you enjoyed it and found it useful, please share that with your colleagues, peers and friends in the Procurement field. Also, I'd very much appreciate it if you'd take the time to let many others know of your experience by writing a positive review on Amazon and other relevant online book outlets or forums.

Please feel free to contact me at www.sigiosagie.com if you have any questions or feedback comments.

REFERENCES AND BIBLIOGRAPHY

Bagshaw, Steve, "Home improvements", *http://www.supplymanagement. com*, 29 September 2008

Bennett, Dean, "The CPO Interview", *http://www-05.ibm.com/tr/gbs/ pdf/supplychainprocurement/johnpatersonpdf_f3409.pdf*, IBM Global Business Services, 2009

Biti, T., Hon. MP, Minister of Finance, Zimbabwe, "The 2011 Mid-Year Fiscal Policy Review – Riding the Storm: Economics in the Time of Challenges", *http://www.zimfa.gov.zw*, 26 July 2011

Blascovich, John, Ferrer, Alejandro and Markham, Bill, "Follow the Procurement Leaders: Seven Ways to Lasting Results", *http://www. atkearney.co.uk/documents/10192/525149/Follow_the_Procurement_ Leaders.pdf*, A. T. Kearney Inc., 2011

Blunt, Elizabeth, "Corruption 'costs Africa Billions'", *http://news.bbc.co.uk/1/ hi/world/africa/2265387.stm*, 18 September 2002

Borg, James, *Persuasion – The Art of Influencing People* 3rd Edition, Prentice Hall 2010

Brass, Richard, "The brains trust", *Supply Management*, 17 January 2008

Checketts, Vance and Dwyer, Christopher J., "The CPO's Strategic Agenda – Managing Performance, Reporting to the CFO", Aberdeen Group Inc., February 2007

"Combating Corruption, Improving Governance in Africa – Regional Anti-Corruption Programme for Africa (2011 – 2016)", Programme Document, UN Economic Commission for Africa and African Union Advisory Board on Corruption

Conger, Jay A., *Winning 'em Over – A New Model for Managing in the Age of Persuasion*, Simon & Schuster, 1998

Covey, Stephen R., *The 7 Habits of Highly Effective People*, Simon & Schuster, 2004

"Create a Culture that Embraces Procurement as a Strategic Business Partner", *http://www.esourcingwiki.com/index.php/Newsletter_Articles*, Iasta Insights, 26 March 2013

Day, Marc and Lichtenstein, Scott, "Exploiting the Strategic Power of Supply Management – Options for creating business-wide strategic alignment", Henley Business School, December 2008

"Delivering on Procurement's Potential", *http://treyaconnectresearch. blogspot.co.uk/*, Treya Partners, 2007

Drucker, Peter F., *The Effective Executive*, William Heinemann, 1967

Ellinor, Rebecca, "We just get on and do it", *Supply Management*, March 2012

Ellinor, Rebecca, "Winning ways", *http://www.supplymanagement.com*, 6 October 2011

Enslow, Beth, "Turning Your CFO into a Supply Chain Cheerleader", Reed Business Information/Aberdeen Group, 2006

Gerstner, Jr., Louis V., *Who Says Elephants Can't Dance? Inside IBM's Historic Turnaround*, HarperCollins, 2002

Goleman, Daniel, *Emotional Intelligence*, Bloomsbury, 1996

Handy, Charles, *Inside Organizations: 21 Ideas for Managers*, Penguin Books, 1999

Handy, Charles, *The Hungry Spirit*, Arrow Books, 1998

Henshall, David, "Raising the esteem of Procurement – Strategies to break into the boardroom", Executive Insight Volume 9, *http://purchasingpractice. com/wp-content/volume-9.pdf*, Purchasing Practice

Hill, Terry, *Manufacturing Strategy – The Strategic Management of the Manufacturing Function* Second Edition, Macmillan, 1993

Houston, Patrick W. and Hutchens, Robert, "Procurement's New Operating Model", *http://www.booz.com/media/file/Procurements_New_Operating_ Model.pdf*, Booz & Company Inc., 2009

Hughes, Jon and Lim, Sarah, "Delivering Against the Promise: Next Generation Skills & Capabilities", The International Procurement Leadership Forum, Odgers Ray & Berndtson and Future Purchasing, 5th October 2006

Impreveduto, Rocco, "A vital partnership", *Supply Management*, October 2012

Jones, Del, "Let people know where they stand, Welch says", *http:// usatoday30.usatoday.com/money/companies/management/2005-04-17-welch-advice_x.htm*, 18 April 2005

Kanter, Jake, "Homeserve team disbanded", *http://www.supplymanagement. com/news*, 27 March 2009

Kim, Miyoung and Jim, Clare, "Japan quake tests supply chain from chips to ships", *http://www.reuters.com*, 14 March 2011

Kushner, Michael, "Reinventing Procurement As a 'Go-To' Organization", *http://www.esourcingforum.com/archives/2012/01/16/*, 16 January 2012

Leach, Adam, "Senior execs unclear on Procurement's role", *http://www. supplymanagement.com/news*, 13 March 2012

Leake, Jonathan and Henry, Robin, "North Face uses down from force-fed geese", *The Sunday Times*, 19 February 2012

Leenders, Michiel R., Fearon, Harold E., Flynn, Anna E. and Johnson, P. Fraser, *Purchasing and Supply Management* Twelfth Edition, McGraw-Hill, 2002

Luft, Joseph, *Group Processes – An Introduction to Group Dynamics* Third Edition, Mayfield Publishing Company, 1984

Masters, Sam, "Horsemeat discovered in beefburgers on sale at Tesco and Iceland", *http://www.independent.co.uk*, 15 January 2013

"Mattel recalls millions more toys", *http://news.bbc.co.uk/1/hi/6946425. stm*, 14 August 2007

Mitchell, Pierre and Dowling, Peter, "The CIPSA-Hackett Group Procurement Value, Performance and Capability Study", *http://www. cips.org/Documents/CIPSAWhitePapers/2011/CIPSA_Hackett.pdf*, CIPS Australasia, October 2010

Moody, Patricia E., "Discovering the Incredible Payback – Innovative Sourcing Solutions That Deliver Extraordinary Results", *CSCMP Supply Chain Comment* Volume 39, Council of Supply Chain Management Professionals, May/June 2005

Mullins, Laurie J., *Management and Organisational Behaviour* Fourth Edition, Pitman Publishing, 1996

Osagie, Sigi, "Boost Your Mojo, But Find It First! Strategies for Managing Your Growth and Development", motivational speech delivered at CIPS Bedfordshire & Hertfordshire branch, Hatfield, UK, 24 November 2010

Osagie, Sigi, "Enhancing Procurement Effectiveness – Strengthening Procurement and Raising Awareness", keynote speeches delivered at CIPS member conferences – Harare, Zimbabwe and Ndola and Lusaka, Zambia, December 2011

Osagie, Sigi, "How to fix inefficient processes", *IFPSM ezine*, January 2011

Osagie, Sigi, "Lean Everywhere", *Engineering & Technology*, 28 Feb – 13 Mar 2009

Osagie, Sigi, "Personal Effects", *Supply Management*, February 2012

Osagie, Sigi, "What Do We Think of What Bosses Think of Procurement?", *http://www.sigiosagie.com*, February 2008

Penka, Adrian, et al., "Global Chief Procurement Officer Survey 2010: Achieving sustained business value through procurement", *http://www.uk.capgemini.com/sites/default/files/resource/pdf/Global_Chief_Procurement_Officer_Survey_2010.pdf*, Capgemini Consulting, September 2010

Peters, Thomas J. and Waterman, Jr., Robert H., *In Search of Excellence – Lessons from America's Best-Run Companies*, Harper and Row, 1982

Pikulik, Jeff, "The CFO's View of Procurement: Getting More to the Bottom Line", Aberdeen Group Inc., September 2005

Player Profile – Thierry Henry, *http://www.arsenal.com*, (Accessed: 26 November 2012)

"Procurement Leaders in a Changing World: Will They Decline or Thrive?", *http://uk.hudson.com/Portals/UK/documents/Research/research-procurement-leaders-report.pdf*, Hudson Supply Chain & Procurement, October 2009

Scott, Caroline, "Bread man talking" – A Life In the Day, *The Sunday Times Magazine*, 4 March 2012

"Siemens' first female board member and Fortune magazine's sixth most powerful woman in business. Meet Barbara Kux…", *Supply Management*, 10 June 2010

Snell, Paul, "CIPS Conference 2011 in review", *http://blog.supplymanagement.com*, 7 October 2011

Snell, Paul, "Homeserve wins top award", *http://www.supplymanagement.com*, 15 September 2008

Story, Louise, "Lead Paint Prompts Mattel to Recall 967,000 Toys", *http://www.nytimes.com/2007/08/02/business/02toy.html*, 2 August 2007

"Strengthening Procurement Capacities in Developing Countries – OECD/DAC-World Bank Roundtable", Summary Report, OECD-World Bank, 22-23 January 2003

"Supply Chain Complexity: Managing Constant Change", *http://www.kpmg.*

com/UK/en/IssuesAndInsights/ArticlesPublications/Documents/PDF/ Advisory/Supply-Chain-Survey.pdf, KPMG LLP (UK), May 2011

"The Power of Procurement – A global survey of Procurement functions", *http://www.kpmg.com/UK/en/IssuesAndInsights/ArticlesPublications/ Documents/PDF/Advisory/the-power-of-procurement-a-global-survey-of-procurement-functions.pdf*, KPMG International, February 2012

Tully, Shawn and Sookdeo, Ricardo, "Purchasing's New Muscle", *http://money. cnn.com/magazines/fortune/fortune_archive/1995/02/20/201867*, 20 February, 1995

Tyson, Shaun and Jackson, Tony, *The Essence of Organizational Behaviour*, Prentice Hall, 1992

Wills, Stephen, "Procurement leadership: Dos and don'ts", *http://www. cpoagenda.com*, Spring 2010

INDEX

A

accountability, individual performance and rewards 79
appraisal
feedback 84
individual performance and rewards 83
Approved Vendor List (AVL), supply base management 135
AVL. See Approved Vendor List
awareness of procurement 31

B

benchmarking, functional performance 184
'best-practice' purchasing 232
boardroom representation, procurement 30
brand, procurement. See procurement brand
budget approval 113. See also finance function, purchase-to-pay (P2P) process

C

centralised/decentralised procurement functions, people capability 73
collaborative relationships 146. See also partnerships, Supplier Performance and Relationship Management (SPRM)
communication. See also public relations (PR)
change management 125
effective leadership 55
people capability 76
persuasive communication 203
procurement brand 200
procurement programmes 173
stakeholders 200
technology enablement 125
competency development, people

capability 67
competency models, people capability 68
contracts, supply, supply base management 157
corporate social responsibility (CSR), supply base management 130
'cost savings'. See value-for-money (VFM) improvements
critical stakeholders 213
CRM. See Customer Relationship Management
CSR. See corporate social responsibility
culture 90
culture change, procurement effectiveness 40
Customer Relationship Management (CRM)
procurement brand 200
stakeholders 200
customers. See also end-user adoption; stakeholders
processes 106
stakeholders as 211

D

dashboards, functional performance 182
decentralised/centralised procurement functions, people capability 73
Delegated Purchasing Authority (DPA) mechanisms, purchase-to-pay (P2P) process 115
developing people, people capability 74

E

effective leadership 49. See also leadership styles
effectiveness 20. See also procurement effectiveness
organisational success 22
vs efficiency 21, 35

effective performance management,
individual performance and rewards
80
efficiency improvements, technology
enablement 125
efficiency, vs effectiveness 21, 35
embedding procurement, public
relations (PR) 225
employee engagement, people
capability 74
enablers 102
fit-for-purpose vs best-in-class 102
processes 111
processes vs tools 103
technology enablement 123
end-user adoption. See also customers
processes 106
technology enablement 125
ethical sourcing, supply base
management 130
evaluating prospective suppliers,
discrete sourcing 118
external/internal stakeholders,
procurement brand 201

F
finance function
aligning 214
budget approval, purchase-to-pay
(P2P) process 113
value-for-money (VFM)
improvements 215
financial measures
functional performance 181
key performance indicators (KPIs)
179
functional leadership. See effective
leadership
functional performance 176. See
also individual performance and
rewards; procurement programmes;
Supplier Performance and
Relationship Management (SPRM)
benchmarking 184
dashboards 182
'engine rooms' 177
financial measures 181
goals 176, 179

key performance indicators (KPIs)
181
performance measurement 179
sample measures 180
scorecards 182

G
goals. See also objectives
developing 58
functional goals 57
functional performance 176, 179
objectives vs responsibilities 61
organisational goals 81, 91, 106
processes 106
procurement programmes 168
SMART objectives 62
vision 58
governance 173, 174. See also risk
management, procurement
programmes

H
HR. See human resources
human capital element, procurement
effectiveness 40
human resources (HR), critical
stakeholders 216

I
individual performance and rewards 79
accountability 79
aligning with organisational goals 81
appraisal 83
effective performance management
80
motivation 80, 88
objectives 81
personal effectiveness 87
'soft' issues 79
ineffective processes 104
ineffective procurement organisations
44
inspiring people, effective leadership 49
integrating procurement functions,
procurement brand 194
internal/external stakeholders,
procurement brand 201

K

key performance indicators (KPIs)
balanced approach 180
financial measures 181
functional performance 179
procurement effectiveness 39
sample measures 181

L

leadership, effective. *See* effective
leadership
leadership, functional. *See* effective
leadership
leadership, procurement programmes
168
leadership styles. *See also* effective
leadership
culture 93
effective leadership 53
logos, persuasive communication 204,
218
low-cost country sourcing, supply base
management 131

M

materials price variance (MPV),
functional performance 180
motivation
individual performance and rewards
80, 88
people capability 74, 77
stakeholders 202
MPV. *See* materials price variance

N

New Product Introduction (NPI)
goals 59
vision 59
NPI. *See* New Product Introduction

O

objectives. *See also* goals
individual performance and rewards
81
setting 81, 82
SMART objectives 62, 81, 168
vs responsibilities 61

organisational climate
effective leadership 55
people importance 55
organisational effectiveness
core components 43
people importance 43
organisational goals
culture 91
individual performance and rewards
81
processes 106
organisational positions, procurement
functions 193, 194
organisational success
effectiveness 22
procurement 22, 27
procurement effectiveness 33
'soft' issues 34
vision 34
outsourcing, globalised economy 27

P

P2P process. *See* purchase-to-pay
process
partnerships 161. *See also* collaborative
relationships, supply base
management
people capability 67
communication 76
competency development 67
competency models 68
developing people 74
employee engagement 74
motivation 74, 77
succession planning 73
talent acquisition 67
task orientation vs relationship focus
76
technical skills 67
perceptions, influencing/managing,
public relations (PR) 220
perceptions of procurement 24, 31
shaping perceptions 203
stakeholders 200
performance and rewards, individual.
See individual performance and
rewards

performance dimensions/functional
responsibilities, Supplier Performance
and Relationship Management
(SPRM) 143
performance frameworks 164
fuctional performance 176
key levels 164
performance management of
procurement programmes 166
performance, functional. *See* functional
performance
performance, individual. *See* individual
performance and rewards
performance management. *See
also* functional performance
performance management structure,
Supplier Performance and
Relationship Management (SPRM)
142
procurement programmes 166
vs functional performance 176
performance measurement 176. *See
also* functional performance, vs
performance management
performance, supplier. *See* Supplier
Performance and Relationship
Management (SPRM)
personal effectiveness, individual
performance and rewards 87
personality types
persuasive communication 206
stakeholders 206
persuasive communication 203
credibility 205
flexibility 205
personality types 206
stakeholders 203
POs. *See* purchase orders
PPV. *See* purchase price variance
PR. *See* public relations
processes 111
classifications 110
customers 106
effective processes 107
end-user adoption 106
principles 106
sourcing 111
stakeholders 109

supply base management 111
supply execution 111
processes vs tools, enablers 103
Procurement Ambassadors/Assassins
culture 95
procurement brand 201
stakeholders 201
procurement brand 191
brand perceptions 197
communication 200
customer-centricity 196
Customer Relationship Management
(CRM) 200
integrating procurement functions
194
Procurement Ambassadors/Assassins
201
public relations (PR) 218
repositioning procurement 194
stakeholders 196, 200
procurement effectiveness 23
'doing the right things' 37, 39
enhancing 39, 236
human capital element 40
importance 233
procurement functions
barriers 193
customer-centricity 197
integrating 194
organisational positions 194
procurement effectiveness 34, 37, 41
'soft' issues 34
stakeholders 196
strategic focus vs tactical focus 191
value proposition, procurement 40
procurement leaders, roles 45
procurement programmes
communication 173
governance 173, 174
leadership 168
performance management 166
planning, project 171, 174
progress reviews 172
project management structure 167
project planning 171, 174
risk management 173
SMART objectives 168
steering groups 170

programmes, procurement.
  See procurement programmes
progress reviews, procurement
  programmes 172
project management structure,
  procurement programmes 167
project planning, procurement
  programmes 171, 174
public relations (PR) 218. *See
  also* communication
  aims 219
  awareness of procurement 223
  credibility 230
  driving understanding 225
  embedding procurement 225
  examples 222
  media 220
  messages, shaping content 228
  reputation management 219
  website, procurement intranet 221
public sector
  corruption 29
  developing world 28
purchase orders (POs) purchase-to-pay
  (P2P) process 114
purchase-to-pay (P2P) process. *See
  also* discrete sourcing
  Delegated Purchasing Authority (DPA)
    115
  purchase orders (POs) 114
  sourcing 113, 116
  supplier management 115
  supply execution 112

Q

QBRs. *See* Quarterly Business Reviews
Quarterly Business Reviews (QBRs),
  Supplier Performance and
  Relationship Management (SPRM)
  140

R

relationships, stakeholders 213
relationships, supplier. *See* Supplier
  Performance and Relationship
  Management (SPRM)
repositioning procurement,

procurement brand 194
reputation management
  aims 219
  public relations (PR) 219
requirements specification, discrete
  sourcing 117
responsibilities
  procurement 26
  sourcing and supply 61
  spend management 61
  supply base management 61
  responsibilities vs objectives 61
reviews/reviewing
  individual performance and rewards
    79
  monitoring/reviewing progress, risk
    management 155
  progress reviews, procurement
    programmes 172
  Quarterly Business Reviews (QBRs),
    Supplier Performance and
    Relationship Management (SPRM)
    140
rewards and performance, individual.
  See individual performance and
  rewards
risk management 146. *See
  also* governance
  assessing/evaluating risks 151
  business continuity 147
  categories 149
  identifying/understanding risks 151
  process 151
  procurement programmes 173
  Risk Priority Number (RPN) 153
  risk registers 155
  supply base management 146, 160
Risk Priority Number (RPN), risk
  management 153
risk registers, risk management 155
RPN. *See* Risk Priority Number

S

scorecards
  functional performance 182
  Supplier Scorecard 144
self-leadership, culture 94

Service Level Agreements (SLAs), supply base management 158
SLAs. *See* Service Level Agreements
SMART objectives 62
  individual performance and rewards 81
  procurement programmes 168
'soft' issues
  individual performance and rewards 79
  people capability 67
  procurement effectiveness 34
  procurement functions 34
  sustainable success 34
sourcing. *See also* discrete sourcing; supply base management
  ethical sourcing 130
  low-cost country sourcing 131
  processes 111
  purchase-to-pay (P2P) process 113, 116
sourcing and supply, responsibilities 61
spend management, responsibilities 61
spend under management, supply base management 160
SPRM. *See* Supplier Performance and Relationship Management
stakeholders. *See also* customers
  aligning 210
  as customers 211
  communication 200
  critical stakeholders 213
  Customer Relationship Management (CRM) 200
  finance function 213
  influencing 210
  internal/external 201
  mapping 207
  perceptions of procurement 200, 203
  personality types 206
  persuasive communication 203
  procurement brand 196, 200
  relationships 213
  repositioning procurement 196
strategic focus vs tactical focus, procurement functions 191
succession planning, people capability 73

success, organisational. *See* organisational success
success, sustainable. *See* sustainable success
supplier alignment, Supplier Performance and Relationship Management (SPRM) 137
supplier failure, risk management 149
supplier managemeent, purchase-to-pay (P2P) process 115
Supplier Performance and Relationship Management (SPRM) 136. *See also* supply base management
  aligning suppliers 137
  collaborative relationships 146
  perfomance dimensions/functional responsibilities 143
  performance management structure 142
  Quarterly Business Reviews (QBRs) 140
  relationships, collaborative 146
  Supplier Scorecard 144
  supply base management 136
Supplier Scorecard, Supplier Performance and Relationship Management (SPRM) 144
suppliers, evaluating prospective 118
supply base management 129. *See also* Supplier Performance and Relationship Management (SPRM)
  Approved Vendor List (AVL) 135
  collaborative relationships 146, 161
  contracts, supply 157
  corporate social responsibility (CSR) 130
  ethical sourcing 130
  low-cost country sourcing 61
  processes 111
  responsibilities 61
  risk management 146, 160
  Service Level Agreements (SLAs) 158
  Supplier Performance and Relationship Management (SPRM) 136
  supply contracts 157
  supply partnerships 161
  value, long-term 133

supply contracts, supply base
  management 157
supply execution
  processes 111
  purchase-to-pay (P2P) process 112
supply partnerships, supply base
  management 161
supply pipeline risks, risk management
  149
sustainable success
  goals 47
  long-term performance 47
  procurement effectiveness 33, 47
  'soft' issues 34

T
tactical focus vs strategic focus,
  procurement functions 191
talent acquisition, people capability 67
task orientation vs relationship focus,
  people capability 76
TCO. *See* Total Cost of Ownership
technical skills, people capability 67
technology enablement 123
  change management 125
  communication 125
  efficiency improvements 125
  end-user adoption 125
  executive-level support 124
  focus 125
time management

culture 97
goals 97
objectives 97
'Total Cost of Ownership' (TCO), supply
  base management 134
'total lifecycle value-offering', supply
  base management 134
transformation rogrammes, processes
  107

V
value-for-money (VFM) improvements
  121
  finance function 215
  management process 121
  stakeholders 215
value, long-term, supply base
  management 133
value proposition, procurement
  procurement effectiveness 40
  procurement functions 40
VFM improvements. *See* value-for-
  money improvements
vision
  goals 58
  imagery 59

W
website, procurement intranet, public
  relations (PR) 221

CPSIA information can be obtained
at www.ICGtesting.com
Printed in the USA
LVOW10s1231140617
538062LV00025B/439/P